Campus Speech and Academic Freedom

CAMPUS SPEECH AND ACADEMIC FREEDOM

A GUIDE FOR DIFFICULT TIMES

• • •

ERWIN CHEMERINSKY
AND HOWARD GILLMAN

Yale
UNIVERSITY PRESS
New Haven and London

Published with assistance from the Ralph S. Brown Memorial
Publication Fund.
Published with assistance from the Louis Stern Memorial Fund.

Yale University Press books may be purchased in quantity for
educational, business, or promotional use. For information, please e-mail
sales.press@yale.edu (U.S. office) or sales@yaleup.co.uk (U.K. office).

Set in Adobe Garamond Pro type by IDS Infotech Ltd.
Printed in the United States of America.

Library of Congress Control Number: 2025941400
ISBN 978-0-300-27098-3 (hardcover)

A catalogue record for this book is available from the British Library.

Authorized Representative in the EU: Easy Access System Europe,
Mustamäe tee 50, 10621 Tallinn, Estonia, gpsr.requests@easproject.com

10 9 8 7 6 5 4 3 2 1

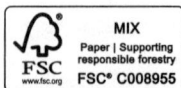

For Catherine and Ellen

Contents

Contents

Campus Speech and Academic Freedom

PROLOGUE

Knowing the Principles Isn't Enough

On Tuesday, December 5, 2023, the Education and Workforce Committee of the U.S. House of Representatives held a hearing focused on antisemitism on campuses. Republicans on the committee called three prominent university presidents to testify: Claudine Gay of Harvard, Sally Kornbluth of MIT, and Elizabeth Magill of the University of Pennsylvania.

The entire hearing was contentious. About four hours in, conservative congresswoman Elise Stefanik tried to get the presidents to agree that the slogan "From the river to the sea, Palestine will be free," was inherently antisemitic. The presidents refused to take a position. Stefanik then asked Gay, "Does calling for the genocide of Jews violate Harvard's rules on bullying and harassment?" "It can, depending on the context," Gay responded.

Stefanik likewise asked Magill whether "calling for the genocide of Jews" would violate Penn's code of conduct. Magill responded: "If the speech turns into conduct it can be harassment, yes." Pressed further, Magill told Stefanik, "It is a context-dependent decision, congresswoman."

Stefanik responded angrily: "The speech is not harassment? This is unacceptable."[1]

The exchange quickly went viral, and the university presidents' testimony was widely denounced. Many found their nuanced answer, that the treatment of calls for genocide depends on the context, deeply unacceptable. Seventy members of Congress sent a letter calling for all three presidents to be fired. "Given this moment of crisis," they wrote, "we demand that your boards immediately remove each of these presidents from their positions and that you provide an actionable plan to ensure that Jewish and Israeli students, teachers, and faculty are safe on your campuses. . . . The university presidents' responses to questions aimed at addressing the growing trend of antisemitism on college and university campuses were abhorrent."[2]

A day after the hearing, Gay publicly apologized for her testimony, saying, "I am sorry. Words matter."[3] Within the week, Magill had been fired by the trustees of the University of Pennsylvania. Soon after, Gay resigned as well, at least in large part based on reactions to her testimony before Congress.

Yet as a matter of First Amendment law, the university presidents' answers were clearly correct. Each of them could have avoided the question by simply saying, "We are a private university. The First Amendment does not apply to us. Of course, we outlaw and punish advocacy of genocide." But like most of the country's private universities, they choose to follow free speech principles, something the two of us very much support as essential to the mission of a university.[4] The First Amendment makes no exception from protection for speech discussing or even advocating genocide. Of course, if the speech rises to the level of incitement or is a threat, then it would not be protected. But that was exactly the point the university presidents were making: it all depends on context.

With the benefit of hindsight, and recognizing how difficult it was to be answering questions in the fourth hour of a tense hearing, it is possible to see that the university presidents made a mistake by giving an answer based on the law to a question calling for an emotional response. In hindsight, they could have denounced advocacy of genocide and described how it violates their campus's principles of community, while then recognizing that whether such speech would be punished depended on context. But it is not clear that such a response would have mattered in the firestorm of outrage about their testimony. Congresswoman Stefanik and those infuriated by the presidents' answers wanted a categorical condemnation, not nuance.

The exchange between Stefanik and the university presidents occurred in a year that posed difficult speech challenges to campus administrators across the country. Immediately after the Hamas terrorist attack on Israel on October 7, some professors and students celebrated the deadly assault. Students for Justice in Palestine called the attack a "historic win" for the "Palestinian resistance." A Columbia professor called the massacre "awesome" and a "stunning victory." A Yale professor tweeted, "It's been such an extraordinary day" while calling Israel a "murderous, genocidal settler state." A Chicago art professor posted a note reading, "Israelis are pigs. Savages. Very very bad people. Irredeemable excrement. . . . May they all rot in hell." A UC Davis professor, noting that "Zionist journalists . . . have houses w addresses, kids in school," wrote, "They can fear their bosses, but they should fear us more" before adding emojis of a knife, an ax, and three drops of blood. A Cornell student was arrested for making threats against a Jewish dining hall and saying he would "bring an assault rifle to campus and shoot all you pig jews."

This all happened before Israel's invasion of Gaza triggered renewed calls for university officials to condemn Israel's actions and to divest from that country. Campus leaders were denounced no matter what they did. Some chose to remain silent and were criticized for that. Balanced messages were attacked for being balanced. Those that seemed too pro-Israel or too pro-Palestinian were criticized as biased.

The tensions increased over the academic year, reaching a climax in April and May when pro-Palestinian demonstrators constructed encampments at many colleges. By May 1, 2024, there were encampments at about eighty universities, and many more were created after that. Some were cleared by police. Some led to violence. Some remained peaceful. Some commencements were cancelled and others were disrupted.

Amid all of this, the Office of Civil Rights of the Department of Education announced that it was investigating incidents of antisemitism and Islamophobia on campus as violating Title VI of the 1964 Civil Rights Act, which prohibits recipients of federal funds from discriminating based on race or national origin. Assistant Secretary of Education Catherine Lhamon said emphatically in speeches and "Dear Colleague" letters that even speech that is protected by the First Amendment could create a hostile environment and require campus action. Dozens of investigations were launched against colleges and universities under Title VI for being deliberately indifferent to antisemitic, anti-Muslim, or anti-Palestinian speech. Many institutions were also sued in federal court.

All of this made free speech on campus a divisive issue at universities across the country. Some suggested that the campus demonstrations in the spring of 2024 were the most extensive protests on campuses since those against the Vietnam War in the late 1960s and early 1970s. But there were key differences. During the Vietnam War, students were largely unified; the antagonists were university administrators who wanted to end the demonstrations. The Hamas attack and the Israeli invasion of Gaza deeply divided students and faculty. There seems to be no middle ground between those who believe that Israel should not exist and those who regard its existence as essential. And for many students and faculty members, the issue engages crucial aspects of their religious and personal identities.

This is just the most prominent instance in which universities have had to deal with issues of free speech over the last several years. There have been many examples of faculty members being disciplined or even fired for their speech. Institutions have faced the question of how much they must spend to protect safety when unpopular speakers are invited to campus, and when they may bar a speaker rather than bear those costs. Some instances of students disrupting speakers have drawn national media attention.

Conservative state legislatures have enacted laws prohibiting the teaching of Critical Race Theory and have abolished diversity, equity, and inclusion initiatives. Some states have sought to eliminate tenure protections for faculty. Republican Party control of all three branches of the federal government in 2025 ushered in a period of even more intense national political scrutiny of the practices and values of American higher education, especially on matters relating to free speech, nondiscrimination, ideological bias, and diversity, equity, and inclusion. And the Trump administration in its first few months dramatically intensified the conservative assault on higher education by using unsupported claims of antisemitism and unethical political indoctrination to withhold hundreds of millions of dollars of medical and scientific research funds while demanding that targeted universities change their governance structure, admissions and faculty hiring practices, recruitment of international students, and oversight of academic programs and schools.[5]

All of this occurs in a time of the ascendancy of the internet and social media. During the anti–Vietnam War protests, demonstrators needed to capture the attention of just a small number of media outlets. Now events are communicated instantaneously, including by the participants themselves. In the past, most people would never know if a student or faculty member had expressed a controversial opinion, but today an outrageous random opinion posted by an otherwise anonymous member of a campus community can become known to millions of people and cause a firestorm of protest.

A decade ago, when we wrote *Free Speech on Campus,* we worried that students were losing faith in freedom of speech. Today's increased activism across the country may have given them a greater appreciation of its importance on campuses and elsewhere. But ironically, just as progressive free speech critics seem to have rediscovered the importance of protecting their rights to express views others abhor, conservatives who once insisted that campuses do a better job protecting free speech have started advocating censorship of protesters and faculty members who say things they don't like. This selective commitment to free speech principles is, sadly, part of our tradition.

The Basic Principles of Free Speech on Campus

Many of the recent controversies have arisen within a context where campuses have a better understanding of the basic principles of free speech and academic freedom than they did even ten years ago. A lot of work has taken place since 2016–17, when many colleges and universities were unprepared even to articulate the reasons for allowing controversial speech on campuses. Today, administrators have adopted clearer statements of these commitments, sometimes following templates like the so-called Chicago Statement, sometimes crafting their own.[6]

Understanding the reasons behind free speech rights is crucial, and campuses should get credit for their progress. It has become clear, however, that appreciating these principles is only the start. Efforts to be faithful to them quickly encounter challenging circumstances that force free speech advocates to move beyond simply repeating basic aphorisms. They must also be willing to tackle the questions that come next.

The reasons to protect free speech and academic freedom do not change, but they are rarely intuitive for most people. People often feel a strong urge to silence speech we dislike. Without knowledge of the arguments for free speech, and of the history of censorship, it is difficult for a person to understand why society should tolerate speech that many consider hateful or harmful. We detailed these arguments and history in our earlier book, but we will briefly review them here before addressing how they should inform the difficult issues campuses have faced this past decade.

First, all ideas and views can be expressed on a campus. This is the core protection of the First Amendment—that the government can never restrict speech based on the viewpoint expressed—and we believe it is central to the mission of a university. Although the First Amendment applies only to government institutions, we believe that all colleges and universities should be committed to this basic premise of open inquiry: never can a college or university ban or punish speech based on the views or ideas expressed.

Second, freedom of speech is not absolute. The Supreme Court has long recognized that some categories of speech are unprotected or less protected. For campuses, the most important of these categories are incitement of illegal activity, true threats, and harassment. The Supreme Court and the lower courts have formulated legal tests for each of these categories that determine whether the speech may be considered unprotected by the First Amendment. It is important to distinguish between the colloquial use of these concepts and the legal test that must be met for the speaker to be punished or held liable.

Incitement requires both that the speech be likely to cause imminent illegal activity and that it be directed at causing that activity.[7] This is a difficult test to meet because it requires that there be *imminent* harm and that the speaker *intended* to cause the harm. For true threat, the Supreme Court has said that a speaker can be punished if he "consciously disregarded a substantial risk that his communications would be viewed as threatening violence."[8] Harassment requires that the speech be directed at a person or be sufficiently pervasive as to materially interfere with educational opportunities based on race, sex, religion, sexual orientation, or gender identity.[9] Importantly, each of these tests requires something other than the mere expression of a viewpoint or idea in order for speech to qualify as unprotected.

This crucial point is often lost in contentious public discussions about freedom of speech.

It is important to remember that hate speech is not among the categories of unprotected speech. As we discuss in *Free Speech on Campus,* the Supreme Court has stated clearly that hate speech is protected by the First Amendment unless it otherwise falls into a category of unprotected expression. This stance distinguishes the United States from many other countries and draws criticism from many prominent scholars.[10] But as a descriptive matter of the law, hate speech is generally constitutionally protected. In the early 1990s, more than 360 colleges and universities adopted hate speech codes. Every one that was considered by a court was declared unconstitutional. In part, this is because of the difficulty of defining hate speech in a way that is not unconstitutionally vague or overbroad. More important, though, is that hate speech always conveys an idea, albeit a very offensive one, and under the First Amendment all ideas and views can be expressed.

Third, because no one believes that free speech means you can express yourself anywhere, at any time, and in any manner you want, campuses may impose reasonable time, place, and manner restrictions on expressive activity. These time, place, and manner restrictions must be content-neutral, serve an important purpose, and leave open adequate alternatives for communication. For public universities, the campus is generally considered a "limited public forum" under the law.[11] This means it can be "limited to use by certain groups or dedicated solely to the discussion of certain subjects." In "such a forum, a governmental entity may impose restrictions on speech that are reasonable and viewpoint-neutral."

Time, place, and manner restrictions may involve prohibitions on sound amplification equipment on campuses, on demonstrations near classroom buildings while classes are in session, and on encampments on campuses. All of these restrictions are content-neutral: they apply to all speech, regardless of viewpoint or subject matter, simply preventing disruption of campus activities and leaving open adequate other places for communication.

Fourth, expressive activity on campuses takes place in two separate "zones," professional and nonprofessional. In places where professors are engaged in their professional activities, such as classrooms and labs, their actions are governed not by general free speech norms but by the protections and obligations of academic freedom. Academic freedom provides faculty members with tremendous discretion in how they use their expertise to discover and transmit higher levels of knowledge, but it also obligates professors to act in ways that reflect high standards of professional competence and ethics. Incompetence or unethical behavior in these professional settings can lead to sanctions for reasons that would not apply in nonprofessional settings. A European history professor who teaches students that the Holocaust never happened could face institutional consequences (such as the denial of tenure for reasons of incompetence), but a member of the public who holds up a sign outside city hall saying the same thing could not be punished, because they are not being held to standards of professional competence. Similarly, when members of the campus community express themselves outside these professional settings, the ordinary rules of free speech typically apply, meaning that a person cannot be sanctioned or censored merely for expressing an opinion, even a flagrantly wrong one. But some people disagree with this general approach and offer reasons why college settings should have no general zone of unrestricted free speech.

An Alternative Model for Free Speech on Campus?

We defend a free speech approach for all colleges and universities, believing that the right to express all ideas and views is crucial to these institutions' mission. But we recognize that there is another perspective.

At the risk of oversimplifying, this view might be labeled the educational mission approach. This says that educational institutions exist to teach and, in some cases, to engage in research. Speech can and should be restricted if it is inconsistent with this educational mission. Yale law professor Robert Post argues forcefully for this approach: "Like all government mission-driven institutions, schools are empowered to regulate the speech of those within the scope of their managerial authority as required to achieve their organizational mission. The purpose of schools is to educate students. The obligation of courts is to review school restraints on student speech to determine, first, whether regulated student speech is within the scope of the managerial authority of a school, and second, whether restraints on student speech are required by the legitimate pedagogical purposes of the school." Post even believes "it would . . . be more accurate to say that student speech is pervasively regulated unless there are reasons to exempt it from the comprehensive authority of the school."[12] Others have also opposed a free speech approach on campuses, arguing that speech should be regulated when doing so serves the educational mission of the university.[13]

Although in many instances these approaches would yield the same result as ours, they would differ on many of the most contentious issues, such as when campuses should be open to protesters, when hate speech should be tolerated, and what speakers should be allowed at schools. The educational mission approach would allow administrators to restrict speech if they considered it inconsistent with the school's mission, while the free speech approach would not allow restrictions unless the speech was unprotected by the First Amendment, violated time, place, and manner rules, or was conducted within campus spaces that are governed by academic freedom norms.

It is always crucial to distinguish a factual description of what the current law is from a normative discussion of what the law should be.

Overall, courts have followed the free expression approach when dealing with colleges and universities, but the educational mission approach when dealing with high schools.[14] In arguing for his approach, Professor Post relies almost entirely on Supreme Court cases that have dealt with speech in high schools, in which the Court has often been very deferential to school administrators.[15] Even when they have ruled in favor of student speech in the high school context, the justices have stressed that expression can be punished when it is disruptive of the educational environment.[16]

The Court has been much more sympathetic to free speech in cases involving colleges and universities.[17] So have most lower courts. As we mentioned, every campus hate speech code that was challenged in court has been declared unconstitutional.[18]

This, of course, does not answer the normative question of which approach *should* be followed, and whether it should be the same for both high schools and universities. There are obvious differences, such as the students' ages and the institutions' missions. Universities have a research mission to which academic freedom is indispensable. Professor Post is certainly correct in noting that speech is restricted in colleges and universities in countless ways: discussion in a classroom is limited to specific topics, student papers are evaluated based on their content, and so are faculty writings when individuals are considered for promotion and tenure. As we will discuss in some detail in chapter 2, the professional activities of university faculty and staff should be restricted in accordance with both the rights and responsibilities associated with academic freedom. But it is a mistake to say that because universities may *sometimes* restrict speech, they therefore may *always* limit speech to serve their educational mission. Of course, a professor can restrict the speech of students in the classroom to ensure that it is pertinent to the subject matter. But this does not justify restricting what can be said outside the classroom.

Our central thesis is that universities cannot achieve their missions in education and research except by allowing all ideas and views to be expressed. In this sense, we agree with Professor Post about the central importance of schools' educational mission, but we disagree that restricting speech on the basis of message advances that mission. Professional norms apply where they should, but it is also part of the educational experience of college students to express themselves and participate in activities that are not directly governed by scholarly norms. As we argued in *Free Speech on Campus*, it is essential that universities be places where all ideas can be expressed. We do not share Professor Post's view that campuses can deviate from this if they believe that the expression will interfere with someone's education. That approach makes it far too easy for any school to suppress speech that some do not like. As administrators, we frequently hear from students that speech they find offensive makes them feel unsafe and must therefore be stopped. Acceding to their demands would undermine the educational mission of the university.

This was the very point of the Berkeley Free Speech Movement, which was triggered by student desire to engage in routine political activities and an administration that denied them access to campus spaces for those purposes because the purposes were not directly related to the university's educational mission. Students argued that in public spaces on a campus they should have the same First Amendment rights they would have in public spaces off campus. Large numbers of them insisted on this, and many faculty members eventually agreed and supported their movement. Without their success, there would have been no civil rights or antiwar demonstrations on campuses in the 1960s and 1970s, and there would be no general rights for political expression or other forms of campus activism today. This would not have been a good result. More than that, it would not have been achievable. If stubborn college administrators had insisted on trying to limit the speech of young adults in the ways Post proposes, the students would not have gone along. This high school model simply will not work in higher education.

We thus believe that the free speech model that we defend in *Free Speech on Campus* and that underlies this book is both descriptively correct, in terms of stating the law, and normatively desirable as to what campuses should do. If it were ever accepted that a campus could punish any speech it deemed inconsistent with its educational mission, there would be no limit on its power to censor. Our central premise is that a university cannot censor or punish the expression of an idea, even though many would say that the viewpoint expressed is inconsistent with the educational mission of the university. The educational mission is best served by allowing all ideas and views to be expressed.

Organization of the Book

We divide this book into five chapters focused on specific issues that have arisen since we wrote *Free Speech on Campus,* investigating the hard questions that cannot be answered simply with reference to basic principles. These issues will certainly keep coming up in the years ahead. Our goal is to examine these current issues and relate them to timeless underlying principles of free speech.

Chapter 1 considers speech on the campus, especially the tensions between protecting speech and preventing discrimination, disruption, and threats to safety. We look again at hateful speech, particularly the tension between Title VI of the 1964 Civil Rights Act and the First Amendment; protests on campus, including the recent encampments; and the ongoing issue of controversial speakers on campuses. We explain our view as to the types of time, place, and manner restrictions that should be enforced and what it means to create effective policies governing "major events" and "disruption" of campus activities. We warn against some troubling suggestions—from campus advocates as well as from national policymakers—that nondiscrimination principles might be a legitimate basis for of censoring or punishing the expression of viewpoints. We oppose arguments that disruptive protests should be considered a form of protected speech, but simultaneously insist that policies regulating expressive activity must be applied in ways that are viewpoint-neutral.

Chapter 2 examines speech in the classroom and other professional settings. We look at academic freedom and its limits, including controversies over pedagogical choices or research programs. We also consider whether professors should attribute to their academic departments and schools certain political viewpoints and also whether campus leaders should make official statements about controversial social and political matters. We finish by discussing whether campuses should require prospective faculty members to submit statements about their commitment to diversity, equity, and inclusion (DEI) goals. We argue in favor of protecting faculty choices in professional settings as long as they are acting within boundaries of professional competence and ethics, which means that certain limits on such speech are a necessary and long-recognized feature of the very concept of academic freedom. We also explain why faculty members should not associate their schools or departments with certain political viewpoints and why campus presidents and chancellors should show restraint when addressing controversial topics unrelated to the core mission of the university. Although we acknowledge that requiring DEI statements might advance important institutional goals, we also argue against across-the-board requirements for the submission of such statements. We prefer instead that disciplines and departments decide on their own what kinds of statements from faculty applicants are best justified on scholarly grounds while also avoiding ideological litmus tests.

Chapter 3 focuses on off-campus or "extramural" speech, and when it should have on-campus consequences. We consider the extent to which academic freedom should safeguard such expression for faculty members and describe the rare circumstances in which faculty might legitimately face sanctions. We discuss protections for students whose social media posts create firestorms of controversy, and examine whether campuses should restrict the speech of senior administrators more closely than that of professors and students. We also discuss the appropriateness of some institutional responses that are not necessarily "sanctions," such as changing teaching assignments or making public statements condemning controversial speech. In general, we argue that, unlike the case with on-campus speech by faculty in professional settings, such off-campus or extramural speech should almost always be considered protected, even if it is also true that there are some responses campuses can make to such controversies that are justifiable when they do not represent efforts to censor or punish the speaker.

Chapter 4 moves away from intra-campus controversies to take up the much more sweeping efforts by government officials to censor or punish campus speech. We pay particular attention to efforts by Republican state legislatures to silence "divisive" discussion or teaching of topics such as Critical Race Theory or gender identity, and to outlaw diversity, equity, and inclusion efforts, which we consider the most sweeping effort to suppress campus speech since the McCarthy era. We will evaluate these government restrictions as well as efforts in the early months of the Trump administration in light of basic principles of free speech and academic freedom. We also look at the litigation surrounding some of these laws and whether they violate either the First Amendment or the equal protection clause, and we draw attention to how these efforts by conservative officials compare with some progressives' efforts to restrict "hate speech" on campus.

Chapter 5 discusses what campuses can and can't do. This reflects our goal in the book both to examine the theoretical underpinnings of free speech on campus and to address the practical realities of what school officials face. We recognize, of course, that many of the questions we discuss do not have clear legal answers. But knowing this can be helpful to campus officials.

We ended *Free Speech on Campus* by stressing the enormous stakes in the debate on this subject. If anything, recent events have made these issues even more difficult and underscored their tremendous importance. We hope our efforts to provide additional guidance will help readers think clearly about the new challenges and questions that are sure to arise.

Speech on Campus: Protecting Speech While Preventing Discrimination, Disruption, and Threats to Safety

Campuses face competing legal duties. On the one hand, the First Amendment imposes a legal obligation on public universities to refrain from infringing freedom of speech. Private universities may be similarly limited, either by statutes or by their own commitments. At the same time, federal laws create a legal requirement to prevent discrimination and harassment based on race and sex, offenses that often occur through speech. There also is a legal duty created by tort law, as well as a moral obligation, to protect the safety of students, staff, and faculty. The tension arises because speech can constitute harassment, and speech events can create risks to safety.

Campuses across the country—public and private, large and small—have struggled with these issues, and there is every reason to believe that the tensions will only grow. In this chapter, we focus on several issues that frequently have arisen concerning speech on campus: disruptions of campus activities, including attempts to silence controversial speakers; responses to encampments and protests; and the tension between Title VI and the First Amendment.

In examining these topics, it is important to distinguish what a campus *may* do from what legally it *must* do. In other words, while the answer for campus administrators is at times provided by the law, there also are situations in which the issue is not legal but involves what is pragmatically and politically most desirable. We also want to state clearly where the law seems settled and where it is in flux.

Controversial Speakers and Disruption of School Events

If campuses are to be places where all ideas and views can be expressed, there will inevitably be controversial speakers. Often their presence inspires others to engage in disruptive activities to prevent them from expressing their views. The thinking, apparently, is that if the campus will not censor the expression of unacceptable ideas, others should accomplish that silencing through direct action.

We wish there were a deeper and more widespread appreciation at colleges and universities of the importance of tolerating the widest possible expression of viewpoints, and of encouraging faculty members and students to respond to disagreeable or hateful opinions through discussion, debate, and engagement rather than by trying to silence them. Although many campuses have offered clear articulations of the fundamental role of free expression for the mission of higher education, we continue to see unfortunate instances of efforts to silence certain speakers or disrupt disagreeable events.

University of California Law, San Francisco (formerly Hastings Law School).[1] Shortly after Judge Ketanji Brown Jackson was nominated to replace the departing Justice Stephen Breyer on the Supreme Court, the Federalist Society organized a discussion about the transition. The event was called "The Battle over Justice Breyer's Seat," and it was supposed to take place on March 1, 2022. The planned speakers were Ilya Shapiro of Georgetown Law School and UC Hastings professor Rory Little. Shapiro had recently been put on leave by Georgetown after he tweeted that federal court of appeals judge Sri Srinivasan would be the "best pick" to replace Breyer, but Srinivasan did not "fit into [the] latest intersectionality hierarchy so we'll get 'lesser black woman.' "

At the event, students chanted, clapped, and banged on desks in an effort to keep Shapiro from being heard. Among other slogans, the students chanted, "I am not lesser" and "Support Black women." Protesters repeatedly interrupted Shapiro, ridiculed his hairline, and called him a coward and a racist. The event was cut short after Morris Ratner, the academic dean and provost at Hastings, was unable to quiet the protesters.

In October 2022, the college updated its policy on events to specifically prohibit "forms of protest that substantially disrupt an in-person or virtual event in a way that has the effect of silencing a speaker" while still protecting peaceful protests such as banner holding, counter events, and engaging in question and answer periods.[2]

Yale Law School.[3] On March 10, 2022, the Federalist Society organized a panel with Kristen Waggoner, general counsel for Alliance Defending Freedom (ADF), and Monica Miller from the American Humanist Association (AHA). ADF is a conservative advocacy organization that is labeled a hate group by the Southern Poverty Law Center, but it has also been very active in federal court litigation. The event, moderated by Yale law professor Kate Stith, was about a case involving a student who was prohibited from sharing his faith on campus due to speech policies. Approximately 120 students held up signs supporting trans rights and other LGBTQ+ causes and interrupted Waggoner while she was speaking. One protester allegedly yelled, "I'll literally fight you, bitch" at Waggoner. After Stith read Yale Law's free speech policies aloud, students left the room but continued to chant in the hallway. The event proceeded to its completion, though after the protesting students left the room they continued to engage in behavior that was disruptive of that event and classes being held nearby.

Stanford Law School.[4] In April 2022, the Federalist Society organized an event called "The Fifth Circuit in Conversation with the Supreme Court: Covid, Guns, and Twitter" featuring Kyle Duncan, a conservative judge on the United States Court of Appeals for the Fifth Circuit. Students protested at the event because of Duncan's conservative advocacy before going on the bench and his rulings as a judge, especially expressing their support for LGBTQ+ rights. Although the judge had been invited by a registered student organization of the law school, the associate dean for diversity, equity, and inclusion, Tirien Steinbach, delivered a speech discussing the harm of the event. She told Duncan, "It's uncomfortable to say that for many people here your work has caused harm." After stating the importance of free speech, she noted, "Again I still ask, is the juice worth the squeeze? Is it worth the pain that this causes? The division that this causes? Do you have something so incredibly important to say about Twitter and guns and COVID that is worth this impact on the division of these people?" Duncan responded to the chanting crowd by telling a member of the audience, "You are an appalling idiot; you're an appalling idiot." He also said, "In this school, the inmates have gotten control of the asylum." The event did not go forward.

After the event, Stanford law dean Jenny Martinez and Stanford University president Marc Tessier-Lavigne issued an apology to Duncan. Stanford leadership stated that it would not discipline any students, but it would require all students to attend a half-day training program on free speech. Both the apology and the required training were considered unacceptable to many students. When Dean Martinez exited her classroom after teaching a course on constitutional law she was met by hundreds of students dressed in black wearing face masks emblazoned with the words "Counter-speech is free speech." The students lined the halls of the law school, creating a corridor of protest for her to walk through.

In the wake of the event, Martinez wrote a long memo to the Stanford Law community in which she argued that "our commitment to diversity and inclusion means that we *must* protect the expression of all views." She noted that Stanford's Statement on Academic Freedom declares, "Expression of the widest range of viewpoints should be encouraged, free from institutional orthodoxy and from internal or external coercion," adding that while protests are often protected by the First Amendment, free speech "does not give protestors a 'heckler's veto'" whereby they are entitled to shout down others. In meeting rooms of the sort reserved for this event, attendees have a right to hold signs and demonstrate disagreement with the speaker as long as the methods used do not "prevent or disrupt the effective carrying out of a University function or approved activity." The protesters, she added, should recognize that "the Federalist Society has the same rights of free association that other student organizations at the law school have."

Dean Martinez explained that while "enforcement of university policies against disruption of speakers is necessary to ensure the expression of a wide range of viewpoints," in this case the administrator responsible for helping to restore order inappropriately "insert[ed] themselves into debate with their own criticism of the speaker's views and the suggestion that the speaker reconsider whether what they plan to say is worth saying. . . . The failure by administrators in the room to timely administer clear and specific warnings and instead to send conflicting signals about whether what was happening was acceptable or not . . . is part of what created the problem in the room and renders disciplinary sanction in these particular circumstances problematic." The lesson for the school was that "a more detailed and explicit policy with clear protocols for dealing with disruptions would better protect the rights of speakers and also those who wish to exercise their right to protest within permissible bound."

Importantly, Martinez also explained that law students in particular must be trained to prepare them "to go out into and act as effective advocates in a society that disagrees about many important issues" with the understanding that "their job is to make arguments on behalf of clients whose very lives may depend on their professional skill [to] confront injustice or views they don't agree with and respond as attorneys."[5]

In July 2023, Martinez announced that Associate Dean Steinbach would leave her role "to pursue another opportunity."

University of North Texas.[6] In March 2022, Young Conservatives of Texas organized an event with Jeff Younger, a candidate for the Texas House who is opposed to gender-affirming care for trans children and has advocated criminalizing sex-reassignment surgery for minors. During the event, dozens of protesters banged on desks and shouted and cursed at Younger. A few hundred protesters stood outside the building chanting, "Protect trans kids." Younger encouraged the protesters, clapping and yelling, "Come on, Communists. Let's go, Commies." The scene grew so raucous that police escorted Younger and Kelly Neidert, chairman emeritus of the university's branch of Young Conservatives of Texas, out of the building and into a police car. Protesters then surrounded the police vehicles in an attempt to block them from exiting. University president Neal Smatresk later sent out a campus-wide email reminding students of the school's free speech policies and extending support to trans members of the university community.

University of New Mexico.[7] In September 2022, Turning Point USA invited Tomi Lahren, a conservative political commentator, to speak on campus. Prior to the event, over one hundred students gathered outside the Student Union chanting, "We don't want you here" and "Shut it down." Protesters then approached the ballroom where Lahren was speaking and proceeded to yell and bang on walls. They held up signs saying, "UNM has no room for racists" and "Fuck white supremacy." University administrators and police barricaded the door to keep the protesters away. Lahren was able to finish her speech, but before the Q&A was completed, police officers escorted her away after protesters knocked a hole in a nearby wall and someone pulled a fire alarm.

In a campus-wide message the following day, the university, in an unsigned statement, clarified that "allowing speakers invited by a student organization on campus in no way implies an endorsement of the content of their speeches or their opinions" and urged those who disagreed with the speaker "to respectfully voice their perspectives." The statement also condemned "the actions of those individuals who intentionally chose to disrupt a scheduled speaker and infringed upon the rights of the speaker and those who attended the event to listen and engage, vandalized University property and unlawfully pulled a fire alarm."[8]

Pennsylvania State University.[9] Uncensored America organized an event, scheduled for October 2022, featuring Proud Boys founder Gavin McInnes. It was billed as a "provocative comedy night" called "Stand Back & Stand By." Prior to the event, opposing groups of protesters gathered outside the building where McInnes was to speak. Violence ensued after Alex Stein, another far-right figure, walked through, taunted the crowd, and recorded their response. Brawls broke out among the protesters, some of whom used pepper spray against one another and the police. A line of police in riot gear approached the demonstrators in an effort to break up the protest, but they were unsuccessful. Eventually the university police department canceled the event, citing "the threat of escalating violence." Penn State president Neeli Bendapudi later commented that "the message too many people will walk away with is that one can manipulate people to generate free publicity, or that one can restrict speech by escalating protest to violence. These are not ideas that we can endorse as an institution of higher education."

University of California, Davis.[10] On March 14, 2023, Turning Point USA invited Charlie Kirk, a conservative commentator, to speak. In a video released prior to the event, UC Davis chancellor Gary May described Kirk as "a well-documented proponent of misinformation and hate . . . who has advocated for violence against transgender individuals," prompting Kirk to threaten to sue him for defamation. Approximately one hundred protesters gathered outside the University Credit Union Center, blocking the main event entrance and at times the pathway to the entrance. They reportedly threw eggs and other objects, pepper-sprayed others in the crowd, and some broke ten glass panes in the doors to the entrance. One police officer was injured when someone jumped on him from behind and pushed him to the ground, and two protesters were arrested for graffiti. At least one of the two people arrested was not affiliated with UC Davis. The event proceeded without cancellation.

University of Iowa.[11] In April 2023, Young Americans for Freedom hosted a screening of Matt Walsh's anti-trans documentary *What Is a Woman?* with Walsh in attendance. The documentary claims to "question the logic behind a gender ideology movement that has taken aim at women and children." University police were present throughout the day, inside and outside of the University of Iowa's Memorial Union. Shortly before the event began, protesters entered the building chanting, "Love is love," "Protect trans kids," and "Trans rights are human rights." They shouted at students who were standing in line for the event, filled the hallway with marbles for attendees to trip over, and attempted to block one of the few exits. Once the doors were closed on the auditorium where the movie was to be shown, police escorted the protesters outside, where the demonstration continued. Over two hundred people shouted, "Hey hey, ho ho, these fascists have got to go!" for approximately two hours. The protesters also marched around a nearby intersection, at times blocking traffic.

University of California, Berkeley.[12] On February 26, 2024, Ran Bar-Yoshafat, a member of the Israeli military who frequently speaks on Israel's behalf, was scheduled to speak on the Berkeley campus. But hundreds of pro-Palestinian protesters, who had been urged on social media by the group "Bears for Palestine" to "shut it down," blocked the venue, smashed windows and, according to some accounts, physically attacked students who had come to hear Bar-Yoshafat. Campus security attempted to move the speaker to a different venue, but the university police decided to evacuate that space and cancel the event, saying that they could not guarantee students' safety in light of the number of demonstrators and the threat of violence. In a joint statement the following day, three student groups—Bears for Israel, Students Supporting Israel, and Berkeley Tikvah—called the demonstration "an appalling display of antisemitism, violence and intolerance resulting in violations of our First Amendment."

University officials called the incident "appalling" and "an attack on the fundamental values of the university." Berkeley's chancellor and provost wrote in a statement, "We deeply respect the right to protest as intrinsic to the value of a democracy at an institution of higher education. Yet, we cannot ignore protest activity that interferes with the rights of others to hear and/or express perspectives of their choosing. We cannot allow the use or threat of force to violate the First Amendment rights of a speaker."

Some of these events attracted national media attention; others did not. We could easily describe many more, but these are enough to allow us to offer thoughts. How should campuses address such situations?

1. Campus policies with regard to speakers and major events that might attract large audiences or crowds must be well established and

clear to the community. They must also be viewpoint-neutral and subject-matter neutral. The Supreme Court has frequently declared that the very core of the First Amendment is that the government cannot regulate speech based on its content. In *Police Department of Chicago v. Mosley,* for example, the Court said: "Above all else, the First Amendment means that government has no power to restrict expression because of its message, its ideas, its subject matter or its content."[13] In countless First Amendment cases, the Court has invoked the content-based/content-neutral distinction as the basis for its decisions. It has declared that "content-based regulations are presumptively invalid."[14] In *Turner Broadcasting System v. Federal Communications Commission,* the Court explained that "government action that stifles speech on account of its message, or that requires the utterance of a particular message favored by the Government, contravenes this essential [First Amendment] right."[15]

It is thus crucial not only that campus policies with regard to speakers be content-neutral, but that they be administered in a content-neutral manner. A campus cannot treat conservative speakers differently from liberal ones, or pro-Palestinian demonstrators differently from pro-Israel ones. Canceling a speaker because of his or her viewpoint is inconsistent with this basic obligation. For example, in fall 2021, Dorian Abbott, a professor of geophysics at the University of Chicago, was invited to deliver the prestigious John Carlson lecture at MIT on the subject of climate and the potential for extraterrestrial life.[16] Professor Abbott is an outspoken critic of diversity initiatives, and his speaking invitation was canceled "in order," he was told, "to avoid controversy." He was accorded another invitation to present his work at MIT, but without the prestige or public aspect of the Carlson lecture. The chair of the department that hosted the Carlson lecture said, "We felt that with the current distractions we would not be in a position to hold an effective outreach event."[17] Canceling a speaker in this situation is inconsistent with a university's commitment to freedom of speech. In this instance, the scheduled speech was canceled not because of what Abbott was going to talk about at MIT, but because of other things he had said on unrelated issues.

2. These cases illustrate the necessity for campuses to clearly articulate their time, place, and manner restrictions with regard to speech. Courts tend to defer to campus officials so long as the rules are content-neutral and administered in a content-neutral manner. For the most part, courts treat campus venues as "limited public forums" within the meaning of the First Amendment.[18] Restrictions of speech in a limited public forum must be both viewpoint-neutral and "reasonable in light of the purpose served by the forum."[19] Reasonableness requires that (1) the restriction be consistent with the purpose of the forum, and (2) the exclusions be based on "definite and objective" standards.[20]

To the greatest degree possible, campus policies governing speakers, events, and protests should be designed both to facilitate speech rights and to prevent violence and disruption. There is not a First Amendment right to use any government property for any speech at any time; therefore, these events may be regulated. Most obviously, campuses can prohibit demonstrations in or near classroom buildings while classes are in session. They can also regulate speech in or near dormitories to protect students' ability to study and sleep.

Campuses can determine where events will be held so long as they do so in a content-neutral manner. For example, in *Young America's Foundation v. Kaler,* the United States Court of Appeals for the Eighth Circuit found no violation of the First Amendment when the University of Minnesota Twin Cities' administrators allowed conservative commentator Ben Shapiro to speak but denied him the large venue he wanted, requiring that he speak in a smaller auditorium.[21] In *Young America's Foundation v. Napolitano,* a federal district court upheld

UC Berkeley's relevant policies—titled the High-Profile Speaker Policy and the Major Events Hosted by Non-Departmental Users Policy—which allowed the campus to restrict speakers if "authorized campus officials determine that the event has a substantial likelihood of interfering with other campus functions or activities."[22] When Shapiro came to speak at Berkeley in 2017, campus officials said that he could speak in the largest auditorium on campus at 7:00 p.m., but not the open area of the campus during the daytime. Using an auditorium allowed for better security, including metal detectors for those entering, while still giving him an opportunity to address a large audience.

UC Irvine's "Major Events Policy" states as its primary purpose "to facilitate free speech and expression and to ensure safe and successful events." It authorizes campus officials to determine whether an event is likely to affect campus safety or services based on the proposed location, the estimated number of attendees, the proximity to other activities or locations, the resources needed to provide adequate security, and any objective and credible evidence regarding disruption or threats to safety. Event planners are expected, whenever possible, to notify the university of the event so that campus police and administrators can make security recommendations to minimize risks and maximize the chance for a successful result.[23]

Following these approaches, campuses should do all they can to ensure that events can move forward safely, but there are times when that may not be possible because of poor planning or unexpected developments. When there is a threat to safety and security, campuses' primary duty is to protect students, staff, and faculty—but this cannot be a pretext for viewpoint discrimination. In January 2017, UC Berkeley officials canceled a speech by Milo Yiannopoulos when the radical group Antifa swarmed the campus with 150 masked and armed agitators, overwhelming the police's ability to keep order. Commercial-grade fireworks and rocks were thrown at police, Molotov cocktails were hurled, and fires were set near the campus book-store and at the construction site of a new dorm. The event was canceled. Doing this, of course, should be a last resort, but there is a point at which safety cannot be maintained any other way. There was no indication that the cancellation was done to stop Yiannopoulos from speaking because of his views.

3. If there are security fees for speakers, the law is well established that campus officials cannot have discretion to set the amount. This discretion inherently risks viewpoint discrimination.

The costs of campus security can be high. In fall 2017, when a student group at UC Berkeley, the Patriots, invited several conserva-tive speakers, the cost to the campus was over $4 million. No courts have yet addressed whether campuses may prevent speakers because they cannot afford, or do not wish, to pay the security costs. Still, there obviously is a point at which the costs are so great that a campus reasonably can say it is unaffordable, and there is no alternative but to cancel an event. But no court has yet dealt with this issue.

The Supreme Court has decided two major cases concerning fee requirements for speakers, although neither arose in a campus context. In *Cox v. State of New Hampshire,* the Court considered a statute that required organizers to obtain a special license before put-ting on a demonstration in a public forum.[24] The statute authorized municipalities, at their discretion, to charge a permit fee of up to $300 for the "maintenance of public order." A group of Jehovah's Wit-nesses held a demonstration without a license and challenged the stat-ute as unconstitutional.

The Supreme Court upheld the statute, stressing that there was no evidence that the statute was administered in a discriminatory manner. The Court declared: "The authority of a municipality to im-pose regulations in order to assure the safety and convenience of the people in the use of public highways has never been regarded as inconsistent with civil liberties but rather as a means of safeguarding the good order upon which they ultimately depend."[25]

The municipality, the Court went on, did not have to charge a flat fee to all applicants, because a flat fee fails to take into account the difficulty of framing a fair schedule to meet all circumstances. "We perceive no constitutional ground," the Court wrote, "for denying to local governments that flexibility of adjustment of fees which in the light of varying conditions would tend to conserve rather than impair the liberty sought."[26]

There is some tension between *Cox* and the Supreme Court's other decision in the area, *Nationalist Movement v. Forsyth County.*[27] In that case the Court invalidated an ordinance that required a permit for a demonstration to occur and that allowed government officials to charge a permit fee of up to $1,000. The licensing law was impermissible, the Court ruled, because "there are no articulated standards either in the ordinance or in the county's established practice. The administrator is not required to rely on any objective factors. He need not provide any explanation for his decision, and that decision is unreviewable."[28] The Court concluded that "nothing in the law or its application prevents the official from encouraging some views and discouraging others through the arbitrary application of the fees. The First Amendment prohibits the vesting of such unbridled discretion in a government official."[29] *Nationalist Movement* did not declare unconstitutional all permit fee requirements; it simply held that such charges are unconstitutional if government officials have discretion as to the amount. In that way, the Court's decision in *Nationalist Movement* is consistent with *Cox v. New Hampshire: Cox* says that permit fee requirements are allowed, but *Nationalist Movement* means that government officials cannot have discretion in setting the amount of the fee in particular instances.

The lower courts have applied this distinction to campuses. In *College Republicans of University of Washington v. Cauce,* a federal court found that the university violated the First Amendment in charging the College Republicans a $17,000 fee as reimbursement for security costs. Relying on *Nationalist Movement,* the court explained that the policy gave administrators inappropriately broad discretion to determine how much to charge student organizations for enhanced security or whether to charge them at all.[30]

Professor Erica Goldberg, in a law review article, identified neutral criteria that universities may consider when assessing security fees, including the size of the audience, whether tickets are being sold, the type of auditorium used, and whether the event is open to the public.[31] She asserts that administrators can charge student organizations different amounts for security costs, even if this has a disproportionate effect on certain types of speech, so long as they use neutral, objective criteria and do not intend to burden unpopular or controversial views. University policies should include the following elements: (1) content-neutral standards for determining security fees, (2) explicit guidelines on how those fees are determined, and (3) a transparent process for student groups to appeal fees that are larger than usual.

UC Irvine's Major Events Policy distinguishes between "Basic Event Security" costs, based on neutral criteria, and "Extraordinary Event Security" arising from a determination that additional security is necessary because of likely protests. The former costs are assigned to the sponsors, but the latter are covered by the university to ensure that fees do not change "based on concerns that the content of the event or the viewpoints, opinions or anticipated expression of the Clients, event performers or others participating in the event might provoke disturbances or response costs required by such disturbances."

4. There is no First Amendment right to shout down or silence other speakers. Institutions can punish such behavior without violating the Constitution.

Many of the incidents we described above involve students attempting to shout down or otherwise silence speakers with whom they disagree. The First Amendment does not contain a "heckler's veto," and if it is allowed, the only speech that will occur is that which no one cares enough about to shout down. On any controversial issue, each side can shout down the other side's speakers. Such silencing is particularly troubling on college campuses, which should be places where all ideas and views can be expressed.

The case law supports this view.[32] As the California Supreme Court stated, "The state retains a legitimate concern in ensuring that some individuals' unruly assertion of their rights of free expression does not imperil other citizens' rights of free association and discussion."[33]

One of the most famous examples involved UC Irvine.[34] On February 8, 2010, Michael Oren, then Israeli ambassador to the United States, was speaking in a large auditorium on campus. Soon after he began, a student stood up and shouted, "Michael Oren, propagating murder is not free speech." The student was escorted out, but each time Oren began to speak, another disruption occurred. The disruptors shouted things like "Michael Oren, you are a war criminal," and "It's a shame this University has sponsored a mass murderer like yourself!" After each statement, the disruptor was escorted out. Eleven protesters, in sequence, disrupted Oren's speech. Ultimately, all left and Oren delivered his address.

The campus brought disciplinary proceedings against the students, the results of which are confidential, and the district attorney of Orange County brought criminal charges against them (earning them the nickname "the Irvine 11") for violating a California law that makes it a crime to disrupt a public meeting. Their free speech defense was rejected by the trial court and they were convicted.

Although we seriously question the desirability of using criminal law in such a situation, the case affirms that there is no First Amendment right to shout others down. Nor, however, does it mean that students must be silent in the face of speakers they find offensive. As administrators, we encourage students to engage in peaceful protests that are not disruptive, and to invite their own speakers in response to those they deem objectionable.

Even when campuses have clear, viewpoint-neutral anti-disruption policies, there are many issues to work through. UC Irvine's "Guidance concerning Disruption of University Activities" describes with some care how the campus can prevent and will respond to disruption of university activities in real time. The policy enumerates eleven factors weighing in favor of a finding that conduct is a disruption, including whether it is violent, incites an immediate breach of the peace, causes physical harm, is intentionally aimed at unduly interfering with an activity, lasts long enough to unduly interfere, or continues after a request to end it is made. The policy also provides examples of conduct that would not be considered disruptive (such as holding a small sign in front of one's body, wearing clothing with words or images, turning one's back on a speaker, or silently kneeling) and conduct likely to be considered disruptive (such as blocking the audience's view, producing loud noises that prevent speakers from being heard, and setting off alarms or turning off lights).

Importantly, the policy also provides direction to organizers and campus officials on how to anticipate and respond to a possible disruption. When there is a concern about a disruption, the organizers are given a script to follow indicating that disagreement with a speaker is welcome so long as it does not unduly interfere with the speaker's ability to communicate with the audience, and that a protester whose actions interfere will be warned and, if the disruption continues, will be held accountable under university policies. Similar directions are provided if a disruptive protest takes place. The importance of clear policies and advance planning were evident in several of the cases discussed earlier, especially the incident at Stanford Law, after which the dean acknowledged that the preexisting policies had not been made sufficiently clear and that this prevented the campus from sanctioning people who violated them.[35]

Encampments and Protests

In the spring of 2024, students on many campuses constructed encampments to protest Israel's actions in Gaza, support Palestinians, advocate against Zionism and the continued existence of Israel as a Jewish state, and demand disclosure and divestment of their institutions' financial ties to Israel and weapons manufacturers. Universities varied in how they dealt with these.[36]

Many experienced campus presidents and chancellors have told us that responding to protesters' efforts to take control of university spaces was one of the most challenging problems they have ever had to manage. Virtually all campuses had rules against setting up encampments, but it was unclear whether these rules should be enforced through the ordinary student conduct process or by using police even when an encampment seemed to pose no threat to campus safety. Should it depend on how large the encampments grew? How well fortified? Whether items were being gathered that could be used as weapons? Whether surrounding police jurisdictions were willing to give "mutual aid" if matters could not be handled by campus police?

Also, how should one weigh competing considerations when protesters avoided direct violence but created spaces that excluded campus members who did not agree with their views? When participants were masked, how could campuses assess whether the protesters were students or nonaffiliated community members (and possibly well-trained community activists)? Should administrators attempt some form of negotiation before calling in police? Does it depend on the nature of the demands, or perhaps on how long the negotiations might take?

Presidents and chancellors confronted a wide variety of specific circumstances and, as always, had to respect both the campus climate and the regional or state political environment. Some quickly called on the police to clear the encampments. Others allowed the encampments to remain without incident. Some allowed them to remain until violence erupted or buildings were occupied. Widespread encampments and protests largely disappeared once students left campuses for the summer.

Columbia University seems to have been ground zero for the encampments in April 2024.[37] On April 17, hundreds of protesters occupied the South Lawn, calling for Columbia's divestment from companies with ties to Israel. That was the day Columbia University president Minouche Shafik testified before Congress on her university's handling of antisemitism on campus. The next day, April 18, she authorized the New York Police Department to clear away the "Gaza Solidarity Encampment." Protesters were arrested and students were suspended. Another encampment was soon constructed, and in the early morning hours of Tuesday, April 30, dozens of protesters occupied Hamilton Hall. The encampment spread to other areas of the campus.

Hundreds of NYPD officers entered the campus that evening, taking down the encampment and arresting dozens of protesters both inside and outside Hamilton Hall. The police later confirmed the arrest of 109 individuals.

On May 31, a new encampment was constructed at Columbia and was quickly cleared by the police.[38] But the precedent established on April 17 of erecting encampments quickly spread around the country. By April 24 more than a dozen campuses had encampments, including Emerson College, MIT, Tufts, Yale, NYU, and UC Berkeley.

Washington University in St. Louis shut down an attempt to build an encampment before it got off the ground.

Police at Yale arrested forty-five protesters, and the university canceled classes for a period of time. The president explained that many protesters left the encampment voluntarily when given the opportunity, but others refused. Campus officials described them as "defying the directives of university officials, staying in campus spaces past allowed times, and [committing] other acts that violate university policies and guidelines [and] create safety hazards and impede the work of the university. . . . Yale will pursue disciplinary actions according to its policies." NYU arrested 120 people, both faculty and students, outside the Stern School of Business after professors encircled a small encampment in an effort to protect students from arrest. A university spokesperson explained that "we witnessed disorderly, disruptive, and antagonizing behavior that has interfered with the safety and security of our community."[39] The University of Florida used police to break up a five-day-old encampment; they arrested nine people, seven of whom were students. Declaring that the campus was "not a daycare," the university said that protesters had been warned over many days of the consequences of violating university rules.[40]

On April 25, Pro-Palestinian students at Northwestern University set up an encampment in a large open area, Deering Meadow, in the middle of the campus. In negotiations with campus officials, an agreement was reached after four days. The encampment was taken down, except for one tent, in exchange for university leaders' promising to answer questions from students and faculty members about Northwestern's investments, establish an affinity space for Middle Eastern and North African students, and pay to educate five Palestinian undergraduates.[41] The Midwest chapter of the Anti-Defamation League and two other Jewish organizations issued a press release labeling the deal "reprehensible and dangerous" and calling for the president's resignation. A university spokesperson said the president was "proud" that the university had achieved "what has been a challenge across the country—a sustainable de-escalated path forward, one that prioritizes safety, safety for all of our students."[42] Encampments at Brown University, UC Riverside, and Rutgers also ended after negotiations that were met with varying degrees of criticism about some of the terms.[43]

On Monday, April 25, pro-Palestinian demonstrators created an encampment at UCLA in an open area between Royce Hall and Powell Library. A counterprotest began a few days later. The situation was essentially nonviolent, but over the next few days the encampment grew significantly, strongly fortified with wooden pallets and other barricades. Helmets and material that could be used as weapons also proliferated within the encampment, underscoring the impression that the protesters were claiming this part of the campus as their territory— and planning to defend it. Protesters also occasionally used metal gates and human walls to control access to campus walkways and entrances. Videos circulated on social media of Jewish students being denied access to places that were normally considered open spaces for all UCLA students.

After five days of growing tension and counterdemonstrations— with counterprotesters constructing stages, large screens, and loudspeakers near the encampment—UCLA declared the encampment unlawful and directed those within it to leave or face discipline. Later that night, the encampment was attacked by a violent mob of sixty pro-Israel demonstrators. The few police officers on duty were quickly overwhelmed, and the violence continued for three hours. UCLA then called in the police to dismantle the encampment. More than 250 California Highway Patrol officers, supported by officers from the Los Angeles Police Department and the Los Angeles County Sheriff's Department, systematically dismantled the barricades and tents and pushed out protesters, arresting more than two hundred people. The chancellor acknowledged that the community was in "deep pain" after the incidents and explained that despite an initial desire to support students and free expression, "ultimately, the site became a focal point for serious violence as well as a huge disruption to our campus."[44]

At Dartmouth in the early evening hours of May 1, students erected tents surrounded by more than a hundred supporters who linked arms. After warning the protesters to leave, campus safety officials turned the situation over to the Hanover Police Department, the New Hampshire State Police, and other local agencies. Arrests began before 9:00 p.m. Eighty-nine people were arrested, including two faculty members, one of whom was knocked to the ground as she tried to grab her phone from a police officer. After the arrests, Dartmouth's president said that taking over the campus's common spaces is "exclusionary at best and, at its worst, as we have seen on other campuses in recent days, can turn quickly into hateful intimidation where Jewish students feel unsafe." The executive director of Dartmouth's chapter of Chabad applauded what she called a "very principled stand." Some faculty members said that "sending the police on protesters is the exact opposite of engaging each other in good faith." A few weeks later, the Faculty of Arts and Sciences adopted a motion to censure the president by a vote of 183-163. The chair of the board of trustees responded, "The board unequivocally and unanimously supports President Beilock."[45]

On April 29, one of us (Gillman) was faced with an encampment at UC Irvine, established in the early morning by approximately fifty people on a plaza near science research buildings and a science lecture hall. Because the participants were masked, it was at first impossible to identify them, or to know how many were students and how many might be from the surrounding community. The campus immediately reached out to inform the protesters that the encampment violated its policies and offered to work with students in the encampment to find a space in a mutually agreeable location, but they declined.

By that evening the number of people in the encampment had decreased and the protesters took up a relatively small space of the plaza. Campus leaders had seen how UCLA's encampment had grown larger and more fortified, becoming a magnet for counterdemonstrators, but that had not yet happened at UC Irvine. We administrators believed we needed to enforce our policies, since if we did not, it would later be nearly impossible to stop others from establishing encampments in support of other causes—time, place, and manner restrictions must be applied in a viewpoint-neutral way. The only question was whether we would enforce university regulations using police or through the university's normal administrative processes. Since we do not normally enforce violations of university regulations with sworn officers, we decided to focus on our ordinary administrative options. We explained to the campus that police would not be used if the protesters acted to ensure "that the encampment remains peaceful and minimally disruptive of university activities, that it is relatively small, that there have been no efforts at building out 'fortifications' or amassing material that could be used as weapons, and that there appears to [be] no conduct that violates the rights of any other member of the campus community to have an equal educational experience free from discrimination and harassment."[46]

We could not negotiate a quick settlement. Protesters changed their demands, adding some that challenged the core values of the institution, including the academic freedom rights of faculty and the free speech rights of students. For example, they demanded restrictions on programs about Israel and antisemitism that might express views that conflicted with the opinions of the protesters. The campus message also reiterated that "just as we have consistently safeguarded the right to express all viewpoints on our campus, we remain committed to preventing any actions that may silence or intimidate those with differing opinions. Individuals on our campus will continue to have the freedom to express their support of Zionism, their allegiance to the State of Israel, and their concerns regarding antisemitism. Academic programs and centers dedicated to Jewish Studies, Israel Studies, and Antisemitism Studies will continue their work under the principles of academic freedom. . . . Embracing a range of perspectives is fundamental to our identity as an institution of higher education in a free society. It underscores the principle that all members of our diverse community are entitled to participate fully in the vital activities of this university."

Because the UC Irvine encampment, while distressing to many students, never got much larger or more disruptive and did not become a magnet for violent counterdemonstrations like those at UCLA, it was allowed to persist, with student conduct sanctions imposed on identified participants who had violated campus rules. Then, after seventeen days of relative calm, the protesters used social media to gather large numbers of community members to the site, suddenly dismantled the barricades of their encampment, and used them to "liberate" a nearby science lecture hall.

At that point, the protesters were directly assaulting the rights of other students to their education. Because the number of students and community members participating in this takeover overwhelmed the capacity of our student affairs professionals and campus police to resolve the situation, we administrators decided to call in aid. Large numbers of regional police came to the campus. An unlawful assembly was declared, and within a few hours the takeover was ended. Everyone who wanted to avoid arrest was allowed to leave the scene. Still, forty-seven people were arrested, including twenty-six students, two faculty members, and ten who were not affiliated with the university.[47] Despite the campus's restraint toward the encampment, and despite our belief that reclaiming a major lecture hall on behalf of our faculty and students was not only well justified but imperative for protecting the university's core mission, the use of police was deeply distressful to the campus. A no-confidence vote against the chancellor was defeated by the Academic Senate, but it did receive a significant plurality of support.

These are just a few of that spring's many incidents. One summary said: "During the spring 2024 academic term, college students set up roughly 121 protest encampments at 117 universities. Approximately 18% of these encampments ended with the university agreeing to at least some of the protesting students' demands. Half (50%) were forcibly disbanded by local or campus authorities."[48]

When chancellors and presidents faced criticism for enforcing anti-encampment rules and other campus policies, the argument (from protesters or their allies) was often that the encampments were "free speech," and efforts to end them amounted to the silencing of legitimate protest. So let us start with the basics. As a matter of law, does the enforcement of viewpoint-neutral time, place, and manner restrictions violate free speech rights?

To state the question is to answer it. As we have already shown, the right to express any viewpoint one wishes without punishment does not imply a right to say whatever one wants at whatever time and in whatever manner. States, municipalities, and campuses can enforce reasonable time, place, and manner restrictions as long as they are enforced in a viewpoint-neutral way. No one—including those who defended the encampments as "free speech"—actually thinks that free speech principles allow any group of people, associated with a campus or not, to simply set up a space on a campus and claim the right to decide who can enter the space and who cannot. As a matter of law, campuses clearly had the right to prohibit encampments on campus property, and therefore to clear such encampments if they wished to do so. Beyond that, some of what occurred, such as occupying buildings and acts of vandalism, violated the law and obviously can be punished.

The Supreme Court has explicitly held that the government can prohibit camping on public property as a form of expression. In *Clark v. Community for Creative Non-Violence,* the Court approved a federal regulation and Park Service decision to keep a group protesting the plight of the homeless from sleeping in Lafayette Park and the Mall in Washington, D.C.[49] The National Park Service allowed the Community for Creative Non-Violence to erect a tent city there as a symbolic protest, but it refused to allow the demonstrators to sleep in the tents because of a regulation prohibiting camping in these parks. The Supreme Court accepted the contention that overnight sleeping as a part of this protest was a form of expressive conduct, but it upheld the regulation as a reasonable time, place, and manner restriction. It emphasized that the restriction was content-neutral, that it served the important purpose of preserving the parks' attractiveness, and that it left adequate alternative ways for protesters to express their message.

The choices for campus administrators concerning encampments are thus less about the law than about what is practically and politically desirable. Campuses may lawfully order that encampments be ended, use law enforcement to accomplish this, and arrest and discipline those who disregard the orders. The question for campus administrators is not what the First Amendment allows but what action is best for the university community. Likewise, those who disrupt commencements can certainly be removed and punished, but the question is whether and when this is desirable.

Some argue that ending encampments, building takeovers, or disruptive activities violates "free speech" not because the First Amendment protects these activities as a matter of law but because the tradition of protest, especially on college campuses, contemplates that protesters will (and even should) create some amount of disturbance or discomfort for authorities. The view, as the *Michigan Daily* put it, is that "protests are only meaningful when they are disruptive. . . . Acting like the protesters are doing something 'wrong' because of their disruptiveness completely misses the purpose of protest in general. . . . The protesters want to hold their institutions accountable. To seek permission to protest from those same institutions would be illogical." Moreover, "Using state-enforced violence to get rid of these protesters is nefarious because these protests, while disruptive, have generally been peaceful."[50] Among those who support student protests, the proper question is not whether they technically violate campus regulations but whether they are (in the eyes of these advocates) "peaceful."[51]

If protesters are to be permitted to violate any university regulation without sanction as long as they are not using violence, then campuses would be prevented from enforcing any of their time, place, and manner restrictions. These restrictions, however, are almost all designed to protect the institution's ability to perform its mission of research and learning, and to protect the rights of all faculty, staff, and students to perform their roles in advancing that mission.

If a group of protesters enters a classroom during instruction and uses bullhorns to shout slogans, they could be described as "peaceful," but their actions would violate the rights and privileges of faculty members and other students. Encampments that physically disrupt students' access to the common spaces of the campus might be "nonviolent," but they have negative consequences for others. The unauthorized use of amplified sound can prevent research and teaching. Columbia professor John McWhorter was teaching a section in his humanities class on the composer John Cage's famous piece *4'33"*, which directs an audience to listen in silence to surrounding noise for exactly that amount of time. "I had to tell students we could not listen to that piece that afternoon," he wrote in the *New York Times,* "because the surrounding noise would have been not birds or people walking by in the hallway but infuriated chanting from protesters outside the building."[52] At UC Irvine, managing the encampment and related protests cost in excess of $2 million—resources that could have been used to support students and the school's academic mission.[53]

Nevertheless, there are those on campuses who use the language of "peaceful" to argue that campuses should not enforce their policies. As a practical matter, administrators understand that even if the law does not treat rule-breaking disruptive protests as protected speech, some people on campus believe the protests should be allowed to go on. How should campus leaders take this into account?

One thing the law does not allow is selective enforcement of regulations based on the protesters' viewpoints or motives. We think it is self-evident that if encampments were constructed by MAGA mobs, anti-immigrant activists, or pro-life advocates, few of the people currently demanding tolerance of disruptive but "peaceful" activities would take that position.

The fact that rules prohibiting encampments were adopted after the pro-Palestinian encampments in spring 2024 does not, by itself, show that the rules are impermissibly motivated. When a new challenge arises, new rules can be adopted. Under the First Amendment what is crucial is that the rules be strictly content-neutral *and* that they be enforced in a content-neutral manner. The Supreme Court's decision in *Hill v. Colorado* is instructive.[54] The Court upheld a Colorado law that prohibits approaching without consent within eight feet of a person who is within one hundred feet of a health-care facility for purposes of oral protest, education, or counseling. The law was undoubtedly adopted to deal with protests outside abortion clinics. But in upholding the law, Justice Stevens, writing for the Court, emphasized the content neutrality of the law as the basis for upholding it. He quoted the determination by the Colorado Supreme Court that the "restrictions apply equally to all demonstrators, regardless of viewpoint, and the statutory language makes no reference to the content of the speech."[55] So long as the restrictions on encampments are written in a content-neutral manner (and that is true for the rules we have seen, such as for the University of California) and administered in a content-neutral manner, there is no violation of the First Amendment.

The question, therefore, is not whether time, place, and manner regulations should exist and be enforced, but whether this should be done through campus disciplinary procedures or by the police. It is not whether to enforce the rules, but how and when.

We can offer some criteria for campus officials to consider as they decide on their response.

How much is the activity disrupting the campus and its educational and research mission? Some encampments were small or in areas of campus where they did not interfere with its functioning. Others have been large and very disruptive. Some encampments, for example, were positioned where commencement ceremonies were scheduled. They had to be cleared or else commencement—an enormously important event for most students and their families—could not happen. The larger and more disruptive an encampment is, the greater the urgency for its speedy dismantling. Smaller and more isolated ones might be allowed to persist while administrative enforcement approaches work themselves out.

How great is the risk of violence and destruction of property? Campuses have a duty to protect the safety of those in the community. The First Amendment never includes a right to endanger others or destroy property. Where the presence of protesters and counterprotesters creates too great a danger of escalation into violence, campus leaders cannot wait until the violence occurs before taking action. The difficulty for officials is in predicting what is likely to ensue in an inherently volatile situation. After UC San Diego officials witnessed the violent clashes between protesters and counterprotesters at UCLA, the university's chancellor decided to use police to end their encampment before the situation deteriorated.[56]

How much harassment is happening? As we discuss below, schools also have a legal and moral duty to prevent students from being harassed based on their race, religion, ethnicity, sex, or sexual orientation. At some schools, those in the encampments have harassed Jewish students going by or refused to allow them to enter certain areas of the campus. That cannot be tolerated. Encampments at other campuses have not posed this problem.

When Jewish students sued UCLA on the grounds that the encampment prevented them from accessing the campus's ordinary common spaces, a federal judge issued a strongly worded preliminary injunction blasting the university for not addressing those exclusions immediately. His opinion began: "In the year 2024, in the United States of America, in the State of California, in the City of Los Angeles, Jewish students were excluded from portions of the UCLA campus because they refused to denounce their faith. This fact is so unimaginable and so abhorrent to our constitutional guarantee of religious freedom that it bears repeating, Jewish students were excluded from portions of the UCLA campus because they refused to denounce their faith. UCLA does not dispute this. Instead, UCLA claims that it has no responsibility to protect the religious freedom of its Jewish students because the exclusion was engineered by third-party protesters. But under constitutional principles, UCLA may not allow services to some students when UCLA knows that other students are excluded on religious grounds, regardless of who engineered the exclusion."[57]

What have been past practices, and what are the implications for the future? This does involve a basic legal requirement: campuses cannot discriminate among speakers based on their message. If a campus allows protesters in a particular area or manner, it will be obligated to do the same for other protesters in the future. By the same token, the campus cannot accommodate encampments or building takeovers by pro-Palestinian protesters if it has refused similar accommodations to other groups in the past. Consistency is vital, both for legal reasons and to avoid accusations that campuses have a double standard.

What actions will be necessary and what are the likely consequences of taking them? Will the use of police be necessary, and what will be the reaction? There are times when a school has no choice but to use law enforcement to prevent disruption and even violence. But there also are times when the harms of using police outweigh the benefits. These determinations depend on the traditions and culture of the institution and the larger political context within which the campus is embedded. Different campus leaders will inevitably make different judgments, even when faced with identical circumstances, because steps that would be tolerated by most campus stakeholders at one institution may not be tolerated at another. Consistency in enforcement is an empty accomplishment if the result is ever-escalating tension and violence.

That being said, campuses should never shy away from doing what is necessary to protect the rights and interests of those not involved in a particular protest, especially when protest activities or demands are intimidating or marginalizing others on the campus. What some call "putting down a peaceful protest" can sometimes be better described as defending the civil rights of other members of the campus community.

Campus officials must make these judgments knowing that whatever they do, they will be criticized—for not doing enough or for doing too much. Often the criticism will come simultaneously from both sides.

Of course, the law of the First Amendment must be the starting point and it must be adhered to by public universities and by private schools that choose to follow it. But it may be merely the starting point, and we need to think through how to apply it in these enormously difficult circumstances.

The Tension between Title VI and Freedom of Speech

Title VI of the 1964 Civil Rights Act says that recipients of federal funds cannot discriminate on the basis of race, color, or national origin. Virtually every college and university receives federal money and is thus covered by this law. The prohibition of discrimination in Title VI also extends to harassment.

Although Title VI does not prohibit discrimination on the basis of religion, in 2004 the Office of Civil Rights (OCR) of the Department of Education released guidance explaining that religious discrimination could, in some circumstances, overlap with racial or national origin discrimination, bringing it within Title VI and the Department of Education's purview. On November 7, 2023, OCR released a letter explaining how it applies Title VI to claims of religious discrimination, including claims by Jewish, Muslim, and Sikh students. As OCR interprets the law, religious discrimination is illegal under Title VI if it is based on a group's "(i) shared ancestry or ethnic characteristics; or (ii) citizenship or residency in a country with a dominant religion or distinct religious identity." Discrimination may include "ethnic or ancestral slurs"; harassment based on how students "look, dress, or speak in ways linked to ethnicity or ancestry (e.g., skin color, religious attire, language spoken)"; and actions grounded in "stereotype[s] based on perceived shared ancestral or ethnic characteristics."[58] As examples of religious discrimination overlapping with racial or national origin discrimination, OCR cited "Muslim students targeted for wearing a hijab," "Sikh students taunted and called terrorists," and Jewish students targeted with swastikas, Nazi salutes, and Holocaust jokes.

The Supreme Court has not yet ruled on whether this interpretation of Title VI is consistent with the statute. But it has said of a different statute—42 U.S.C. § 1981, which prohibits race discrimination in contracting—that discrimination against Jews and Muslims fits within that law's prohibitions.[59]

The Office of Civil Rights has said that "to establish a violation of Title VI using this analysis, OCR must find that: 1) a hostile environment based on race, color, or national origin existed; 2) the school had actual or constructive notice (i.e., the school knew or should have known) of the hostile environment; and 3) the school failed to take prompt and effective steps reasonably calculated to: i. end the harassment, ii. eliminate any hostile environment and its effects, and iii. prevent the harassment from recurring."[60]

As one court put it, "A Title VI hostile environment claim has five elements: (1) plaintiffs were 'subject to "severe, pervasive, and objectively offensive" . . . harassment'; (2) the harassment 'caused the plaintiff to be deprived of educational opportunities or benefits'; (3) the school 'knew of the harassment'; (4) the harassment occurred 'in [the school's] programs and activities'; and (5) the school 'was deliberately indifferent to the harassment such that its response (or lack thereof) is clearly unreasonable in light of the known circumstances.' "[61]

Under Title VI, administrators must address two crucial questions: What constitutes harassment? And what action is sufficient to meet a school's obligations to avoid liability? At the outset, we must emphasize that the law does not provide a clear answer to either question.

As for the former question, harassment is generally regarded as conduct that is directed at someone or that is sufficiently pervasive as to materially interfere with a student's educational opportunity. The OCR Fact Sheet addresses this as well: Generally, unwelcome conduct based on race, color, or national origin creates a hostile environment under Title VI when, based on the totality of the circumstances, it is: subjectively and objectively offensive; and so severe or pervasive that it limits or denies a person's ability to participate in or benefit from the recipient's education program or activity.

Harassing conduct need not always be targeted at a particular person to create a hostile environment. . . . Additionally, a single victim may experience a hostile environment when the conduct of multiple offenders, taken together, meets the definition above. Whether harassing conduct creates a hostile environment on the basis of race, color, or national origin must be determined based on the totality of the circumstances. Relevant factors for consideration may include, but are not limited to, the context, nature, scope, frequency, duration, and location of the harassment, as well as the identity, number, age, and relationships of the persons involved. Generally, the less pervasive the harassing conduct, the more severe it must be to establish a hostile environment under Title VI.

This definition is in accord with how courts have defined harassment in other contexts, such as employment. The difficulty, both in the workplace and on campuses (and campuses, of course, are workplaces too), is when speech is sufficient to constitute harassment. After October 7, the issue arose as to whether chants such as "From the river to the sea, Palestine will be free," or "We don't want no two state, we want 48" should be deemed harassment. These slogans clearly communicate ideas that are protected by the First Amendment. During the 2023–24 academic year, OCR did not expressly rule on whether they constituted harassment, but in letters to several universities that were under investigation, the organization implied that they created a hostile environment for Jewish students. Writing to Brown University, OCR noted reports of a complaint that a group screened a movie and invited a speaker "that were allegedly anti-Semitic," and also stated in a poster that it held Israel and its allies "unequivocally responsible for all suffering and loss of life, both Israeli and Palestinian." In a part of the letter to the University of Michigan discussing harassing conduct, OCR described protests at the graduation ceremony on May 4, 2024, in which graduates "held Palestinian flags, chanted pro-Palestinian messages and held pro-Palestinian signs."

In fall 2023, Catherine Lhamon, assistant secretary of education for civil rights, said on several occasions that speech protected by the First Amendment can be a basis for finding that there was a hostile environment. This does not mean that a school can or should punish the harassing speech. For public universities, Title VI does not create an exception to the First Amendment. As the OCR fact sheet says, "Nothing in Title VI or regulations implementing it requires or authorizes a school to restrict any rights otherwise protected by the First Amendment. Neither Title VI nor its implementing regulations require schools to enact or enforce codes that punish the exercise of such rights."[62]

Rather than punish speakers, the duty of the campus is to not be "deliberately indifferent" when such speech occurs. The OCR Fact Sheet states: "To redress a hostile environment based on race, color, or national origin, a school has a legal duty to take prompt and effective steps that are reasonably calculated to: (1) end the harassment, (2) eliminate any hostile environment and its effects, and (3) prevent the harassment from recurring. OCR evaluates the appropriateness of the school's responsive action by assessing whether it was reasonable, timely, and effective."[63]

But it is unclear what action will satisfy this requirement. Doing nothing, clearly, is being deliberately indifferent. For example, in *Feminist Majority Foundation v. Hurley,* the United States Court of Appeals for the Fourth Circuit found that the University of Mary Washington—a public university in Virginia—was deliberately indifferent when it did nothing in response to harassment of women students on campus.[64] The case arose when several women students wrote an op-ed in the school newspaper against allowing fraternities on campus, arguing that the presence of fraternities leads to more sexual violence against women.

The authors of the op-ed were then targeted over the social media platform Yik Yak with hundreds of messages, many vile and some threatening. They also experienced harassment on campus. In response to a complaint from the targeted students, a campus official sent an email to all on the campus saying "that nothing could be done, that is, the University had 'no recourse for such cyber bullying.' Instead, she encouraged UMW students to report any threatening online comments to Yik Yak or other platforms where such comments were made."[65]

The students sued under Title IX, a federal civil rights statute providing that "no person . . . shall, on the basis of sex, be excluded from participation in, be denied the benefits of, or be subjected to discrimination under any education program or activity receiving Federal financial assistance." Title IX, like Title VI, also forbids harassment and requires that universities not be deliberately indifferent.

The United States Court of Appeals for the Fourth Circuit rejected the claim that there was nothing that the campus could do, concluding that the university had been deliberately indifferent. "UMW," it explained, "could have exercised control in other ways that might have corrected the hostile environment. For instance, UMW administrators could have more clearly communicated to the student body that the University would not tolerate sexually harassing behavior either in person or online. The University also could have conducted mandatory assemblies to explain and discourage cyber bullying and sex discrimination, and it could have provided anti-sexual harassment training to the entire student body and faculty. In these circumstances, we are satisfied that the Complaint sufficiently alleges UMW's substantial control over the context in which the alleged harassment occurred."[66]

In the spring of 2024, OCR offered some guidance as to what campuses might do to avoid being deemed "deliberately indifferent." Assistant Secretary of Education Catherine Lhamon wrote in a "Dear Colleague" letter in May:

> Schools have a number of tools for responding to a hostile environment—including tools that do not restrict any rights protected by the First Amendment. To meet its obligation, a university can, among other steps, communicate its opposition to stereotypical, derogatory opinions; provide counseling and support for students affected by harassment; or take steps to establish a welcoming and respectful school campus, which could include making clear that the school values, and is determined to fully include in the campus community, students of all races, colors, and national origins.[67]

But what is sufficient, and under what circumstances, remains unclear. There also may be a difference between OCR's idea of "deliberate indifference" and that of a court. For example, in July 2024, a federal district court in Massachusetts found that MIT was not deliberately indifferent in responding to protests that allegedly had created a hostile environment for Jewish students. The court stressed that deliberate indifference is "a stringent standard of fault. [A] claim that an institution could or should have done more does not establish deliberate indifference. Rather, plaintiffs must allege facts showing that MIT's response to the incidents was so lax, so misdirected, or so poorly executed as to be clearly unreasonable under the known circumstances. The test is not to be viewed through the lens of hindsight; instead, the court must consider whether MIT responded in a clearly unreasonable manner based on what it knew at the time." Using this standard, the court rejected the claim that MIT had been deliberately indifferent to antisemitism. It noted the great tensions on campus and stressed that "MIT's evolving and progressively punitive response largely tracked its increasing awareness of the hostility that demonstrators directed at Jewish and Israeli students [and] shows that MIT did not react in a clearly unreasonable manner."[68]

A few weeks later, that same federal judge permitted a lawsuit to proceed against Harvard University on the grounds that Harvard's alleged disregard for antisemitic behavior on its campus might plausibly meet the standard of deliberate indifference. The court noted that some of the Jewish plaintiffs during the spring of 2024 were prevented from entering a study room by demonstrators, were "surrounded and intimidated" by protesters, avoided clothing that might identify them as Jewish, and ceased attending Jewish-sponsored events on campus. There was also evidence that the university had a double standard in enforcing its various policies in ways that skewed against Jewish students. "For example, after student groups protested for two weeks in Caspersen lounge, a common student area in the Harvard Law School, Jewish students asked Harvard deans and administrators if they could also hold a demonstration in the lounge. Only after that request was made did Harvard Law Dean of Students Stephen Ball email the student body that the lounge area is reserved for 'personal or small group study and conversation.' " Even then, Harvard allowed pro-Palestinian protests to continue in the lounge. "Harvard required Chabbad, a campus Hasidic Jewish community center, to remove its Hanukkah menorah from campus each night to prevent it being vandalized, but it provided

24/7 security to PSC's 'Wall of Resistance.' " In sum, "Harvard's reaction [to antisemitic incidents] was, at best, indecisive, vacillating, and at times internally contradictory," and "in many instances, Harvard did not respond at all. . . . The law expects reasonable and proportionate acts by university officials—the standard is not faultless perfection or ultimate success. Liability attaches only when a school's response is 'so lax, so misdirected, or so poorly executed as to be clearly unreasonable under the known circumstances.' "[69]

It may be that OCR is more willing than the courts to reach a finding of deliberate indifference. Different administrations may also put political pressure on OCR to reach certain conclusions or pressure campuses to agree to wide-ranging settlements or risk millions of dollars of federal grant funding. If so, it should be remembered that ever since June 2024, when the Supreme Court overruled the so-called *Chevron* doctrine, courts are no longer required to defer to federal agencies when they interpret ambiguous statutes.[70] This could become important if there is a disagreement between OCR and judges over the meaning of deliberate indifference.

As campuses contemplate how to avoid deliberate indifference, one possible avenue—bias response teams—has been foreclosed by some courts. Over two hundred universities have created bias response teams to handle claims of discriminatory conduct on campus.[71] According to a 2019 review conducted by *Inside Higher Ed,* these teams usually involve representatives from several campus departments and focus on support for impacted students and proactive efforts aimed at reducing incidents of hate or bias. Bias response teams usually do not have the authority to punish students or to impose discipline, although many would engage those who were the subjects of reports in conversations that were characterized as voluntary.[72]

As of this writing, there is a split among the lower courts as to whether such bias response teams violate the First Amendment. In

Speech First, Inc. v. Schlissel, the United States Court of Appeals for the Sixth Circuit found that the University of Michigan's bias response team violated the First Amendment because of its chilling effect on speech.[73] The Court of Appeals for the Fifth Circuit has reached the same conclusion, but the Court of Appeals for the Seventh Circuit has found that bias response teams do not infringe the First Amendment because they do not have the authority to impose sanctions or punishments.[74]

A university's obligation under Title VI can be enforced by OCR and also by the courts. An example of the latter is a suit by the Brandeis Center for Human Rights against UC Berkeley.[75] In August 2022, a student group at Berkeley, Law Students for Justice in Palestine, asked other student groups to adopt a bylaw excluding any speaker who "expressed and continued to hold views or host/sponsor/promote events in support of Zionism, the apartheid state of Israel, and the occupation of Palestine." Nine other student groups in the law school adopted the bylaws, including the Middle Eastern and North African Law Students Association, Law Students of African Descent, Asian Pacific American Law Students Association, Women of Berkeley Law, and the Queer Caucus. Many other students and faculty found this very upsetting. For most Jews, the existence of Israel and Zionism are an important part of Jewish identity, and the bylaw was felt as antisemitism. One of us (Chemerinsky), as dean of the school, wrote a letter to the leaders of all student groups explaining that while their speech rights would be strongly supported, the bylaw was inconsistent with our values as a law school, our commitment that all viewpoints be expressed, and our desire that every student feel equally included in all aspects of the school.

At the same time, for a student group to exclude any speaker on the basis of race, religion, sex, or sexual orientation would violate law school and campus policy as well as state and federal law. Berkeley

Law has an all-comers policy: all student groups, and all events by student groups, must be open to all law students. This practice was approved by the United States Supreme Court in *Christian Legal Society v. Martinez* (2010), which upheld the decision by Hastings College of the Law to decline to recognize the Christian Legal Society as a registered student organization because the group wanted to limit membership to people who held certain religious beliefs. Similarly, in *Alpha Delta Chi v. Reed,* the Court of Appeals for the Ninth Circuit upheld San Diego State University's requirement that registered student organizations not restrict membership "on the basis of race, sex, color, age, religion, national origin, marital status, sexual orientation, physical or mental handicap, ancestry, or medical condition."[76]

Many students and faculty demanded that Berkeley Law adopt a position that student groups cannot exclude speakers based on their viewpoint and that the student groups that adopted the bylaw be punished. But this cannot be reconciled with the First Amendment, or even common sense. Of course student groups can decide what speakers to include based on their views. Obviously, a college Republicans' group could decide to invite only conservative speakers. Requiring student groups to invite speakers whose views they loathe would violate the First Amendment as a form of compelled speech.

Under well-established First Amendment law, a group holding an event may choose speakers based on their views. The Supreme Court's decision in *Hurley v. Irish-American Gay, Lesbian, and Bisexual Group of Boston* is particularly relevant.[77] Every St. Patrick's Day, the Veterans Council, a private organization, puts on a parade in Boston. The Veterans Council refused to allow the Irish-American Gay, Lesbian, and Bisexual Group of Boston to participate in its parade. The group sued in Massachusetts state court based on the state's public accommodations law, which prohibits discrimination by business establishments because of sexual orientation. The Massachusetts Supreme Judicial Court sided with the Irish-American Gay, Lesbian, and Bisexual Group.

The United States Supreme Court unanimously reversed this decision. In an opinion by Justice Souter, the Court said that organizing a parade is an inherently expressive activity and that it violated the First Amendment to force the organizers to include messages that they find inimical to their values. Compelling the Veterans Council to include the Irish-American Gay, Lesbian, and Bisexual Group, Souter wrote, "violates the fundamental rule . . . under the First Amendment, that a speaker has the autonomy to choose the content of his own message.[78] The Veterans Council clearly decided to exclude a message it did not like from the communication it chose to make, and that is enough to invoke its right as a private speaker to shape its expression by speaking on one subject while remaining silent on another."[79]

This ruling establishes that those putting on an event get to decide what viewpoints will be expressed there, including what speakers to include. To force students to invite speakers with views they disdain would be impermissible compelled speech. For this reason, the law school decided that it could not prohibit student groups from adopting the bylaw, or deny funding to groups that did so. By contrast, though, Berkeley Law took the position that the university would not continue to publish law journals that refused to publish authors who supported the existence of Israel or required members to participate in a training by the Law Students for Justice in Palestine. The law school would not allow a viewpoint-based litmus test as a requirement for earning academic credit for participating in such journals. When credit is awarded, the law school is integrally and irreducibly involved in determining that the activity is pedagogically sufficient and appropriate for academic credit, including by setting requirements and appointing a faculty member to determine that each student has done the requisite work.

The controversy over the student group bylaws escalated when, on September 28, 2022, Kenneth L. Marcus, who had been the civil rights chief of the U.S. Department of Education during President Trump's first term, published an opinion column in the *Jewish Journal* titled "Berkeley Develops Jewish-Free Zones." Comparing the bylaw to laws in 1930s Germany that barred Jews from public spaces, he claimed, "Anti-Zionism is flatly antisemitic. . . . The real issue here is discrimination, not speech." Chemerinsky responded in a letter to the *Jewish Journal* pointing out that the article was incredibly misleading, noting that the law school has an "all-comers" policy and "I know of no instance in which this has been violated or there has been any discrimination against Jews. . . . It is important to recognize that law student groups have free speech rights, including to express messages that I and others might find offensive."[80]

That November, two attorneys filed a complaint against Berkeley Law with the Department of Education's Office of Civil Rights, claiming the school had violated Title VI of the Civil Rights Act by failing to take action against Law Students for Justice in Palestine members for their anti-Zionist bylaw. "By discriminating against 'Zionists,' the registered student groups, and by extension UC Berkeley Law School are discriminating against the Jewish community." In December, OCR announced it would open an investigation.[81] A year later the campus was sued by the Louis D. Brandeis Center, a Jewish legal advocacy group that Marcus headed, which reiterated the claim that the bylaws are "tantamount to an exclusion of Jews" since "Zionism is a central tenet of the Jewish faith and a recognition that the Jews are a people with an ancestral heritage rooted in the land of Israel. . . . These bylaws—or any other mechanism—that treat Zionists in an inferior manner to non-Zionists are a guise for anti-Semitism."[82]

In its motion to dismiss the lawsuit, the University of California argued that as a public institution, it must balance "the right of students of all faiths and backgrounds to receive the many benefits of a University of California education, and the foundational constitutional principle that government cannot punish speech due to its viewpoint." The motion pointed out that "aware that these bylaws were perceived by many in the Berkeley Law community to be antisemitic, the University swiftly denounced the policies, expressed support for Jewish students, and explained that the University would not incorporate the bylaws into its own curricular standards and would therefore not grant academic credit for participation in any student organization that adopted the bylaws. Consistent with long-established constitutional principles, the University did not discipline the student organization for their political speech. But Plaintiffs now ask this Court for an unconstitutional order requiring the University to do so."[83]

The lawsuit against Berkeley is predicated on the assumption that exclusion based on being a Zionist does not reflect the ordinary First Amendment right of an organization to choose what viewpoints it will support, but should be considered discrimination against a protected class. If the university allowed a Jewish student organization to declare it would not invite anti-Zionists, could it be sued for being indifferent to anti-Palestinian discrimination? If a student organization founded on anti-abortion principles were to declare that it would not invite pro-abortion speakers, could there be a civil rights claim on the grounds that most women favor abortion rights and the viewpoint restriction is an attempt to discriminate against women speakers? What about a student organization focused on bringing attention to the Armenian genocide? Could the university be sued for discrimination on the basis of (Turkish) nationality? The possible examples are easily produced and endless.

When campuses protect the rights of students and others to express viewpoints, and to denounce or disassociate themselves from viewpoints, they are upholding a fundamental value of a modern university. To implicate the university in the perceived hatefulness or discriminatory nature of the viewpoints being expressed by campus affiliates would invert what it means for an institution to be dedicated to the free expression of all ideas, even ideas the institution or its employees might abhor. There could be no free speech or academic freedom if campuses were held liable for disagreeable or discriminatory opinions expressed by members of the community.

As of September 2025, the Brandeis Center suit against the University of California remains pending in federal district court.

Where does all this leave campuses in dealing with their competing duties under Title VI and the First Amendment? The law is uncertain and still being developed. We offer a few thoughts.

1. Title VI forbids harassment based on race, which has been defined by OCR to include discrimination on the basis of religion against Jews and Muslims and on the basis of ethnic ancestry. Title IX also forbids harassment based on sex—defined by OCR and in many court cases. It is clear that speech can be a basis for harassment, and OCR has taken the position that this can include speech protected by the First Amendment.

We hope that OCR and courts will be restrained in finding that speech expressing a viewpoint by itself can be a basis for determining harassment. The Education Department has previously said that universities may be legally obligated to respond to protected speech that expresses "persistent and pervasive derogatory opinions about a particular ethnic group." But the elaboration of that position in the current context highlights the challenges of imposing liabilities on universities for defending protected speech.

Universities have been advised that statements from protesters such as "From the river to the sea, Palestine will be free" likely create a hostile environment for Jewish students that undermines their equal opportunity to an education and therefore requires investigations and mitigation efforts. But this is speech protected by the First Amendment, and we know that some Muslim, Arab, and Palestinian students also feel threatened by protesters who chant "We stand with Israel." Do those chants also require investigations and mitigation efforts?

It is easy to imagine endless examples of students complaining about a hostile environment as a result of being exposed to protected speech. What should universities do when conservative Christians advocate against transgender rights and transgender students complain that the statements create a hostile environment? Conversely, what about conservative Christians who complain that pro-abortion or pro-trans rights advocates create a hostile environment for them?

The Department of Education during the Biden administration made it clear that universities should not attempt to censor or punish constitutionally protected speech. Instead they should take additional steps, including speaking out against certain viewpoints or reaching out to those who are saying controversial things to discuss the impact they are having on other members of the academic community. But should universities speak out against the statement "We stand with Israel" because some students believe it creates a hostile environment? How do administrators determine which constitutionally protected speech should be publicly denounced and which should not?

2. When there is harassment, Title VI and Title IX require that a campus not be "deliberately indifferent." But it is not clear what action is sufficient to avoid a finding of deliberate indifference. OCR has said explicitly that schools are not required to prohibit or punish speech that is protected by the First Amendment. For public universities, that

would not be an option; Title VI and Title IX do not create an exception to the First Amendment.

From OCR guidance letters and court decisions, it is apparent that doing nothing in response to harassment is deliberate indifference. Several possible courses of action have been identified, including campus officials speaking out against the harassing speech, counseling and support for affected students, educational programs, training, safety and security measures, and bias response teams (which some courts have declared unconstitutional).

In one sense, the issues universities face regarding speech on campus are not new. There always have been controversial speakers at universities, and campus protests have a long history. Yet the context is different. Students as well as faculty seem more divided than ever before. Many have compared the current protests to those during the Vietnam War. But in the 1960s and the 1970s, our perception is that students on most campuses were unified. (We recognize that we may be too readily generalizing from our own experiences and perceptions.) Now there is a deep, seemly intractable division between those who believe Israel should not exist and those who believe its existence is essential—positions that are closely tied to many students' and faculty members' identities, including their religion and ethnicity. And everything that occurs is immediately visible to all over social media.

The Trump administration in its first months cut off funds to campuses, including Columbia, Harvard, Princeton, Cornell, and Northwestern, allegedly because of antisemitism on those campuses. In these actions, it did not follow the law requiring notice, hearing, finding of facts, and advance notice to both houses of Congress before the cutoff of funds. There was no finding of "deliberate indifference" as required by federal law. Nor was the cutoff of funds limited to specific programs found to violate Title VI, as required by law. Some universities challenged the illegal cutoff of funds. All of this adds enormous uncertainty for campus officials in knowing what it is they must do to avoid Title VI sanctions. Indeed, the Trump administration cutting off funds to universities because of constitutionally protected speech that occurred on their campuses should be deemed to violate the First Amendment.

In such divisive times, the issues of speech on campus are, to say the obvious, enormously difficult. But the basic principles remain the same: universities must be places where all ideas and views can be expressed; campuses may have time, place, and manner restrictions with regard to speech so long as they are content-neutral and leave adequate alternative places; campuses cannot be deliberately indifferent when harassment occurs.

2

Speech in Professional Academic Settings

When outside speakers come to campus and create tumult, or when protests occur in campus spaces, the activities sometimes distract us from what should otherwise be the temperate and respectful enterprise of scholarly inquiry and education. But universities cannot blame intruders or protesters for controversies arising from statements made by professors and students in teaching settings, by academic departments, or by officially recognized student groups.

Many of these on-campus dynamics are not governed by the hurly-burly free speech norms available to most citizens, but rather by the professional rights and privileges of faculty members and other scholars under the concept of "academic freedom." The basic tenets of the concept are easily summarized: consistent with professional competence and ethics, professors are entitled to full freedom in research and in the publication of results, freedom in the classroom to teach and discuss the topics in which they have professional expertise, and freedom to convey their knowledge and expertise to the public at large. These tenets, codified early in the twentieth century, are central to the creation of modern American universities. Colleges and universities could not do the important work of creating and transmitting advanced knowledge unless there were robust protections for scholarly inquiry and expression, bounded by professional expectations of competent and ethical behavior. More than the general principles of universal free speech, these norms anchor the distinctive work of higher education.

We will begin this chapter by describing how academic freedom differs from free speech. This will set the stage for an assessment of recent high-profile cases where faculty members have made decisions in professional settings that triggered demands for sanctions against them. We will look at examples of faculty members using their association with schools or academic departments to attribute certain political viewpoints to those schools or departments. We then focus on the recent issue of when or whether "campuses" or their administrative units as entities should make official statements about controversial social and political matters. We end by considering whether a requirement that prospective faculty members submit statements about their commitment to diversity, equity, and inclusion is an appropriate exercise of academic freedom.

The Protections and Boundaries
of Academic Freedom

The debate about whether and how campuses should protect "free speech" obscures a fundamental aspect of free expression at colleges and universities: the professional spaces for teaching and scholarly work on campuses—which represent these institutions' core activities—are also governed by academic freedom principles that do not apply to others in society or to other open spaces on campuses.[1]

When we talk about free speech protections generally, we mean that the government cannot censor or punish a person merely for the expression of an idea. Of course, there are many things a person can do with "speech" that the government can regulate or sanction, such as rob a bank, commit fraud, incite violence, harass or threaten another person, or libel someone. But what these exceptions to protected speech all have in common in American constitutional law is that it takes something other than the mere expression of a viewpoint for the speech activity to become unprotected. For example, even if a viewpoint is so inherently dangerous that it may lead some people to engage in violent or unlawful behavior, the expression of that viewpoint still does not become illegal "incitement" to lawlessness unless it is directed to eliciting immediate lawless behavior and is done in a context where that result is likely to occur.[2] Also, as we have seen, while the government cannot punish the mere expression of an idea, it can impose reasonable time, place, and manner restrictions on how and where ideas can be expressed, provided those restrictions are applied equally regardless of the viewpoints people are expressing. No one thinks that free speech means you can say anything you want anywhere you want in any manner you want.

The notion that any idea can be expressed without censorship or sanction does not apply to the professional speech of faculty members. When they are engaged in their on-campus activities within classrooms or expressing views within their scholarly work, faculty members enjoy "academic freedom" rather than "free speech" rights.

"Academic freedom" refers to the rights and privileges enjoyed by the professoriate as highly qualified professionals who should be trusted to make decisions about how best to generate and transmit advanced knowledge within their disciplines. The assumption is that colleges and universities will do a better job creating new knowledge and communicating it to students and the public if the quality of teaching and scholarship is determined not by governing bodies, administrators, or politicians but by experts committed to norms of professional competence, ethics, and peer review. To this extent, the privileges of faculty members are comparable to what is granted to experts in other professions. Physicians, for example, are expected to use their expertise and best judgment to determine what is in their patients' best interests, subject to review by other physicians.

As the then-new American Association of University Professors (AAUP) put it in their original *Declaration of Principles on Academic Freedom and Academic Tenure* in 1915,

> If education is the cornerstone of the structure of society and if progress in scientific knowledge is essential to civilization, few things can be more important than to enhance the dignity of the scholar's profession. . . . It is highly needful, in the interest of society at large, that what purport to be the conclusions of men trained for, and dedicated to, the quest for truth, shall in fact be the conclusions of such men, and not echoes of the opinions of the lay public, or of the individuals who endow or manage universities.

This deference to the judgment of professional scholars also depended on the commitment of faculty members to ensuring that their colleagues acted in ways consistent with the highest standards of their profession; thus,

> Since there are no rights without corresponding duties, the considerations heretofore set down with respect to the freedom of the academic teacher entail certain correlative obligations. . . . The liberty of the scholar . . . is conditioned by there being conclusions gained by a scholar's method and held in a scholar's spirit; that is to say, they must be the fruits of competent and patient and sincere inquiry.[3]

According to the University of California's official policy on academic freedom, "Freedom of inquiry and research, freedom of teaching, and freedom of expression and publication . . . enable the University to advance knowledge and to transmit it effectively to its students and to the public. . . . The exercise of academic freedom entails correlative duties of professional care when teaching, conducting research, or otherwise acting as a member of the faculty."[4]

It is these duties of professional care that distinguish academic freedom from general free speech protections. The government cannot sanction a member of the public who holds up a sign outside city hall proclaiming that the moon is made of green cheese, because free speech rights mean that any idea, even a wrong one, is expressible. In a professional academic setting, however, an aspiring astronomy professor who teaches that the moon is made of green cheese and advances that idea while applying for tenure or promotion will have that view assessed by experts in planetary geology, and if they determine that the view is incompetent (as they should!) that person could be sanctioned by the institution (and probably lose their job).

In campus settings, therefore, there are two spheres of speech activity, regulated by different norms: the academic freedom sphere, which applies to faculty members in their professional settings, and a free speech sphere, which governs nonprofessional spaces where general expressive activity is permitted. This means that sometimes faculty members are engaging in academic freedom, and sometimes, when they're "off the clock," they are able to exercise free speech like everyone else.

What a faculty member may say in a classroom setting is thus different than what they may say as part of a campus protest. In classroom settings, faculty members are granted broad latitude to decide what materials should be included in a course, even if those materials may be controversial, if they are acting competently and ethically. They should have discretion in deciding the best method of teaching course materials and of determining what should count as acceptable or exceptional performance by students, provided those criteria are based on scholarly considerations and not extraneous ones. At the University of California, faculty members are expected to "establish conditions that protect and encourage all students in their learning, teaching, and research activities," which include "free inquiry and exchange of ideas; the right to critically examine, present, and discuss controversial material relevant to a course of instruction; enjoyment of constitutionally protected freedom of expression; and the right to be judged by faculty in accordance with fair procedures solely on the basis of the students' academic performance and conduct."[5] And, of course, faculty members are expected to treat all students with respect, establish instructional norms that allow all students to benefit from the learning environment, and ensure that they do not act in ways that create unequal learning environments for some groups of students in violation of Title VI or Title IX.

Put another way, if we were to draw a Venn diagram, freedom of speech and academic freedom are overlapping circles. Some things are protected by academic freedom but not by the First Amendment. At a private university, for example, a professor's peer-reviewed, published scholarship is protected from her college's censure by the principles of academic freedom, but the First Amendment has nothing to say about it. The Constitution does not apply to private entities, only to the government. Other expression is safeguarded by the First Amendment, but not by academic freedom. A professor at a public university has the First Amendment right to attend a controversial rally, and the Constitution would limit the ability of the school to impose sanctions, but this would not likely fall within the domain of academic freedom. And there is much speech that would be protected by both the First Amendment and academic freedom, such as the scholarship of a faculty member at a public university.

Controversies Involving Faculty
Teaching and Research

Independent experts who are tasked with challenging prevailing ways of thinking and with pushing the boundaries of knowledge will often express controversial opinions. Academic freedom has been embraced by American universities because extending deference to scholarly experts has been shown to generate better results for society than the historic practice of requiring faculty members' adherence to the opinions of campus administrators, boards, or politicians. But this also means that professors will sometimes take controversial positions. When they do, when should the campus defend that choice, and when should it determine that the faculty member acted outside of the boundaries of professional competence and ethical behavior?

There are several recent controversies that, in our judgment, demonstrate the importance of academic freedom protections.

The painting depicting the Prophet Muhammad. Erika López Prater was an adjunct professor of art history at Hamline University, where she was teaching a course on global art history. She was aware that many Muslims have deeply held religious beliefs that prohibit depictions of the Prophet Muhammad, but she felt it was important to show a fourteenth-century painting that depicted the Prophet receiving revelation from the Angel Gabriel because of its status as a masterpiece of Persian manuscript painting. In the syllabus for her course in fall 2022, she warned students that images of holy figures would be shown and invited them to raise concerns with her, but none did. In class, before showing the image, she told the students that anyone who wanted to leave could do so, and none did. But after she showed the image, a campus and community firestorm broke out.

A senior in the class who was the president of the university's Muslim Student Association complained to the administration, and other Muslim students, who were not in the class, joined the criticism, claiming that Dr. López Prater had attacked their religion. The executive director of the Minnesota chapter of the Council on American-Islamic Relations said there was no legitimate reason to show the depiction and the university "cannot have incidents like this happen." (The national chapter of the Council on American-Islamic Relations later disagreed.)[6] Campus officials informed Dr. López Prater that her services next semester were not needed, and in emails to students and faculty, they said that the incident was Islamophobic and that respect for Muslim students "should have superseded academic freedom."[7]

A historian of Islamic art wrote an essay defending Dr. López Prater and started a petition that attracted twenty-eight hundred signatures, which was submitted to university officials in December 2022. Academic freedom organizations issued blistering criticism of the administration. On January 17, 2023, the chair of the university's board of trustees released a statement saying that respect for Muslim students should not have superseded academic freedom. This was certainly the more appropriate position for the university to take. Dr. López Prater's decision to show the painting was clearly within the scope of academic freedom: it was based on an academic judgment of the kind of material that should be shown to art history students. She also demonstrated a strong professional ethic of respect for Muslim students' sensitivities. One can imagine countless situations in which certain students might be offended by a course's content. For example, a Christian conservative might object to material in a geography course about the age of the Earth or material in a course on evolution about the origins of human life. But higher education obviously would not work if campuses censored all material that might offend students, or if professors needed to fear discipline any time they upset some of their students.

The university and Dr. López Prater eventually settled a lawsuit for undisclosed terms.[8]

The blackface Othello. One of the University of Michigan's most celebrated faculty members, composer Bright Sheng (a two-time Pulitzer finalist and winner of a MacArthur "genius" grant), wanted students to learn about the process of adapting a classic literary text into an opera, so in an undergraduate music composition seminar in fall 2021 he played a video of the 1965 movie version of Shakespeare's

Othello, in which Laurence Olivier notoriously played the title role in blackface. Even before the class period ended, messages were circulating about how offended many students were and Professor Sheng's lack of an explanation for why he had chosen this video. Within hours, he issued the first of what would be two apologies.

After weeks of canceled classes, emails, open letters, and potential investigations, the campus announced that Professor Sheng was voluntarily stepping back from the class. He eventually released a statement saying that "it feels uncomfortable that we live in an era where people can attempt to destroy the career and reputation of others with public denunciation." He later wrote, "Times have changed, and I made a mistake in showing this film. That was insensitive of me, and I am very sorry."

One of the students in the course eventually published a widely circulated blog post in which he explained his strong negative reaction and opined that, after four years of studying classical music, he realized that "this overwhelmingly homogenous industry operates by its own set of rules." He noted that he was initially told he should discuss his concerns with the professor, but he felt "this was a conversation that could never take place" because "he's had tenure since before my classmates and I learned to read" and "there was no way we could voice our feelings about this incident without fearing for the professional repercussions." He complained that "when it comes to incidents like this blackface video that don't warrant termination, tenure prevents administrators from issuing meaningful consequences that will deter similar behavior in the future."[9]

It is certainly true that academic freedom, combined with the protections of tenure, "prevents administrators from issuing meaningful consequences" to faculty members when they are acting within the boundaries of professional competence and ethics. Was Professor Sheng within those boundaries? While he later came to view his decision as a mistake, there was no indication that his choice was based on anything other than his view that the film "was one of the most faithful to Shakespeare" and that Olivier's performance was consistent with operatic traditions that valued the quality of the performers over physical resemblance. If he had not later voluntarily removed himself from that classroom, he should have expected the university to stand by his rights as a faculty member despite the controversy. The university was correct to reject calls to open a formal investigation.

This is not to say that his decision could not be criticized. It was clear from the class's response that the choice of the film was not adequately justified, and there was no effort to help students understand that they would be shown a practice that no one would venture today. But the professor's choice to show the movie was unquestionably within the scope of his academic freedom. Institutions of higher education must be allowed to expose new generations of students to historic practices and assumptions that would be denounced today, whether they be conventions in film and acting, language in novels published many years ago, or views expressed in historical documents. Although we do not believe campuses can require "trigger warnings" (in which professors warn students in advance about potentially disturbing content), there are circumstances where the space of learning can benefit by helping students understand, in advance, what they will be seeing and why it is being shown. But whether to give trigger warnings or expose students to material without them is a choice protected by academic freedom.

Also, it should always be possible for students to take issue with professors' choices, and to talk to their professors about their concerns. Expressing contrary views and inviting members of the university community into dialogue should be standard practice at institutions of higher education, both so that teachers can teach the students and so that students can teach the teachers. Campus officials can and must take a stand against efforts by students to use disruptive protests to shut down classes they object to, as occurred at Reed College while students were demanding changes to a first-year humanities course.[10]

The mention of a racial epithet. In February 2022, San Diego State University professor J. Angelo Corlett was teaching a class entitled "Philosophy, Racism and Justice" when he showed a slide listing racial epithets. He later explained that he was teaching students about the difference between racist and nonracist language and to appreciate the distinction between "using" an epithet (with racist intent) and "mentioning" one (in contexts presumably without racist intent). In March, a student who was not in the class came to his office to discuss the slide. On the same day, the university suspended Professor Corlett from teaching based on student complaints, explaining that the issue "is not about free expression or academic freedom."

The professor later wrote an op-ed in a local newspaper in which he said that the point of the lesson was to expose students to what philosophers call the "use-mention" distinction. He wrote, "I have been teaching this material essentially the same way for over two decades while receiving stellar student and department reviews" and "the language was clearly relevant to the subject matter of the lesson." Several national organizations dedicated to academic freedom agreed. They criticized the university on the grounds that "preemptively removing a professor from the classroom is a serious sanction" that "is wholly uncalled for as a response to a professor's classroom speech demonstrably protected by academic freedom, even if that speech is found offensive or troubling by some listeners." Over 150 professors nationwide signed a petition that read in part:

> The various signers of this letter might have approached Professor Corlett's material differently, and may have differing personal views

and practices when it comes to the treatment of racial and ethnic slurs in the academic context. We're joined, however, in recognizing that Professor Corlett's expression is well within the bounds of his academic freedom when viewed in the context of his teaching, which endeavored to illustrate for students, by way of example, when the usage of certain terms is properly considered racist—all during a lecture on a course on critical thinking. Students are free to register criticisms of Corlett's pedagogical methods, as Corlett undoubtedly recognizes. But mere offense over a professor's exercise of academic freedom falls far short of the threshold for disciplinary action.[11]

San Diego State University's decision to impose administrative disciplinary action against Professor Corlett under these circumstances was inconsistent with academic freedom principles. Exposure to offensive words or hateful content in a pedagogical context should not be a sanctionable offense. As noted in the AAUP's 2007 report on freedom in the classroom, "Ideas that are germane to a subject under discussion in a classroom cannot be censored because a student with particular religious or political beliefs might be offended," and it would be "inimical to the free and vigorous exchange of ideas necessary for teaching and learning in higher education" if professors could be sanctioned because of students' reaction to words or ideas being discussed.[12] At the same time, there are obvious sensitivities about referencing racial epithets that may not have been in the minds of faculty decades ago, in different social contexts, when the student body was much less diverse. At least one prominent First Amendment scholar, who for decades believed he could not teach the boundaries of free speech without mentioning racial epithets in a class of advanced law students, has publicly said that he will stop using at least some epithets, explaining, "I'm persuaded that the value is offset by the distraction and the harm it causes."[13]

Because standards of professional behavior in a classroom evolve over time, there will be ongoing debate about when references to racist language can be justified on pedagogical grounds and when they are gratuitous. If an English professor is teaching texts, even by African American writers, that include the n-word, is it a legitimate exercise in a college course to have the students hear and react to the word? Should students be assigned readings that use the word? What if the text has great historical significance? What if the point of the text is to force people to reconsider their views of how language is used? What if the material is supplemented by a scholarly article by a Harvard law professor arguing in favor of referring to that word in proper academic contexts?

When an English professor at the University of Rochester was suspended from a class for taking this approach, the Academic Freedom Alliance objected to his suspension and to the claim by the professor's dean that any use of the word in class was "demeaning" and never appropriate.[14] The professor commented, "Silencing teachers and honoring all discomforts of students will not contribute to the ending of racism in the United States." We agree that the professor's suspension was inconsistent with academic freedom principles. Academic freedom protects the instructor's ability to choose how to teach the material, even if the choice offends some students. That said, we would advise faculty to think very carefully about the controversy that will result from using certain words, and whether it advances or undermines their pedagogical objectives

Redacted racial insults on a law exam. In December 2020, Jason Kilborn, a law professor at the University of Illinois at Chicago, asked in an exam for his "Civil Procedure" course whether a hypothetical company must disclose to a plaintiff that a former employee told the company's lawyer "that she quit her job at Employer after she attended a meeting in which other managers expressed their anger at

Plaintiff, calling her a 'n——' and 'b——' (profane expressions for African Americans and women) and vowed to get rid of her." The exam did not spell out the words; they appeared exactly as they do here. As a hypothetical situation that actual lawyers may face, the prompt does not seem exceptional, since parties to a lawsuit often must decide whether to disclose very disturbing or inflammatory information. (One could argue that if the information at issue was not inflammatory and potentially devastating to the lawyer's client, it would not be an interesting question to ask on an exam.) Still, one student was very upset by the question, and before long, the Black Law Students Association demanded that Professor Kilborn be stripped of his committee assignments, denounced him on social media, and filed a complaint with the university's Office for Access and Equity (OAE). He was placed on administrative leave, and OAE sent a notice of "investigation into allegations of race-based discrimination and harassment."

The case eventually became mired in other accusations, but an investigation characterized the exam question as "harassing conduct." When Professor Kilborn objected to the criticism, the school responded that his "reactions to minority students' expressions of extreme disappointment in the exam question demonstrated racial insensitivity and even hostility to those voicing concerns about a racially charged topic."[15] The law school eventually reached an agreement with him that allowed him to resume his professional activities, but the steps taken against him on the basis of the exam question are clear violations of academic freedom principles. In March 2025, the United States Court of Appeals for the Seventh Circuit ruled in favor of Kilborn, concluding that his exam question and in-class remarks were protected by the First Amendment.[16]

There are times when campus administrators need to take immediate action in response to a controversy, but this was not one of them.

The language used on the exam should have been viewed as clearly protected by academic freedom even if some students took offense. Their concerns did not have to be disregarded, but the engagement with them should not have included the imposition of an administrative leave and the launching of an investigation at least partly predicated on the complaints about the exam.

Research on "adult-child" sex. Not all academic freedom controversies arise in classroom settings. Professors are also entitled to full freedom in conducting research, publishing their results, and conveying their expertise to broader audiences. SUNY Fredonia philosopher Stephen Kershnar, a distinguished teaching professor, specializes in applied ethics and the philosophical foundations of bad or immoral behavior. He has written on several highly controversial topics, including an academic book entitled *Pedophilia and Adult-Child Sex: A Philosophical Analysis,* for which he was positively evaluated as a faculty member.

In 2022, after he discussed his work on the respected philosophy podcast *Brain in a Vat,* there was a major social media controversy over his claim "It's not obvious to me that it's in fact wrong" for an adult to have sex with twelve-year-olds and "exploring why it's a mistake will tell us not only things about adult child sex and statutory rape, but also about fundamental principles of morality." To be clear, Kershnar has said that adult-child sexual activity should be criminalized. In response to the public attention, the university president issued a statement saying that the campus was aware of the video and that the views expressed "were reprehensible and do not represent the values of SUNY Fredonia. . . . The matter is being reviewed."[17] The university later suspended Kershnar from teaching, banned him from campus, and prohibited him from contacting "the campus community."[18] A student-led petition with some fourteen thousand signatures (which later grew to sixty thousand) demanded that Fredonia fire him. Some students said they did not feel safe on campus if he was present.[19]

When the university first announced that the matter was under review, the Academic Freedom Alliance wrote to the president to argue that "there is, quite simply, nothing for the university to review" since the statements were protected by the First Amendment and academic freedom principles. The organization's public letter emphasized that the university had an obligation to protect faculty members rather than contribute to a potentially menacing environment for them. "A member of your faculty under such public scrutiny is likely to be targeted for abuse and threats, and the university's responsibility is to shelter the faculty member from that harassment and not add to it." More generally, the letter argued that a university "should be a place where such questions can be boldly and honestly investigated. If a scholar's analysis is mistaken, then it should be rebutted or ignored. But the scholar should not be driven from campus for challenging widely held beliefs or for reaching the wrong or unpopular conclusions."[20]

If Kershnar's views had come out of the blue or were assessed as incompetent scholarship, then a response that separated him from the academic community might have rested on a firmer foundation. But the university's ordinary processes of assessing academic merit included evaluations of his long-standing views on these issues (and others), and far from condemning this work, the university determined, after peer review, that it represented high-quality scholarship. Standing by scholars whose work, while controversial, meets the criteria for expert knowledge is precisely the basis for insisting that the institution defend academic freedom against political or social demands for censorship and punishment.

To return to our Venn diagram, this is an instance where there was both a First Amendment issue—because he was a faculty member at a public university who was disciplined for his speech—and an issue of academic freedom, because the punishment was for his scholarly work.

Faculty members serving as expert witnesses. Three members of the political science department at the University of Florida requested permission from their dean (as they were required to do) to serve as expert witnesses in a lawsuit against the state on the constitutionality of a recently enacted voting rights law. The request was denied on the grounds that such activity "may pose a conflict of interest to the executive branch of the state of Florida" and that full-time employees could not undertake "outside paid work that is adverse to the university's interests as a state of Florida institution."[21]

The prohibition seemed clearly inconsistent with long-standing principles of academic freedom, which state that professors should be free to convey their expertise to the public at large. According to the AAUP's 1940 *Statement of Principles on Academic Freedom and Tenure,* when professors "speak or write as citizens" in ways not related to their scholarly expertise, they have the same free speech rights as everyone else. They also have the right to speak in a professional capacity by sharing their expertise with the public, but when doing so they "should at all times be accurate, should exercise appropriate restraint, should show respect for the opinions of others, and should make every effort to indicate that they are not speaking for the institution."[22] If those conditions and responsibilities are met, academic freedom protects their right to share their expertise. Florida believed it could censor them as employees of a government institution because they did not recognize the special protections of academic freedom and instead believed that the government should be able to control the job-related speech of its employees, including professors. Ironically, the University of Florida's own policies guaranteed the academic freedom of the faculty "as essential to the integrity of the university."

After a public outcry, the university reversed its decision.[23] But the professors sued to ensure that the restriction would not be reimposed. A federal district court judge eventually ordered the university "to take no steps to enforce its conflict of interests policy with respect to faculty and staff requests to engage as expert witnesses or provide legal consulting in litigation involving the State of Florida." The judge's opinion noted the shocking similarities between this case and the "demise of academic freedom" at the University of Hong Kong, where campus administrators fearful of the Chinese government took it upon themselves to silence students and faculty.[24]

The judge's order did not convince other university overseers of the importance of this academic freedom protection. The politically appointed chair of the University of Florida Board of Trustees later denounced the faculty members, saying that "our legislators are not going to put up with the wasting of state money and resources, and neither is this board. And we shouldn't. This behavior is unacceptable."[25]

We understand that political officials seeking to exert political control over faculty members oppose any independence of thought and action by faculty members. But we should keep in mind that it was *precisely* in reaction to the problematic efforts of late nineteenth-century politicians and board members to exercise control over what professors teach, study, and profess that the concept of academic freedom was devised in the first place.

There have also been several controversies that reflect decisions by faculty members that we believe should not be protected by academic freedom principles because they are outside the boundaries of professional competence or ethical behavior.

Dissuading conservative students from taking a class. While the following incident is not recent, it shows us how to think about what may fall outside of the boundaries of academic freedom. More interestingly, it led the University of California to change its policy on academic freedom in important ways.

In spring 2003, a graduate student instructor at Berkeley posted a description of a freshman writing course entitled "The Politics and

Poetics of Palestinian Resistance." The course description explained that students would examine the creation of Palestinian literature "under the brutal weight of the [Israeli] occupation" and ended with the suggestion that "conservative thinkers are encouraged to seek other sections" of the course. Even in an age before social media, news of the course circulated widely, with criticism directed both at the politically charged description and the attempt to certain dissuade students from enrolling.[26]

Berkeley's chancellor ordered the instructor to remove the last line of the course description, but discussions of other parts of the listing generated renewed attention to the University of California's 1930s-era policy on academic freedom, which required faculty to be "neutral" and "dispassionate" in addressing matters of public concern. Many faculty members agreed that it was unprofessional to use a course setting to engage in political "indoctrination," but it also seemed impossible to expect faculty members to express themselves only in "neutral" or "dispassionate" ways. It certainly seemed that faculty members could hold strong viewpoints and yet act in accordance with the highest professional standards.

University of California president Richard Atkinson set in motion a process by which the existing policy might be updated, enlisting Berkeley law professor Robert Post to provide an assessment and a set of recommendations. Post's recommendations reiterated that academic freedom entails "correlative duties of professional care," including a commitment to fostering in students "a mature independence of mind, and this purpose cannot be achieved unless students and faculty are free within the classroom to express the widest range of viewpoints in accord with the standards of scholarly inquiry and professional ethics." At the same time, "academic freedom requires that teaching and scholarship be assessed only by reference to the professional standards that sustain the University's pursuit and achievement of knowledge" rather than additional amorphous criteria like "neutrality" or "dispassion." The standards of defensible academic judgment may lead a scholar to conclusions that would not be seen as dispassionate in ordinary political debate, but the protections of academic freedom still attach so long as the viewpoint is justified by ethical expert opinion.[27]

While much of the national attention to the controversy focused on the opinion articulated in the course description, the actual problem with that description was the last sentence, which cast doubt on the instructor's willingness to follow the university's course enrollment policies, to evaluate students without discrimination or harassment, and to allow them to express their honest views.

In our judgment, it is not possible to make faculty experts refrain from articulating any political viewpoint. But it is possible to require that they limit the viewpoints expressed in classes to those that are academically justifiable and germane, and to create a space in class where other defensible positions can be expressed. This requires difficult judgments about when opinion shades into unethical political indoctrination. Here are some examples of faculty crossing that line.

Singling out Jewish students in a classroom. A few days after the October 7, 2023, Hamas attacks in Israel, a Stanford lecturer in a required class for first-year students reportedly asked Jews and Israelis to identify themselves in class and then asked them to stand separately from their classmates in order to make the point that their segregation depicts how Israel as a "colonizer" treats Palestinians. The following day, the university announced that an unnamed instructor had been removed from the classroom and was being investigated because he was "reported to have addressed the Middle East conflict in a manner that called out individual students in class based on their backgrounds and identities." The statement continued: "Academic freedom does not permit the identity-based targeting of students." There is no definitive public report of what precisely happened, including whether a number of Jews or Israelis were asked to separate themselves or whether a volunteer was used to make a point about occupation and power imbalances. But Stanford later announced that the instructor's employment would not continue.[28]

Although we don't know precisely what happened in this circumstance, it is clear that academic freedom does not allow what occurred: identity-based targeting of students. A classroom benefits from a study body that represents a range of backgrounds and perspectives, and encouraging students to add their voices to a discussion can elevate everyone's learning experience. It is hard to see how singling out students of certain backgrounds or identities to make a point, or giving them politically charged labels based on their identities or nationalities, contributes to a supportive learning environment. Whether or not the activity was protected by academic freedom norms would be fact-specific, but faculty members who consider identity-based targeting of students in classroom environments should not expect that their choices will be supported.

Class credit for protesting against a Supreme Court nominee. Academic freedom also does not permit a faculty member to use their position in a course to make students participate in an instructor's preferred political activities. In 2018, a faculty member at the University of Southern Maine offered course credit if students joined a bus full of people planning to protest Brett Kavanaugh's nomination to the Supreme Court and lobby Maine senator Susan Collins to vote against it. The campus president announced that the professor had been barred from teaching "for her role in listing and promoting an unauthorized class that advanced her personal political agenda. The course was promptly rescinded and university officials took immediate steps to ensure that institutional resources were not . . . used to support one-sided political activism."

The instructor objected to these actions, protesting that "if you're willing to stand up and fight for social justice . . . you will be attacked and vilified." But this reflects her confusion about how faculty members' professional responsibilities differ from their broader free speech rights. No campus can prevent or sanction a faculty member who, on their own time, participates in political activism. But faculty members are not engaging in free speech rights when they are teaching students: they are engaged in the practice of their profession, with all the attendant responsibilities and obligations. The classroom is not a forum where faculty members can say or do as they please; it is a space for teaching an approved curriculum in a professional manner.[29]

Events after October 7. In the wake of the Hamas October 7 attacks, faculty members and graduate instructors around the country tried to use their positions in the classroom to encourage or incentivize students to participate in pro-Palestinian demonstrations, some by offering class credit for participation, others by canceling classes to allow for participation.[30] Campuses had an obligation to preempt such activity and intervene when such efforts were discovered. At one of our campuses, UC Irvine, a message was sent to all faculty to remind them of university policies regarding political advocacy in the classroom. The message stated, "While instructors enjoy considerable freedom and all individuals, when acting as private citizens, enjoy free speech rights, University policy does impose limits on using the classroom or one's course for purposes of political advocacy. As a public institution we have a particular obligation to preserve the public's trust." Among the policies we referenced were the rights of students to have their classes held as scheduled, the prohibition on "misuse of the classroom by, for example, allowing it to be used for political indoctrination," and prohibitions against "significant intrusion of material unrelated to the course and the use of the position of a faculty member to coerce the judgment or conscience of a student."[31]

Refusal to use preferred pronouns. In 2016, Shawnee State University developed a policy requiring faculty members to refer to students by their preferred pronouns. Nicholas Meriwether, a philosophy professor and self-identified devout Christian, wrote that he believes that "God created human beings as either male or female . . . [and] it cannot be changed, regardless of an individual's feelings or desires." On the first day of class in January 2018, while using the Socratic method to question students, Meriwether referred to a transgender woman as "sir." When the student demanded after class that the professor use her preferred pronouns, Meriwether explained that he could not do that because of his religious convictions. He was reprimanded and told he could face termination if he continued to create a "hostile educational environment."

Surprisingly, in the case *Meriwether v. Hartop* (2021), the United States Court of Appeals for the 6th Circuit ruled that (1) the First Amendment protects the academic speech of university professors, and (2) the campus's pronoun policy violated the First Amendment because it imposed "compelled speech" on an unwilling speaker and cast a "pall of orthodoxy" over the classroom. Any other result would permit a university to "require a pacifist to declare that war is just, a civil rights icon to condemn the Freedom Riders, a believer to deny the existence of God." The court also expressed the view that academic freedom covers "all classroom speech related to matters of public concern, whether that speech is germane to the contents of the lecture or not."[32] Shawnee State eventually settled the lawsuit with Meriwether, agreeing to pay him $400,000 in damages and attorneys' fees and allowing him to choose when to use titles or pronouns when addressing students.[33]

The court's opinion improperly assumes that academic freedom rights are similar to First Amendment free speech rights, and that campuses cannot discipline a faculty member for violating university policy about the respectful treatment of students. The classroom is a space created for the purpose of teaching a particular subject matter, not for faculty members to express whatever ideas they wish on areas of public concern. It is also necessarily a space where norms of decorum and respectful interaction can be required if they do not interfere with a faculty member's professional judgment about effective pedagogy, since these norms are central to the creation of an effective learning environment. To create supportive learning environments, campuses can also require faculty to take a variety of steps, such as including in course syllabi learning outcomes, warnings about plagiarism, contact information for counseling services, or information about disability services and accommodations. Generally, courts have consistently upheld limits on the rights of faculty both in choosing the content of courses and in how that content is administered, including the university's right to require faculty members to clearly communicate with students about grading policies and to require that teaching philosophies comport with university standards.[34]

Academic freedom certainly protects Meriwether's decision to use the Socratic method to teach philosophy, and it would protect his right to criticize the campus's pronoun policy on pedagogical grounds or to publish scholarship criticizing the concept of preferred pronouns. He also has a free speech right to advocate, outside the classroom, against accommodating the pronoun preferences of transgender students.

But he did not defend his choice to violate the pronoun policy on the grounds of effective pedagogy or other professional scholarly considerations. Instead, he argued that his personal religious objection should take precedence over a university policy designed to prevent discrimination against a particular class of students. Yet just as academic freedom does not protect a professor who treats students of different races differently out of a personal or religious view that some races are superior to others, so too does it not protect a choice to misgender students in violation of campus policies. Violating the university's policy on respecting students' gender preferences does not contribute to an effective learning environment, does not demonstrate respect for students as individuals, and does not reflect the obligations of professional competence or ethics in the transmission of higher knowledge.

Imagine that the professor, whenever calling on a Black student, had said, "You, n-word, you can speak now." Surely no court would say that such behavior in a classroom is protected by the First Amendment. Refusing in professional settings to call students by their chosen gender pronouns should not be deemed protected by the First Amendment because it involves expectations of professional conduct and ethical behavior as governed by principles of academic freedom rather than the anything-goes boundaries or ordinary free speech considerations.

At other times, Meriwether said he was opposed to "the juggernaut of political correctness."[35] But as we saw in earlier examples, academic freedom does not protect faculty members in using classroom spaces as forums for their personal political agendas or, by extension, to promote their personal religious views.

The point of these examples is that although what is protected by academic freedom is often hard to define, doing so is essential. Instances such as these, which clearly fall on each side of the line, can help us assess the myriad of new situations that are likely to arise.

When Should Academic Departments or Campus Leaders Make Statements on Social or Political Matters?

In recent years, faculty members at some institutions have claimed that academic freedom or free speech principles support their right to associate their departments with certain political positions. We believe this is a mistaken understanding of both academic freedom and free speech.

Such a controversy arose in May 2021, following an escalation of Israel-Hamas hostilities, when UCLA's Asian American studies (AAS) department posted a "Statement of Solidarity with Palestine" that characterized Israeli violence against Palestinians as "the latest manifestation of seventy-three years of settler colonialism, racial apartheid, and occupation." The statement claimed that Asian American studies as a discipline "has long advanced a critique of imperialism, militarism, and settler colonialism" and condemned (among other things) "how Israel has too often upheld its support of Asian and Asian American individuals as proof of multicultural democracy, over and against ethnic cleansing of Palestine via a process of 'yellow-washing.'" The statement saluted Palestinian uprising throughout all of historic Palestine and lent its voice "to uplifting the struggle of the Palestinian people."[36]

A number of UCLA professors spoke out against the statement at a meeting of the UC Board of Regents. Professor of computer science Judea Pearl said the statement "violates campus norms of discourse, and amounts to character assassination of many students and faculty whose identity is bonded to Israel." Other professors noted they had research collaborations with Israeli colleagues, "yet the AAS statement uses the good name of UCLA to admonish and denigrate such cooperation." One commented that the statement was "crude propaganda" and noted that "individual faculty members are of course free to spout whatever malicious nonsense they wish, but it's morally unacceptable for departments to do so in the names of all their members. . . . There are potential legal issues based on nationality and religious discrimination since the statement is saying to anyone thinking of enrolling in a course or applying for a staff or faculty position, that they are not welcome if they disagree."[37]

An "Ad Hoc Faculty Committee for Academic Integrity" also wrote to UC president Michael Drake to express "outrage" at the statement and to complain that it violated UCLA Policy 110, which states that faculty cannot use "University Assets or their affiliation with the University in any manner that suggests or implies University support, endorsement or advancement of, or opposition to, any issue, activity or program, whether political, religious, economic or otherwise" without obtaining appropriate approvals. The committee also claimed that the statement violated California Education Code section 92000, which states that the "name 'University of California' is the property of the state" and no person shall use this name in connection with "any propaganda, advertising, or promotional activity which has for its purpose . . . the support, endorsement, advancement, opposition, or defeat of any strike, lockout, or boycott or of any political, religious, sociological, or economic movement, activity, or program." The committee also argued that the statement "does harm to students and to the environment of mutual respect, diversity and inclusion that should characterize all academic programs."[38]

Similar statements of solidarity with Palestinian resistance, premised on the view that from its beginning, the creation of the State of Israel was an illegitimate and oppressive act of settler colonialism and ethnic cleansing, proliferated among many university departments throughout the country, including gender studies, ethnic studies, Middle East studies, and anthropology.[39] In August 2021, after the gender studies department at USC brought out a statement similar to the one from UCLA's AAS department, several USC faculty members, who held "wide and diverse perspectives on the Israeli-Palestinian conflict," wrote an open letter to university leadership claiming that "the errors and polemic tone of this Statement are cruelly alienating to many students, staff, and faculty." The letter argued that the statement was unethical, improperly conveyed that it represented the views of the entire department, and implied endorsement by USC itself. "If USC's implicit support stands, many Jewish students and others who believe in Israel's right to exist will be reluctant to attend our university." Such polemical proclamations also created "an unwelcoming, even toxic, atmosphere for students who disagree with them," and most Jewish students who might be enrolled in that department's classes "might now expect, quite reasonably, that they are not welcome as peers and that their academic careers will be harmed because of their beliefs or identity."[40]

Following these controversies, several universities set up working groups to assess whether faculty members should be able to officially associate their departments with controversial political statements.

In December 2022, the Academic Senate of the University of Illinois Urbana-Champaign (UIUC) approved guidelines governing the issuing of "political" department statements. They first clarified that "the right of faculty as individuals to express such positions is protected by academic freedom" but added that "the rights of individual faculty and the rights of departments are not the same in this context" because of "the need to respect the academic freedom rights of all members of a department or other academic unit, including those who disagree with them." The Senate's guidelines were premised on the AAUP language that when communicating to external audiences, faculty members "should exercise appropriate restraint" and "make every effort to indicate that they are not speaking for the institution." The Senate also indicated that departments should be mindful that when they advocated issuing such statements, some faculty might "unwittingly coerce . . . vulnerable department members" such as nontenured faculty, "risk creating an unwelcome environment for potential students" and, even worse, "be viewed as hostile or even discriminatory toward members of particular groups. . . . While faculty as citizens have the same rights of free speech as anyone, in their capacity as faculty they have responsibilities toward students and others that need to be weighed when supporting such statements."

The UIUC Senate's recommendations included a requirement that units create bylaws and a process to be followed before such statements may be issued. The Senate also said that faculty members who believe their academic freedom was infringed by such a statement should have a right to appeal. Another recommendation was that statements be issued with a list of signatories rather than simply as a department's position (with opportunities for the views of dissenters to be similarly promulgated). The Senate recommended that such statements include an explicit disclaimer that they do not represent the university as a whole. It also urged the university to issue a directive that statements not be promulgated through department websites or official social media sites since "a department does not own its website," which is "by definition University property." Even beyond these recommendations, the Senate advised that departments limit their statements to their core academic mission.[41]

That same year, UC Berkeley set up a joint Senate-Administration Workgroup, "Report on the Role of the University and Its Units in Political and Social Action." It was formed "partly in response to concerns that have arisen over the past few years when both administrative and academic departments at Berkeley have posted statements on their websites that expressed the political perspectives of staff, faculty and/or students [but] were presented as . . . positions adopted by the department itself, and not just of individuals affiliated with the department. Given their placement on digital platforms belonging to the university, these statements raised concerns that they could be mistaken for official positions." Even though the report recognized that "messaging about controversial issues has the potential for adverse impacts on members of the community and on the reputation of the institution as a whole," a majority of the workgroup concluded that such statements were permissible but advised that they should "always indicate whose views are represented by the statement, and should ensure that dissenting views can be expressed on the same platform." It was also suggested that statements on subjects outside the governance and pedagogical concerns of the department "should be issued sparingly."[42]

Two members of the workgroup dissented. One argued that because of the diversity of the public served by the institution, any actual or perceived politicization of the institution "comes with great costs to our mission, our reputation, and our academic integrity." It would be difficult "to explain to our stakeholders, and ourselves, when a departmental or school statement on a departmental or school website signed by those presumed to be leaders is not somehow an expression of an institutional position." A second member, a co-author of this book (Chemerinsky), said, "I do not believe that departments or schools as entities have the authority to do this or should do this." As we explain below, this remains our position.

We should once again emphasize that individual faculty members, or groups of faculty members, are unquestionably free to express any point of view they choose on any topic. At issue is whether they are free to associate their political views with an administrative unit of the university, either by claiming that the statement is the official position of a school or department or by using the school's or department's official channels of communication. We believe they are not. There are four main reasons for this.

First, departments and schools are subdivisions of the larger corporate entity that is the university, and typically only a few designated people may speak authoritatively on behalf of the institution. For example, within the University of California, only the regents can associate the university with certain official positions, although the president is also authorized to speak on behalf of the entire university and chancellors are authorized to speak on behalf of their respective campuses. The websites and official channels of communication of an administrative unit are the property of the institution as a whole and are not intended as open public forums for the political views of people affiliated with the unit. They exist to convey the unit's official business.

Departments and schools, as administrative units of the university, do not belong to whatever group of faculty happens to constitute a majority of the unit at any particular time. Departments and schools are created by the institution as a whole for specific curricular and research purposes, and the speech conveyed by the unit should therefore be limited to expressing and explaining its academic policies and procedures. For example, at the Berkeley Law School, faculty members often file briefs in courts on behalf of themselves or their clients, but they cannot file a brief on behalf of the University of California or on behalf of the University of California, Berkeley School of Law. Only the regents can do that. Similarly, the law school can require all students to take a course about race and the law as a condition of graduating, and explain why that requirement was adopted, but it cannot, as the law school, issue statements criticizing a Supreme Court decision even if every member of the faculty disagrees with it.

Second, when acting in their professional capacity—as they are doing when claiming policies and statements come from their departments—faculty members are governed by academic freedom principles and not general free speech principles. In other words, attempting to speak on behalf of a department, rather than as an individual expressing political views, is no more a matter of "free speech" than speaking in a classroom setting is a circumstance of free speech. What does academic freedom say about such matters? The canonical AAUP statement about the academic freedom to convey opinions "as scholars and educational officers" is that "they should at all times be accurate, should exercise appropriate restraint, should show respect for the opinions of others, and should make every effort to indicate that they are not speaking for the institution."[43]

It is hard to imagine a clearer violation of the responsibility to separate one's personal views from the institution's view than to claim that one's personal political opinions should be considered the official position of a formal administrative unit of the university. No reasonable member of the public could be expected to separate "official department statements" from the institution's position, unless central campus administrators were to publicly distance the institution from its own departments and schools—which would create the confusing impression (in the words of the other Berkeley workgroup dissenter) of "a house publicly divided against itself."

Third, department political statements risk *undermining* academic freedom and free speech by coercing faculty who might disagree with the dominant opinion. As the University of California's Academic Senate Committee on Academic Freedom noted in a May 2022 report on the issue, "departmental statements can threaten or violate the academic freedom of members of the department who do not share the views of a majority of their colleagues." Minority viewpoints might be suppressed, especially for those, such as students, staff, and untenured faculty, who have less power and authority. And even if their opinions are not suppressed, "the departmental statement may have a chilling effect on their speech that can infringe on academic freedom." Moreover, "unless the department has undergone a process to secure agreement from all of these individuals, it is possible the statement ascribes to members of the department who do not agree with the statement . . . a viewpoint they do not actually share" or choose not to speak about.[44]

This is another reason why it is better that faculty members make statements under free speech principles using their own names and affiliations, rather than try to associate their views with a department and all of its affiliates.

Fourth, associating academic departments and programs with controversial political views risks alienating students who disagree with those views and making them feel unwelcome within those departments and programs. It is widely acknowledged that professors have a professional responsibility to show restraint and welcome all legitimate views within a classroom setting, precisely because they are expected to create a supportive learning environment for students who have different viewpoints and come from different backgrounds. The management of an academic department is governed by precisely the same considerations. Faculty members who express controversial political views in nonprofessional settings can reasonably say that those views have no impact on how they perform their academic duties, but they cannot credibly say this while attempting to formally link their political views with their professional setting. This is especially problematic when the statements being associated with the academic program are extremely strident and aggressive, implying strong personal denunciations of, and disrespect for, those who dare believe otherwise.

The pro-Palestinian and anti-Zionist positions that have been most common in the past few years, especially in the wake of the Hamas attack in Israel on October 7, 2023, risk not only alienating individuals who have different views but also creating a discriminatory educational environment for Jews whose religious beliefs compel them to support the existence of Israel as a Jewish state. Jewish Zionists are properly considered a protected class within the meaning of Title VI of the Civil Rights Act, and formal declarations that stridently associate academic departments and schools with anti-Zionism contribute to a hostile environment that can be severe, pervasive, or persistent enough to interfere with the ability of those students to benefit from the services, activities, or privileges provided by the campus. These conditions may violate federal law.[45] Upon reading UCLA's Asian American studies statement in May 2021, how could most Jewish students at UCLA believe they would be as welcome to study in that department as declared non-Zionists?

For these reasons we believe the information provided on administrative units' official channels of communication should be limited to the established purposes, responsibilities, and activities of the unit. Academic units should communicate their curricular offerings, traditional mission statements or strategic plans, administrative activities or resources, news announcing events or opportunities, and news related to faculty or student research, teaching, and public service. Even at institutions that do not have a policy imposing such restrictions, we urge faculty members to oppose efforts by their colleagues to implicate their programs in controversial, divisive, and potentially exclusionary political statements.

If it seems too difficult or controversial to impose such restrictions within a particular campus setting, we would urge that leaders set up clear policies on the responsibilities of academic campus units when issuing public statements, and clear procedures for doing so. Such a policy was passed by the regents of the University of California in July 2024. It governs when and how academic units can use their homepages to issue "discretionary statements," which are defined as statements that are "not part of the day-to-day, term-to-term operations of the unit, and that comment on institutional, local, regional, global or national events, activities or issues."[46] Taking guidance from the University of California's system-wide Academic Senate evaluation of the issue, the policy requires that all public statements be consistent with applicable law and university policy, including anti-discrimination and codes of conduct. Under the policy, discretionary statements must be accompanied by a disclaimer expressly stating that the statement should not be taken as a position of the university or the campus as a whole. Units that intend to produce and disseminate discretionary statements must comply with an extensive set of rules designed to ensure that all members of the unit enjoy the freedom to speak or not to speak, and not to be misrepresented. Also, importantly, discretionary statements should not appear on the main homepage of a website but should be posted on a separate page reserved for such statements.[47]

The main weakness of this policy is that it only addresses statements on the homepages of websites rather than the broader issue of department statements in general or the use of official channels of administrative communication for such purposes.

When they saw the UC regents' decision regarding political statements on homepages, some faculty members and students claimed it violated free speech and was a "censorship proposal."[48] This is incorrect. No one has a free speech right to use an administrative website of the university to express their political views. Faculty members have academic freedom obligations to ensure that their personal views are *not* presented as representing the institution's views and to ensure a welcoming educational environment for students of many backgrounds and viewpoints. What violates academic freedom responsibilities is the decision to insist on associating controversial political views with a department.

None of this resolves the situation in which an academic program claims that politically controversial statements are not discretionary at all or separate from the department's core activity, but are central to the expertise associated with the discipline and the standards for acceptable curriculum, teaching, and research. Many statements from programs in Asian American studies, gender studies, ethnic studies, and anthropology, among others, claim that their disciplines have anti-racist, anti-colonial, pro-indigenous, anti-militaristic viewpoints as core assumptions. Many of them make arguments that suggest they have the same right to exclude Zionist sensibilities from the curriculum, the classroom, and the assessment of faculty scholarship as an evolutionary biology program has to exclude creationist theories of the origins of humankind. They might claim that in both cases, the decision is based on what the highest standards of scholarly expertise require.

We are skeptical that the only legitimate conclusion that an expert in (say) gender studies can arrive at is that the State of Israel should not exist as a Jewish state and that its creation was such a unique evil that this one state, and no other, deserves to be eliminated, but that question must ultimately be resolved by the scholarly community. We would urge faculty members who are considering such questions to reflect on Keith Whittington's point that "if commenting on social and political controversies is part of the job description of members of the faculty and can appropriately be done through the instruments of university decisionmaking, then it will necessarily put pressure on those who might dissent from the majority sentiment. . . . Indeed, prospective students and faculty will receive the signal that the institution is officially hostile to and unwelcoming of people with their personal political views." Moreover, "it will be all the more difficult to reassure students that professors understand that it would be professionally inappropriate to allow their personal politics to creep into their teaching duties if professors demonstrate that they believe that there is no divide to be maintained between their personal and professional activities. Students would have a reasonable fear that professors will treat students differently depending on their politics if those same professors use the university as their personal political platform."[49] When they are tempted to assert that issuing politically controversial statements is a nondiscretionary part of their scholarly responsibilities, faculties should reflect very seriously about the impact on a politically diverse learning environment.

There is the additional question of whether the leaders who are authorized to speak on behalf of the campus should make statements about local, national, or global events that do not directly flow from their campus's core mission or activities. Of course, there are arguments on both sides, and there will inevitably be disagreement about what is the "core mission" of the university.

Those who advocate that leaders speak out on a range of issues claim that the current generation of campus stakeholders wants to be associated with institutions that articulate and validate their own values. They believe that when leaders fail to speak out on issues, it makes the entire institution complicit in whatever bad statements or policies remain unrebutted. The idea that people feel let down and alienated when organizational leaders fail to "speak out" can be seen not just on campuses but across many organizations. Younger workers especially want their CEOs to take positions and associate their businesses with the "correct" position on many controversial social issues. Many consider this part of being an effective leader.[50] Within campuses, too, many want university leaders to voice their stakeholders' concerns and outrage, such as after the murder of George Floyd, and they see silence itself as a message—at times the wrong message.

Those who advocate more restraint note that university leaders have a responsibility to represent the campus as a whole and not just their personal views, and the university's official position should be to encourage expression of the widest diversity of views and leave it to various stakeholders (faculty, students, staff) to condemn speech they abhor or uplift views they embrace. Unlike most companies, the point of universities is to encourage the expression of ideas, and this might be chilled if campus leaders make strong statements supporting one side of a contentious issue, leaving the impression that those on the other side may be less welcome on campus. Opponents of campus statements also note that a decision to make one is a slippery slope, since a statement about one issue inevitably leads people holding strong views on other issues to expect the leader to associate the university with their position as well. Campus leaders might suddenly face endless pressures and demands from groups on and off the campus to issue statements. Speaking on some issues and not others will lead disappointed advocates to conclude that their concerns are not as valued.

After the Hamas attack in Israel on October 7, college and university leaders found that there was no safe harbor. Those who spoke out to condemn the attack were pilloried for not also putting the attack in the larger context of the history of conflict between Israel and Palestine. Those who referenced the attack but put it in the larger context of suffering on both sides were pilloried for diminishing the unique historic circumstance of the largest mass killing of Jews since the Holocaust. Those who said nothing were pilloried for disrespecting how the event traumatized many on campus and for implying, by their silence, that core campus values had nothing to say about the slaughter.[51]

Debates about whether campus leaders should speak about social and political issues start with the Kalven Report from more than half a century ago. Like many campuses, the University of Chicago in the late 1960s was roiled by unrest over the Vietnam War. People on both sides of the issue wanted the university to take a stand either for or against the war. In February 1967, President George W. Beadle appointed a committee to prepare "a statement on the university's role in political and social action." It was chaired by the noted First Amendment scholar Harry Kalven Jr.

The committee determined that there is "a heavy presumption against the university taking collective action or expressing opinions on the political and social issues of the day, or modifying its corporate activities to foster social or political values, however compelling and appealing they may be." In perhaps its most famous lines, the committee wrote that "the instrument of dissent and criticism is the individual faculty member or the individual student. *The university is the home and sponsor of critics; it is itself not the critic*" (emphasis added). Why?

> A university, if it is to be true to its faith in intellectual inquiry, must embrace, be hospitable to, and encourage the widest diversity of

views within its own community. It is a community but only for the limited, albeit great, purposes of teaching and research. It is not a club, it is not a trade association, it is not a lobby. Since the university is a community only for these limited and distinctive purposes, it is a community which cannot take collective action on the issues of the day without endangering the conditions for its existence and effectiveness. . . . There is no mechanism by which it can reach a collective position without inhibiting that full freedom of dissent on which it thrives.[52]

When a university finds itself pressured by both sides of a contentious issue, a policy whereby its leaders do not (except in rare circumstances) take positions on divisive social or political issues is incredibly useful. The principled arguments in favor of such restraint are easy to understand. If all ideas are expressible on a campus, a campus leader who takes one side of a divisive issue might be signaling that the views of those on the other side will not be as highly respected; the campus has chosen its side. Which is more important: preserving a culture where all views can be expressed, protecting the full independence of thought, and enshrining the right to challenge prevailing opinion? Or having the university community know that, when push comes to shove, the university's leader will articulate the values of the university in relationship to social and political controversies?

When we consider the options available to university leaders it may be helpful to distinguish between the positions of institutional neutrality (the Kalven Report), institutional restraint, and institutional engagement.

As an alternative to the Kalven Report's notion that campus leaders should remain strictly neutral on matters of public debate, Princeton University president William G. Bowen in 1985 advocated a position of "restraint" that allowed for statements to be made when well justified. He noted that Princeton "is a value-laden institution, and it is for that reason that I avoid using the word 'neutrality' to describe its aims." Princeton's current president, Christopher Eisgruber, has reiterated his campus's commitment to the tradition of restraint. He recognizes that his main responsibility is "to ensure that the University remains an impartial forum for vigorous, high-quality discussion, debate, scholarship, and teaching," which requires "a presumption against commenting on social, moral, or political topics." But "this presumption is not . . . absolute" because there are occasions when it is important "to reaffirm or elaborate values that are fundamental to our community or mission," including, for example, its commitments to racial equity and inclusivity. In these circumstances, "silence is untenable" and some statement is necessary to prevent disruption of the university's basic functions.[53]

Other campus leaders believe that institutions should not feel restrained, but should engage with important current events. Brian Rosenberg, the former president of Macalester College, frequently voiced his thoughts on political events. He criticized President Trump's Muslim ban and other policies that conflicted with Macalester's commitment to "internationalism, multiculturalism, and service to society." He has argued that "those who turn it into a simple binary—never say anything or say things—are oversimplifying. Virtually everyone would agree that there are some instances where you need to say something." He views the college president as serving "a kind of pastoral role" in providing students a supportive environment, and this requires leaders sometimes "to say something that acknowledges to the community that you know some people are in pain or that some people are afraid." Speaking out in the wake of George Floyd's murder would be an example of acknowledging the fear and pain on a campus while linking that response to the core values of the institution.[54]

It also is often difficult to distinguish between the positions of institutional neutrality and institutional restraint. Both allow for expression by campus officials regarding matters related to the campus. There is no principled way to draw the line as to what is sufficiently related to the campus to allow for university officials to speak out.

In the wake of the bitter, angry, and unsettling divisions on campus around Israel-Palestine during the 2023–24 academic year, many institutions have adopted or been urged to adopt the Kalven Report's approach to institutional neutrality.[55] We agree with those who argue that such an approach, while tempting amid controversies, when any statement will be vilified by one or both sides, is not viable for value-laden institutions in an era when leaders are expected to articulate and reaffirm their institutions' core values. There are too many circumstances in which silence will be considered heartless or complicity with evil, and will harm the functioning of the institution. Even if some in the university community might disagree with statements in these circumstances, it should not be considered a violation of their rights to free speech and freedom of thought if university leaders occasionally say something they don't like. Continual editorializing by presidents and chancellors may create a chilling effect, but as long as there are no sanctions for people holding different views, the occasional expression of an opinion one disagrees with does not violate anyone's rights. Government officials and institutional leaders are also allowed their points of view.

Campus leaders should mostly speak out to articulate the basic values and mission of the university, celebrate and honor accomplishments that advance that mission, and address issues that directly affect our ability to teach, research, and serve our communities. As a usual principle, presidents and chancellors should not have official views about general social and political matters on which a diverse group of people will naturally disagree. A main responsibility of a campus leader is to ensure that the campus culture welcomes debate and discussion and protects the right of faculty and students to express controversial opinions and challenge prevailing ways of thinking. These responsibilities are even more pressing for leaders of public institutions because they are government entities, and the government should not be telling people what to say or think about matters of public debate. Campus leaders should emphasize that their primary goal is protecting the voice of members of their community. Whether or not the leader adds their own voice to a particular debate is far less important.

One reason campuses should manage expectations about when presidents or chancellors speak is that it is impossible for a leader to satisfy everyone's expectations about which matters deserve to be up-lifted by a campus message. Every campus contains individuals who are deeply committed to a wide range of causes or are desperately trying to draw attention to some circumstances that seem to urgently implicate fundamental human values. They are not wrong, but if leaders are ex-pected to amplify every cause or circumstance that some campus stake-holder deems a matter of great urgency, then presidents and chancellors would spend all their time issuing statements—and inevitably trigger additional demands, counterdemands, and denunciations.

At one of our campuses (UC Irvine), the standard on which these judgment calls are made is whether "the external event affects the ability of UCI (or institutions of higher education generally) to advance our mission of education, research and service; or the external event causes a level of disruption that raises questions about our community's ability to pursue education, research or other operations—or for members of the community to function effectively in their roles—manifesting a need to affirm our commitment to community, mission and/or val-ues."[56] This led one of us (Gillman) to issue statements denouncing candidate Donald Trump's proposed Muslim ban (to reassure the Mus-lim members of the campus that they are supported) and acknowledg-ing the pain and larger issues raised by George Floyd's murder. There was no statement after the Supreme Court overturned *Roe v. Wade* be-cause abortion rights are a deeply contested issue, and it was unclear how the campus could have an official position on the proper interpretation of the due process clause of the Fourteenth Amendment.

In the wake of the Hamas attack on October 7, there was a campus message acknowledging that profound tragedy and giving voice to our common humanity. One line read: "There is no notion of 'freedom fighting' or anti-Zionism that justifies or can rationalize the targeted murder and kidnapping of more than a thousand civilians." It turned out that many people on the campus disagreed with this view and bitterly objected to the statement. As many leaders around the country learned, any statement—or even the refusal to make a statement out of a commitment to institutional neutrality—was going to trigger bitter criticisms. Leaders must, on occasion, stand by what they believe is correct even when they know the criticisms will come. These choices are inevitably matters of judgment, based on expectations within the local campus context.

Ultimately, for both of us, the question is when silence is the wrong message—when it does more harm than good. At those times, it is important to speak out. To be sure, it is inevitably under pressure and at a difficult time. But a policy of never saying anything, while appealing for the way it eliminates choices, will prove unsustainable.

"DEI Statements" for Prospective Faculty Members

It is a routine component of faculty hiring in higher education for job seekers to submit statements describing their contributions to research or disciplinary knowledge, their contributions to teaching (including sometimes their philosophy of teaching), and their contributions to campus or disciplinary service. Starting in the 2010s, a number of universities also began encouraging and sometimes requiring candidates for faculty appointments to submit a personal statement on their contributions to diversity, equity, and inclusion. The new requirement reflected, in part, the growing diversification of student bodies in higher education and a belief that more intentional efforts were needed to expand opportunities for historically disadvantaged groups.

The University of California system was the first to require such statements. As described in the instructions given by the University of California, San Diego, "The purpose of the statement is to identify candidates who have the professional skills, experience, and/or willingness to engage in activities that will advance institutional diversity and equity goals." This requirement was linked to the university's formal documents on appointment and promotion, which included an assessment of "contributions to diversity and equal opportunity" while acknowledging that contributions "can take a variety of forms including efforts to advance equitable access to education, public service that addresses the needs of California's diverse population, or research in a scholar's area of expertise that highlights inequalities."[57] UC Davis's instructions noted that search committees often consider the applicant's "**Awareness** of inequities and challenges faced by underrepresented minority students and faculty; **Track record** (commensurate to career stage) of activities that reduce barriers in education or research for underrepresented minority students and faculty; **Vision and plans** for how their work will continue to contribute to UC Davis' mission to serve the needs of our diverse state and student population and create an inclusive campus."[58] According to a survey by the American Association of University Professors, as of 2022 more than one-fifth of colleges and universities include DEI contributions in tenure standards, including more than 45 percent of large institutions. A survey by the American Enterprise Institute of academic job postings found in 2021 that 19 percent required DEI statements, and elite institutions were more likely to do so.[59]

In the statement from the University of California's Office of the President, the need for such statements was predicated in part on the observation that "removing the barriers that prevent participation of all qualified people . . . in the science and engineering fields as well as in the social sciences, humanities, fine arts, and education is critical to development of an educated workforce" that can address important societal challenges. The document references a 2007 report from the National Academy of Sciences entitled "Beyond Bias and Barriers," which asserted that the United States "must aggressively pursue the innovative capacity of all of its people . . . to maintain leadership in the global marketplace." The UC president's statement argued that traditional efforts to accomplish this goal have yielded only slight improvements in the percentages of new faculty appointments for women candidates and underrepresented minority candidates. "In the coming decades, a more diverse faculty will be an increasingly important measure of a great university."[60]

It is appropriate that institutions dedicated to excellence in research and teaching would take note of the long-standing underrepresentation of historically disadvantaged communities among their students and faculties and make it an institutional mission to expand opportunities for talented people who have been historically excluded. The National Science Foundation refers to the number of people who could be making important contributions to science and engineering as "the missing millions" and calls on campuses to be more intentional about increasing representation of women and underrepresented groups in STEM fields to "help meet the country's STEM workforce needs."[61] Without a more intentional culture addressing these issues, faculty hiring can easily become "self-replicating," with established professors consciously or otherwise preferring candidates whose backgrounds resemble their own. Campuses that have achieved more diverse student bodies also understand that successfully teaching promising students from many different backgrounds and life experiences can be more challenging than teaching more homogeneous and privileged groups of students. Hiring faculty who can be successful teachers in such an environment is a commonsense job requirement. All of this is consistent with a simultaneous commitment to assessing an applicant's record without considering their race, ethnicity, or other categories that would violate constitutional and legal requirements prohibiting discrimination. The focus on such statements is assessing how a faculty candidate will teach a diverse student body.

Even though colleges and universities may have good reasons to assess the commitment of faculty members to these goals, the use of DEI statements in hiring is controversial, including among university professors. In a survey of college and university faculty commissioned by the Foundation for Individual Rights and Expression (FIRE), half of all respondents said that the use of such statements was "a justifiable requirement for a job at a university" and half said they represented "an ideological litmus test that violates academic freedom." Three-fourths of faculty who described themselves as liberal said they were a justifiable requirement, while 56 percent of moderate faculty and 90 percent of conservative faculty considered them an ideological litmus test.[62]

Critics claim that forcing applicants to make strong statements in favor of DEI initiatives inevitably leads to hiring decisions based on the applicant's political opinions, which would constitute unconstitutional viewpoint discrimination in violation of basic free speech principles. Abigail Thompson, a mathematician at the University of California, Davis, wrote in an opinion piece in the *Notices of the American Mathematical Society* that while "the professed purpose is to identify candidates who have the skills and experience to advance institutional diversity and equity goals," in reality "it's a political test, and it's a political test with teeth."[63] Considering whether universities should ask candidates to sign on to a particular vision of diversity as a condition of employment (for example, the premise that structural racism and sexism are serious challenges that must be proactively addressed), law professor Brian Leiter compares such requirements to loyalty oaths: "In a free and democratic society, citizens should not be penalized in the workplace for their lawful political opinions and expressions." Courts have agreed; one court concluded that "the state can neither directly nor indirectly interfere with an employee's or potential employee's rights to association and belief."[64]

Then again, a candidate's viewpoint is often relevant to their fit for a particular program. Scholarly peer review in the context of academic freedom is not blind to the substance of one's arguments; assessing the suitability of a candidate's viewpoints to a particular program or discipline is commonplace. As law professor Brian Soucek puts it, "When a university hires someone to run an asylum clinic, or to direct its program on entrepreneurship, it can reject an immigration restrictionist for the former search, but not the latter, and favor someone who is pro-capitalism for the latter search, though not the former."[65] When conservative lawmakers mandate new university centers focused on civics and "classical liberal education," they certainly expect that the leaders of such centers will have positive views about the canon that such centers will teach and promote.[66] By extension, if a university believes its "core mission" includes ensuring that a diverse students flourish in the classroom, how could it be irrelevant to the hiring of professors whether they are likely to contribute to that part of the mission?

Soucek agrees with critics that in evaluating the quality of a DEI statement, it would be inappropriate to attach higher or lower scores on the basis of political ideology or a declaration of beliefs that has no relationship to the qualifications for the position. He believes campuses should develop rubrics of evaluation that focus on what candidates have done or plan to do, not what they believe, when it comes to advancing diversity in their fields or at the institution. Focusing on actions rather than beliefs makes it "harder to fake" a commitment by repeating the right buzzwords; it also gives faculty members "the space to express dissenting views about their school's DEI commitments somewhere outside the diversity statement."

These reassurances have not quieted critics of the practice. One UCLA professor wrote, "If you doubt this is likely to be used as an ideological screening tool, imagine UCLA replacing 'equity, diversity, and inclusion' with [requirements to indicate one's support for] capitalism, freedom, and patriotism."[67] Others have called the statements "a form of virtue signaling" and "just another performative measure institutions take to convey their commitment to social justice ideas regardless of whether their policies and practices on the ground reflect these values."[68] Professor Steven Pinker, a co-president of Harvard's Council on Academic Freedom, wrote in an op-ed that the statements "purge the next generation of scholars of anyone who isn't a woke ideologue or a skilled liar."[69] Undoubtedly, some will not apply for jobs that require DEI statements.

After reviewing how Harvard's Bok Center suggests answering questions such as "Do you know how the following operate in the academy: implicit bias, different forms of privilege, (settler-)colonialism, systemic and interpersonal racism, homophobia, heteropatriarchy, and ableism?," Professor Randall Kennedy concluded that as a practical matter, these statements "will essentially constitute pledges of allegiance that enlist academics into the DEI movement by dint of softspoken but real coercion: If you want the job or the promotion, play ball—or else. . . . It does not take much discernment to see, moreover, that the diversity statement regime leans heavily and tendentiously towards varieties of academic leftism and implicitly discourages candidates who harbor ideologically conservative dispositions. . . . I am a scholar on the left committed to struggles for social justice. The realities surrounding mandatory DEI statements, however, make me wince."[70]

These concerns have led some leading organizations advocating for campus free speech and academic freedom to oppose mandatory DEI statements. The Foundation for Individual Rights and Expression claims the risk is too great that the statements will be used by faculty members to discriminate against applicants "for holding ideologically disfavored views." Some campus policies expressly penalize faculty applicants who question the effectiveness of racial affinity groups, measures that compel faculty to embed "anti-racist principles" in their curricula, or other DEI initiatives. If the statements are evaluated in ways that reward prospective faculty who promote DEI views in their teaching or research, they may violate the academic freedom of professors.[71] The Academic Freedom Alliance called for an end to the use of such statements on the grounds that an "academic seeking employment or promotion will almost inescapably feel pressured to say things that accommodate the perceived ideological preferences of an institution . . . notwithstanding the actual beliefs or commitments of those forced to speak." The group claims that the demand for these statements "enlists academics in a political movement, erasing the distinction between academic expertise and ideological conformity. It encourages cynicism and dishonesty." The statements also "distract search committees from fair and unbiased evaluation of candidates' merit as scholars and educators."[72]

A number of universities that formerly required the statements have now stopped. In the spring of 2024, both Harvard and MIT announced they would no longer require them of applicants for faculty positions. A former dean of medicine at Harvard said that many professors on hiring committees had been reluctant to voice their concerns about the requirement, but now the "silent majority of faculty who question the implementation of these programs and, in particular, these diversity statements—these people are being heard."[73] MIT president Sally Kornbluth explained that while MIT remained committed to tapping into the full scope of human talent, "compelled statements impinge on freedom of expression, and they don't work."[74] Many conservative state legislatures have also attacked "woke" activism and the ideology of DEI and have prohibited public campuses from requiring DEI statements.[75] In 2025, the Regents of the University of California prohibited requiring diversity statements for faculty applicants. The Trump administration has emphatically opposed DEI programs and statements, with threats to universities that they will lose federal funds if they maintain them.

We agree that it is an impermissible violation of free speech and academic freedom for DEI statements to be used as ideological litmus tests in hiring decisions. The criteria by which departments recruit new faculty members must focus exclusively on their professional qualifications as scholars with a mastery of disciplinary knowledge, a plan for making ongoing contributions to knowledge, and a capacity for transmitting that knowledge to students. As we have seen, scholars are not expected to be politically "neutral." But just as students are to be evaluated only on the basis of their scholarly competence, not their political viewpoints, so too must prospective faculty members be assessed only on the quality of their teaching and scholarship, as determined by experts in their fields of study. Academic freedom also protects faculty members from retribution if they publicly take issue with the policies of the campus or campus administrators, and this freedom would mean very little if applicants for faculty positions were pre-screened for their support of a particular set of DEI initiatives.

We believe it is possible, in theory, to require DEI statements and yet avoid unethical (likely unconstitutional) viewpoint discrimination, and also fully protect faculty who disagree with institutional policies. The prohibition against using DEI statements to screen for applicants' political views should be stated in no uncertain terms, and the rubrics for analysis should be sufficiently clear as to focus attention strictly on professional experiences and goals that contribute to the university's mission. In such circumstances can we be confident that applicants for faculty positions who express in such statements commitments to color-blind nondiscrimination and merit-based mentoring would not be put at a disadvantage? It is theoretically possible, but the suspicions about DEI statements being impermissibly used are widespread.

Campuses should keep in mind that faculty members are hardly unified on the legitimacy and efficacy of such requirements. At the same time, there may also be programs or disciplines in which these issues are more salient as a matter of scholarly reflection (such as hiring a professor of education with an expertise in advancing opportunities for historically underrepresented groups) and others where it is mainly a problem of the demography of the profession (such as engineering or chemistry).

A disadvantage of campus-wide requirements is that engagement with questions of diversity and equity often seems unrelated to specific disciplinary circumstances. We would urge departments to use more carefully tailored recommendations for prospective faculty, similar to the routine requirements for statements regarding research, teaching, and service. Also, given the controversies that now surround this issue, we urge campuses to create mechanisms to monitor whether hiring decisions are being made on irrelevant political grounds rather than on disciplinary mastery and scholarly and teaching excellence, and to create a culture whereby faculty who are involved in the hiring process may raise concerns outside of their programs if they believe improper considerations played a part in recommendations or decisions.

The Trump administration in its initial months has strongly opposed all efforts at DEI. It is imperative to separate the goals of diversity, equity, and inclusion from the means used to achieve them. We strongly believe that diversity, equity, and inclusion are essential goals

for educational institutions. Nothing from any Supreme Court decision or any law prohibits universities from pursuing being diverse,
equitable, and inclusive communities. Some means–such as preferences in admissions based on race–are prohibited. Giving a preference
in hiring based on views about diversity would be problematic. But
nothing in the law keeps schools from pursuing diversity through
lawful means.

Going Forward

Most controversies about what should and should not be said on
college campuses are framed as matters of free speech. But it is often
overlooked how much expressive activity on campuses is not governed
by general free speech principles. Universities are places dedicated to
the pursuit, achievement, and transmission of higher knowledge. For
all the attention given to protests and controversial speakers, the core
professional work of the university—in classrooms, labs, theaters, and
other places where professors interact with students—is governed not
by free speech but by the principles of academic freedom, a concept
that is central to the modern research university. These principles
give wide latitude to the decisions made by highly qualified experts in
their disciplines, but that deference is premised on their commitment
to perform their professional responsibilities both competently and
ethically.

Higher education is inevitably affected by the broader culture.
We live in turbulent times when social media encourages nasty, demeaning, and aggressive expression. But for universities to perform
the mission society has assigned them, campuses must embrace the
norms of a scholarly community and create relationships of mutual
respect and tolerance of diverse viewpoints. Campuses must be places
where, at the core, we work out our differences through civil debate
and deliberation. Professors must continue to model what it means to

engage the world with a scholarly frame of mind—asking hard and sometimes uncomfortable questions, expecting courage when confronting disturbing ideas, requiring more thoughtful and rigorous responses, and improving students' minds by demonstrating how to marshal stronger evidence or develop better arguments. It seems indisputable that the goal must be to create an environment where in every classroom, department, or school it is clear that all students are welcome to participate in the endeavor of mastering an academic discipline.

"Extramural" Speech

In addition to their on-campus and professional activities, professors, students, and administrators also express themselves in places other than the campus. They have outside lives, and like anyone associated with any organization, they reasonably assume that the organization will not claim an interest in everything they do when not at work.

Yet we have seen how a person's private expressions can lead to serious consequences in their professional environment. There may not be a generally accepted meaning of "cancel culture," but one dimension of it is when a person who has expressed themselves in ways considered unacceptable becomes the object of ostracization, boycotting, shaming, or bullying, often including the use of social media to pressure the person's social or professional circles to disassociate themselves from the offender.[1] This is, of course, not a new phenomenon. Communities have shunned and targeted people forever, powerful people have a habit of finding internal enemies to ostracize and isolate, and activists have organized boycotts to achieve political goals. But since the 2010s, the widespread use of social media has dramatically increased the number of people who share their opinions not just with relatives, friends, and neighbors but with large numbers of strangers. Cell phone videos can now capture anyone's bad behavior. In ways not previously imaginable, many people who would otherwise be anonymous are just a few clicks away from angry denunciation by thousands if not millions. Social media creates an unprecedented ability to reach a mass audience instantaneously.

Universities are not immune. Like anyone else, some professors and students have always had strange or unsettling private opinions, but for most of the history of higher education, who would know? Faculty members who say outrageous (or merely unpopular) things on social media can now expect their institutions to receive pressure to rebuke, sanction, or fire them. Students who have received acceptance letters may find their plans changed when campuses revoke the acceptance after controversial statements or actions are revealed. Institutions of higher education are, after all, deeply mission driven and anchored in frequently recited aspirational principles of honest exploration, curiosity, integrity, discovery, mutual respect, toleration of difference, progress, enlightenment. Should not such principled institutions care whether those who affiliate with them embrace beliefs that deeply offend these values? Despite commitments to free expression, should they not banish the unworthy from their midst? Then again, what if a student or faculty member is merely worried that they have opinions that, in the real world, would be viewed as ordinary, but that are inconsistent with the prevailing views of some righteous colleagues?[2]

In this chapter we explore the circumstances under which universities should address, even sanction, statements made by its members that are considered outrageous, and conversely, the circumstances in which outrageous external utterances should be tolerated even in the face of pressure campaigns for sanctions or banishment. We begin by describing some established general principles governing the external or "extramural" speech of faculty members, as laid out over the decades in canonical discussions of academic freedom and its relationship to the ordinary free speech rights of the professoriate. We also discuss how campus statements about "principles of community" or norms of student conduct affect students' free speech rights. We then review some cases of controversial speech that, in our judgment, should be considered protected despite demands for sanctions—and then some more difficult cases in which speech may justify an institutional response. Along the way we discuss whether there is a difference between the steps that may be taken against professors or students and those that may be taken against administrators who hold their positions "at will" and are expected to be representatives of the institution. We also look at some institutional responses that are not necessarily "sanctions," such as changing a professor's teaching or service assignments.

General Considerations for Faculty, Students, and Administrators

Before getting to more complicated questions, we should begin with a straightforward point. Speech that would be considered a violation of university policy or law if it occurred on campus is also a violation of policy or law if it takes place off campus or on social media. Students could harass other students either in person or on social media. The same is true, of course, of serious threats, incitement, or other categories of speech not protected under First Amendment law.

We previously discussed the case *Feminist Majority Foundation v. Hurley* to make the point that institutions cannot be deliberately indifferent to the harassment of women students on the campus.[3] One aspect of that case was that some of the harassment took place over the social media platform Yik Yak, which facilitated anonymous online postings within a limited geographic range. The women, students at the University of Mary Washington, had documented "nearly 200 examples of students using Yik Yak to post either violent, vitriolic hate or threats against [them]" and asked the administration for help. The university responded with a schoolwide message saying that viewpoints expressed on social media platforms were matters of free speech and therefore it could provide "no recourse for such cyber bullying"; instead, it encouraged the students to report their concerns to the social media company.

The United States Court of Appeals for the Fourth Circuit ruled that "although that harassment was communicated through cyberspace, the Complaint shows that UMW had "substantial control over the context of the harassment because it actually transpired on campus." Some of the posts were created "using the University's wireless network" and "specifically targeted UMW students." UMW, the court said, cannot "turn a blind eye to the sexual harassment that pervaded and disrupted its campus solely because the offending conduct took place through cyberspace."

Simply put, speech that otherwise would be a basis for university sanctions is not more protected because it occurs over social media. The more difficult question is whether speech that would otherwise be protected by First Amendment principles may nevertheless be a basis for institutional responses against professors or students. It would be easiest to simply say that constitutionally protected speech is always protected, but more needs to be considered before we can reach that conclusion.

We begin with factors related to extramural speech by faculty members, because the boundaries of such speech have long been a subject of discussion among advocates of academic freedom.

At the beginning of the twentieth century, there were countless examples of professors being fired or threatened with termination for expressing controversial ideas in public.[4] That is why the 1915 *Declaration of Principles on Academic Freedom and Academic Tenure* included protections for "extramural" (externally directed) speech. After discussing the importance of the freedom to promote inquiry and advance the sum of human knowledge and the freedom to provide general instruction to the students, the declaration turned to the third major category of academic freedom: the social importance of having expert scholars share their knowledge with the public.[5]

The authors of that document were trying to break free from the traditional American practice of having college leaders, boards, and politicians control what faculty members were permitted to study, teach, and discuss.[6] To justify deference to the professoriate, the authors needed to convince their audiences that a professional, scholarly faculty could be trusted with that responsibility, just as well-respected professionals were trusted in fields such as law and medicine. It was in the interest of society if "men of high gift and character should be drawn into [this] profession by the assurance of an honorable and secure position," including the "freedom to perform honestly and according to their own consciences the distinctive and important function which the nature of the profession lays upon them."

In describing the importance of developing "experts for the use of the community," the declaration noted that the audience for such expertise—whether legislators, administrators, or the public—must "enjoy their complete confidence in the disinterestedness of [their] conclusions." Therefore, with regard to professors' extramural utterances,

> it is obvious that academic teachers are under a peculiar obligation to avoid hasty or unverified or exaggerated statements, and to refrain from intemperate or sensational modes of expression. But, subject to these restraints, it is not . . . desirable that scholars should be debarred from giving expression to their judgments upon controversial questions, or that their freedom of speech, outside the university, should be limited to questions falling within their own specialties. . . . "It is neither possible nor desirable to deprive a college professor of the political rights vouchsafed to every citizen." . . . [Still, it is] in no sense the contention of this committee that academic freedom implies that individual teachers should be exempt

from all restraints as to the matter or manner of their utterances, either within or without the university. Such restraints as are necessary should in the main . . . be self-imposed, or enforced by the public opinion of the profession. But there may, undoubtedly, arise occasional cases in which the aberrations of individuals may require to be checked by definite disciplinary action. What this report chiefly maintains is that such action cannot with safety be taken by bodies not composed of members of the academic profession.

The authors emphasized that they were not advocating the "absolute freedom of utterance of the individual scholar," but rather "the absolute freedom of thought, of inquiry, of discussion and of teaching, of the academic profession." They acknowledged that it was "conceivable that our profession may prove unworthy of its high calling, and unfit to exercise the responsibilities that belong to it." But the "existence of this Association . . . must be construed as a pledge, not only that the profession will earnestly guard those liberties without which it cannot rightly render its distinctive and indispensable service to society, but also that it will with equal earnestness seek to maintain such standards of professional character, and of scientific integrity and competency, as shall make it a fit instrument for that service."

A social contract was thus being proposed: in exchange for recognition of their rights and privileges, members of the scholarly community would take responsibility for maintaining standards of professional character in their utterances "either within or without the university." Hence the language in the classic 1940 *Statement of Principles on Academic Freedom and Tenure*: when faculty members "speak or write as citizens, they should be free from institutional censorship or discipline, but their special position in the community imposes special obligations," including the responsibility to "remember that the public may judge their profession and their institution by their utterances," and hence "they should at all times be accurate, should exercise appropriate restraint, should show respect for the opinions of others, and should make every effort to indicate that they are not speaking for the institution."[7]

There is a tension between the claim that professors have all the expressive rights of citizens yet also have "special obligations" when their speech should be considered an extension of their professional identities as scholars whereby "the public may judge their profession and their institution." A political scientist who has an expertise in gerrymandering might have a social media account in which she reviews local restaurants, new music releases, or video games, and no one would confuse those utterances with her work as a scholar. In such cases, there are no "special obligations" and ordinary free speech rights apply, including the right to be irresponsible, unserious, or wrong. But if this same scholar were called to testify as a scholar about legislative redistricting, she would have an obligation to "be accurate," "exercise appropriate restraint," "show respect for the opinions of others," and so on. Similarly, as Keith Whittington has put it, "an engineering professor who makes a hobby of Holocaust denial might expect to be shielded from professional repercussions, but a historian of twentieth-century Europe espousing the same views should expect closer scrutiny and likely adverse professional consequences."[8]

Yet these obligations do not necessarily mean that college and university administrators have unilateral authority to monitor faculty members' public expressions or to sanction speech they consider insufficiently accurate, restrained, or respectful. Whittington argues that "we should be comfortable giving the faculty freedom to engage in idle speculation and boisterous public debate because we want to give them the freedom to speak their minds and to develop the habits of thought that allow them to think in ways that are creative and unorthodox, sometimes ingenious but sometimes just wrong. Cultivating a professoriate willing to speak its mind on any topic and in any forum is a necessary precondition for intellectual progress."[9] In the early twentieth century, Harvard president A. Lawrence Lowell recognized that extreme or injudicious public utterances by professors could "shock public sentiment" and harm the affiliated institution. Yet it would be even riskier, he warned, if universities tried to censor what professors said in public, since the university then "assumes responsibility for that which it permits them to say."[10] The institution would be better protected if it distanced itself from the expressions of individual professors and emphasized that they were speaking for themselves, not the institution.

How to reconcile professors' general rights as citizens from their "special obligations"? In 1964, the AAUP's Committee on Academic Freedom wrote that the "controlling principle is that a faculty member's expression of opinion as a citizen cannot constitute grounds for dismissal unless it clearly demonstrates the faculty member's unfitness to serve. Extramural utterances rarely bear upon the faculty member's fitness for continuing service."[11]

We agree with this summary. It should happen very rarely that a faculty member's extramural speech would constitute grounds for sanction or dismissal by the institution. But there could be extreme cases where public expressions clearly demonstrate "the faculty member's unfitness to serve." In such cases, the process for considering sanctions should be similar to the ordinary processes of peer review of a scholar's contributions; that is, the claim of unfitness to serve should (in the words of the original 1915 report) be judged initially by bodies "composed of members of the academic profession." This puts professional scholars in the same position as physicians and lawyers in those rare circumstances when their utterances raise questions about their fitness to serve in those professions.[12]

Other members of the campus community may also have some "special obligations" to refrain from public commentary that casts doubt on their professional fitness. For example, physicians in clinical settings have an ethical obligation to "do no harm" and to convey that all patients will get the care they deserve.[13] But for students and most staff, there generally are no obligations associated with their status that require them to be careful about their public expressions. This, too, is not absolute. If a medical or law student in a clinical setting were to publicly reveal confidential information, that could be a basis for sanctions.

Do students have other obligations that would justify campus sanctions based on their off-campus utterances?[14] Most campuses articulate "principles of community" that are designed to create an atmosphere of civility, honesty, integrity, mutual respect, and other norms central to the work of a scholarly community. The University of California's principles of community are fairly typical. They emphasize a commitment to "offering all its members a safe, supportive, responsive and equitable environment." They recognize that "diversity contributes to the university's strength" and state that the university "rejects all forms of discrimination." The document also asserts that the university "commits to fostering an atmosphere of respect and empathy" and expects every faculty and staff member "to behave in ways that support these principles and to do what he or she can to improve life at UC."[15]

But at most public and secular universities that are not governed by religious or (for example) military honor codes, these statements of principle are aspirational declarations rather than enforceable regulations. They typically stand alongside a parallel commitment to "defend the right to free speech." As one statement clarifies, "Even though speech may contravene the school's principles of community, the speaker cannot be punished for such a violation, unless the speech falls into one of the specific content- or conduct-related exceptions to the First Amendment. As such, while speech may be hurtful and offensive, and may oppose the Principles of Community, it may still be protected by the First Amendment."[16] This does not prevent campus officials from denouncing outrageous speech or urging greater attachment to that institution's principles of community. But a commitment to free speech principles prevents campuses from using aspirational statements as a basis for punishing extramural student speech that is otherwise protected by the First Amendment.

Finally, campuses have more flexibility to take steps against the extramural speech of campus officials who have higher-level administrative positions, such as presidents/chancellors, vice presidents/vice chancellors, deans, department chairs, and executive directors. These officials typically have "at-will" appointments, meaning they can be terminated from these positions without cause so long as the dismissal is not otherwise illegal. By virtue of their positions, they are seen as representing the institution and in general are not permitted to make public statements that would harm the institution's reputation. No college or university would be expected to continue a dean's appointment if they were making racist remarks on social media or disparaging women students. The executive director of student enrollment should not publicly speak out against the university's special programs providing outreach to historically underrepresented student populations if these programs are a campus priority. Larry Summers the economist may speak publicly about the gender disparity in the sciences, but Larry Summers the university president might get in trouble if he makes remarks about gender that the Board of Overseers considers unpresidential.

This expectation of higher-level administrators should not be pushed too far. Insisting that every administrator toe the line and never publicly disagree with a president or a board would be inconsistent with maintaining a highly qualified leadership team.[17] Moreover, when faculty members are serving in administrative positions, a statement that might lead to their removal from the at-will administrative position should have no bearing on their faculty position, as long as the statement does not rise to the rare level of demonstrating professional incompetence as a professor.[18] In general, administrators are less immune from sanction for controversial public speech than faculty members and students.

The Boundaries of Faculty Members' Extramural Speech

How should these general considerations apply in specific circumstances? We begin with examples of controversial speech by professors that, in our judgment, deserved to be protected despite pressure on institutions to impose sanctions.

Steven Salaita's anti-Zionist tweets. In the fall of 2013, Steven Salaita was offered a position as associate professor with tenure in the American Indian studies program at the University of Illinois Urbana-Champaign, with a start date of August 2014. Like all offers, it was conditioned on the approval of the board of trustees. In July 2014, a major conflict broke out between Hamas and Israel in Gaza, with many Palestinians killed. Salaita used his Twitter account to post hundreds of messages about the conflict, including statements such as "Let's cut to the chase: If you're defending #Israel right now you're an awful human being"; "This is not a conflict between #Israel and 'Hamas.' It's a struggle by an Indigenous people against a colonial power"; "The logic of 'antisemitism' deployed by Zionists, if applied in principle, would make pretty much everybody not a sociopath 'antisemitic' "; and "If it's 'antisemitic' to deplore colonization, land theft, and child murder, then what choice does any person of conscience have?"[19]

These posts caused an uproar, with right-wing publications like the *Daily Caller* writing that the university "has continued its bizarre quest to employ as many disgusting scumbags as possible by acquiring the services of Steven Salaita, a leading light in the movement among similarly obscure academics to boycott Israel."[20] In late July, the university's chancellor, Phillis Wise, discussed the situation in a closed session with the campus's board of trustees. On August 1, having received hundreds of letters from alumni, students, parents, and members of the local Jewish community—and well after Salaita had quit his previous job and was preparing to move to Illinois—Wise informed him that the university had decided not to present his appointment to the board because it was "unlikely" to win their approval.

On August 22, Wise released a statement explaining that while robust, intense, and provocative debate and disagreement are deeply valued by the university, "what we cannot and will not tolerate at the University of Illinois are personal and disrespectful words or actions that demean and abuse either viewpoints themselves or those who express them."[21] On September 11, the trustees voted 8-1 to support Wise's decision to reject Salaita. Some four hundred faculty members signed a letter supporting the decision, while fifteen academic units voted "no confidence" in her. The president of the Illinois system, Robert Easter, backed Wise, explaining, "I have come to the conclusion that Professor's Salaita's approach indicates that he would be incapable of fostering a classroom environment where conflicting opinions could be given equal consideration." Easter also expressed concern that "his irresponsible public statements" would make it more difficult to attract the best students, faculty, and staff.[22]

A college senior and former intern for the American Israel Public Affairs Committee collected more than thirteen hundred signatures on a petition opposing the appointment. "Hate speech," the petition read in part, "is never acceptable for those applying for a tenured position. . . . There must be a relationship between free speech and civility." But the head of the UIUC English department said that there were times in public discourse "when we may need to expand our notion of what constitutes an acceptable tone so that it is commensurate with the events at stake," and the director of the American Indian studies program called the decision "despicable."[23] A year later, after a number of lawsuits and the chancellor's resignation, Salaita settled with the university for $875,000.[24]

Assuming, for the sake of argument, that Salaita was properly considered hired by the university and should have been treated as a tenured professor, his tweets expressing strong opinions about Israel, Zionism, Hamas, and colonialism should be considered protected speech and therefore could not be a basis for sanctioning him, much less firing him. In almost all such cases, these sorts of public statements fall under the category of professors speaking or writing as citizens rather than operating in professional settings, and this means they have all the free speech rights enjoyed by everyone else. Even if such statements occasionally affect assessments of professionalism, we should recall that according to the AAUP's Committee on Academic Freedom's 1964 statement cited earlier, the assumption is that "extramural utterances rarely bear upon the faculty member's fitness for continuing service." It should be presumed that during the recruitment process, the University of Illinois evaluated Salaita's record as a teacher and judged it consistent with the high standards expected of its faculty members. More generally, it is improper to infer from strong or even intemperate public statements that a scholar is incapable of maintaining an appropriate classroom environment. If every over-the-top social media post by a professor were sufficient to show that they are unfit for service, then there would be essentially no protections for faculty members to challenge orthodoxy in their public statements, and one of the key goals of academic freedom would be eviscerated.

Since the advent of social media, we have discovered that people everywhere, including in university communities, express opinions that others find unacceptable. But campuses cannot excommunicate everyone who expresses controversial opinions if their work within campus settings meets all standards for professional and ethical behavior. Campus stakeholders must accept that some of their colleagues may hold views they would consider outrageous. Otherwise, the witch hunts would be endless, and the views targeted by those witch hunts would constantly evolve, until nobody would feel safe to utter anything except banalities.

The monkeypox tweet. On July 15, 2022, Timothy Farage, a computer science professor at the Jonsson School of Engineering and Computer Sciences at the University of Texas, Dallas, tweeted from his personal account a response to an article stating that most monkeypox patients in New York City were gay men. He asked, "Can we at least try to find a cure for homosexuality, especially among men?" The incident sparked an outcry among LGBTQ+ students and allies, who demanded that administrators take "substantive action" against the professor and reaffirm the university's commitment to diversity and inclusion. They noted that UT Dallas had earned a reputation for being LGBTQ+ friendly and that many students had chosen to attend because they believed it offered an environment free from homophobia. To remain true to this reputation, should the campus sanction a professor who held contrary beliefs?

No, it should not. The public views expressed by this computer science professor raised no questions about his behavior in professional settings or his expertise or competence in computer science; thus it was a matter of free speech rather than academic freedom. The university announced it was starting an investigation into Farage based on complaints over his tweet. But that decision—while perhaps understandable given the Department of Education's expectations that campuses treat accusations of discrimination seriously—was not justified because the statement at issue was clearly protected by the

First Amendment. Launching investigations into faculty members whenever they express controversial opinions would clearly have a "chilling effect" on professors' willingness to express views in public.[25]

Instead of imposing sanctions or launching an investigation, the campus should have focused on speaking out against Farage's views, reasserting its commitment to its values, and finding ways to address the students' concerns. A campus announcement said: "We unequivocally denounce statements that disrespect groups or individual members of our community. UT Dallas is committed to providing an educational, living, and working environment that is welcoming, respectful and inclusive." The dean of the Jonsson School also wrote in a message that "over the weekend, a faculty member . . . expressed some thoughts about homosexuality on his personal Twitter account. We are personally appalled by those comments. Many of you, in direct messages to us or in public comments, have expressed disappointment, not feeling safe and concern for yourself or classmates. . . . As part of our immediate response, we can share that tomorrow we are opening up additional sections of the fall classes taught by the professor to include at least one other professor to provide more options for students."[26]

Rather than sanction a professor for constitutionally protected speech, the campus correctly used its institutional voice to articulate its values. Rather than change Professor Farage's conditions of employment, it addressed students' concerns by offering them the option of taking classes with another professor. The campus was not obliged to change the teaching schedule, but doing so was a way of acknowledging the concerns that students conveyed to the administration. This is inevitably a judgment call. It would be unreasonable for campuses to set up other course sections every time students found a faculty member's views unacceptable. For example, one of us (Chemerinsky) faced a situation where students in a required class demanded to be transferred to another section when they found a ten-year-old article that a professor had written criticizing Critical Race Theory. The students said it made them feel "unsafe" in the professor's class. But their request was denied because the article was a scholarly discussion that expressed no bias; nor was there any indication or allegation of racial bias in anything the professor had written or said. Never had there been an allegation of racial bias against the teacher in many years of instruction. Students cannot refuse being assigned to classes simply because the teacher has expressed views they disagree with. It also is important for administrators to distinguish between students disagreeing with what a professor wrote and their plausibly feeling "unsafe." Often disagreeing or being offended is presented as feeling "unsafe."

In the example of Farage, would it have been acceptable to cancel his classes or assign him to different classes because of his extramural speech? In principle, no faculty member is entitled to teach any particular class during any particular academic term, although they are entitled to be assigned courses in their areas of expertise or as described in their offer of employment. Teaching schedules are typically set at the discretion of deans and department chairs, who must take many factors into account, including faculty members' preferences, the need to cover required classes, and student evaluations of how well particular professors teach certain classes. If a faculty member was not especially good at teaching large required introductory courses, it would be normal for a department chair to assign a better teacher. If a faculty member is controversial for the kinds of reasons Farage was controversial, it would not be a violation of academic freedom to assign that person to elective courses or to offer options for students regarding required courses.

Farage eventually issued a statement saying he had "no intention of offending anyone" and "I deeply apologize to those who were. Students who have taken courses from me know that I harbor no ill will towards anyone, and especially not because of their sexuality, or race, or country of origin. Please forgive me."[27]

The tweet while Queen Elizabeth II was dying. In September 2022, reports started circulating that the queen of England was on her deathbed. Upon hearing that news, Dr. Uju Anya, a Nigerian American linguistics professor at Carnegie Mellon University, tweeted: "I heard the chief monarch of a thieving, raping genocidal empire is finally dying. May her pain be excruciating." This drew the predictable flood of condemnations, which were then supercharged when the world's richest man, Jeff Bezos, wrote, "This is someone supposedly working to make the world better? I don't think so. Wow." Piers Morgan called Professor Anya a "vile, disgusting moron." Her original tweet was taken down by Twitter and she was locked out of her account. There were many demands that she be fired.

But she faced no formal discipline. Instead, the university released a statement calling her message "offensive and objectionable" while acknowledging the importance of protecting free expression. "Free expression is core to the mission of higher education, however, the views she shared absolutely do not represent the values of the institution, nor the standards of discourse we seek to foster." In turn, Anya received letters of support from Carnegie Mellon faculty members and students, some of whom said that the university could have acknowledged that her views do not represent the institution without the additional step of criticizing her speech.

Anya later explained that fifteen years into the reign of Queen Elizabeth II, civil war broke out in Nigeria, a former British colony, creating a humanitarian catastrophe. "We lost half of our relatives. That's the legacy of this war. It was a genocide, a slaughter, a holocaust. If anyone expects me to express anything but disdain for the monarch who supervised a government that sponsored the genocide that massacred and displaced half my family and the consequences of which those alive today are still trying to overcome, you can keep wishing on a star." She also said that she understood why the university distanced itself from her words, adding, "I'm grateful that my university reiterated my right to freedom of speech and expression."[28]

People may object to the fact that the university said anything critical of her remarks, but the most important point is that there was no effort either to launch an investigation or to consider sanctions against Anya for exercising her free speech rights.

The tweet about "Black privilege." A little over a week after the videotaped murder of George Floyd by Minneapolis police officer Derek Chauvin, University of Central Florida psychology professor Charles Negy, who had written a book titled *White Shaming: Bullying Based on Prejudice, Virtue-Signaling, and Ignorance,* tweeted, "Sincere question. If Afr. Americans as a group, had the same behavioral profile as Asian Americans (on average, performing the best academically, having the highest income, committing the lowest crime, etc.), would we still be proclaiming 'systemic racism' exists?" A few minutes later he tweeted, "Black privilege is real," naming affirmative action as an example.

In the wake of a flood of outraged responses and calls for Negy to be fired, the university denounced his remarks but acknowledged his free speech rights. "We are aware of Charles Negy's recent personal Twitter posts, which are completely counter to UCF's values. We are reviewing this matter further while being mindful of the First Amendment." The university's interim provost explained in a meeting with angry students that tenured faculty can be removed only for job-related misconduct, not controversial speech. "We can act when people's conduct is in the course of their job, when it's in their classroom, when it's with their colleagues. People's behavior is something we can act upon. But we can't act on people's speech outside the university." He also urged students to report racist, intolerant, or demeaning behavior in any professor's classroom.

They did. Not long thereafter, the university announced that it was opening an investigation into Negy because "we have been receiving complaints alleging bias and unfair treatment in Dr. Negy's classroom. . . . Everyone has the right to their personal beliefs, but no university employee may mistreat or discriminate against students in their classes or in any other setting. No student should fear they will be treated differently because of others' personal biases."[29]

While launching an investigation based solely on the views expressed in Negy's tweet would be improper, a campus must obviously investigate a professor if it is receiving "complaints alleging bias and unfair treatment" in his classroom. Even though Negy had received campus awards three times for his teaching, and his recent evaluations rated him "outstanding," the university was obligated to take seriously any new reports of improper behavior. Investigators reviewed thirty-seven hours of classroom recordings, heard from hundreds of witnesses, and interviewed Negy for nine hours. He admitted to making some crude comments in class that were designed to be humorous, including a conversation about race and penis size during which he "jokingly" high-fived a Black student.

In a 244-page report of its findings, the Office of Institutional Equity concluded that Negy's tweets were protected under the First Amendment and that many of his classroom comments were protected by academic freedom. Nevertheless, the investigator concluded that he had created "a hostile learning environment" with his comments and actions associated with the "high-five" and by using a multiple-choice question on an exam that forced students to accept that a "rational person" would equate a religious upbringing with "child abuse." Negy received a formal Notice of Intent to Terminate. In response, he claimed the investigation was just a ruse to fire him for his unpopular speech.[30]

More than a year later an arbitrator ruled that the university had to reinstate Negy because the institution failed to show "just cause" for his termination and had not given him a chance either to correct his conduct in the classroom or, alternatively, to show that he was incapable of changing his behavior. "There is no evidence that U.C.F. gave him reason to believe he was anything but as highly esteemed as his evaluations and treatment, with no reason to perform differently," the arbitrator wrote, and he should not be sanctioned for what the institution "retroactively sees as serious misconduct." UCF responded that it "stands by the actions taken following a thorough investigation that found repeated misconduct in Professor Negy's classroom, including imposing his views about religion, sex and race. However, we are obligated to follow the arbitrator's ruling." Negy applauded the ruling, saying that "it was a fraudulent firing from the beginning" and "just because George Floyd died, which was a national tragedy, doesn't mean the social mob gets to go around demanding people get fired just because they are offended by controversial comments."[31]

Throughout this controversy, the university appropriately emphasized that Negy's external speech could not be the basis for sanctions and that an investigation was warranted only after new accusations were made regarding his professional conduct in the classroom. Given that the university had praised his teaching over several years and that the accusations arose only after the uproar over his public statements, it is understandable that the campus and the arbitrator might interpret the record differently. The arbitrator's emphasis on providing someone with Negy's record an opportunity to either change his behavior or show that he was incapable of changing is a legitimate consideration before making a decision about termination under academic freedom principles. And in cases such as these, the determination of whether the record demonstrates a lack of professional competence or ethics should include an assessment by faculty peers.

The professor who wondered if women were destroying academia. Eric Rasmusen, a tenured economist at Indiana University's Kelley

School of Business, had caused controversy for years with his public comments, including a claim that gay men should not be hired as schoolteachers because they might prey on children. In 2019, he tweeted a link to an article titled "Are Women Destroying Academia? Probably" and quoted a line from the article that claimed, "Geniuses are overwhelmingly male."[32]

The university's provost, legal scholar Lauren Robel, decided she needed to say something about what it meant to have a professor with such views on the campus. Her long statement was both an assertion of university values and a frank explanation to the campus community, including infuriated students, about what universities can and cannot do under these circumstances. We consider her statement exemplary.

Robel noted that Professor Rasmusen "has, for many years, used his private social media accounts to disseminate his racist, sexist, and homophobic views." She called these views "stunningly ignorant, more consistent with someone who lived in the 18th century than the 21st." But she made it clear that "we cannot, nor would we, fire Professor Rasmusen for his posts as a private citizen, as vile and stupid as they are, because the First Amendment of the United States Constitution forbids us to do so. That is not a close call."

Referencing the university's nondiscrimination policy, she wrote that "we demand tolerance and respect in the workplace and in the classroom, and if Professor Rasmusen acted upon his expressed views in the workplace to judge his students or colleagues on the basis of their gender, sexual orientation, or race to their detriment, such as in promotion and tenure decisions or in grading, he would be acting both illegally and in violation of our policies and we would investigate and address those allegations according to our processes." She noted that it was "reasonable" that students who are women, gay, or of color could be concerned that, given the strength of his views, he might "not give them a fair shake in his classes."

Therefore, Robel announced, "No student will be forced to take a class from Professor Rasmusen. The Kelley School will provide alternatives" to his classes and "Professor Rasmusen will use double-blind grading on assignments." If some components of the course could not be subject to double-blind grading, then the school "will have another faculty member ensure that the grades are not subject to Professor Rasmusen's prejudices." She ended her statement:

> The First Amendment is strong medicine, and works both ways. All of us are free to condemn views that we find reprehensible, and to do so as vehemently and publicly as Professor Rasmusen expresses his views. We are free to avoid his classes, and demand that the university ensure that he does not, or has not, acted on those views in ways that violate either the federal and state civil rights laws or IU's nondiscrimination policies. . . . But my strong disagreement with his views—indeed, the fact that I find them loathsome—is not a reason for Indiana University to violate the Constitution of the United States. This is a lesson, unfortunately, that all of us need to take seriously, even as we support our colleagues and classmates in their perfectly reasonable anger and disgust that someone who is a professor at an elite institution would hold, and publicly proclaim, views that our country, and our university, have long rejected as wrong and immoral.[33]

One might question whether the campus should have changed Rasmusen's teaching assignments and required double-blind grading if there was no evidence that he had in fact treated students unfairly. But the campus was not responding to fleeting comments that some found inappropriate. It was the strength and long-standing nature of these views that made concerns about fair treatment reasonable. Moreover, we do not think these adjustments in teaching responsibilities constitute the kinds of "sanctions" that would violate Rasmusen's free speech or academic freedom rights. But reasonable scholars may disagree, and if Rasmusen claimed violations of his rights, he was entitled to an assessment of the issue by his faculty peers.

A few months later Rasmusen was informed that he was under investigation for making "unwelcome comments based on race, sex, sexual orientation, and religion" in professional settings. News of the investigation led him to send an email to students taking stock of the accusations against him and soliciting comments about the charges. "Most of you have been interviewed by the investigators—thirteen out of the seventeen of you in the class, it seems." Eventually the university concluded that he had violated university policies; it also viewed his emails as "witness retaliation." The campus informed him that he was free to speak and write as he wished "outside of class and the university," but "you do not have the right to treat students or colleagues in a derogatory or stereotypical manner when performing your roles as an employee of the university." The university cut his pay by 10 percent and barred him from teaching required courses or participating in faculty hiring. He retired soon after.[34]

The tweet about "lesser" Black women Supreme Court nominees. When Supreme Court justice Stephen Breyer announced his retirement, President Biden responded in January 2022 that "the person I will nominate will be someone with extraordinary qualifications, character, experience and integrity—and that person will be the first Black woman ever nominated to the United States Supreme Court."[35] A few days later, Ilya Shapiro, a constitutional law expert at the conservative Cato Institute and the incoming executive director of the Georgetown Law School Center for the Constitution, tweeted: "Objectively best pick for Biden is Sri Srinivasan, who is solid prog[ressive] & v smart. Even has identity politics benefit of being first Asian (Indian) American. But alas doesn't fit into latest intersectionality hierarchy so we'll get lesser black woman. Thank heaven for small favors?"[36] The next day, Shapiro deleted the tweet and apologized for his "poor choice of words" while reasserting his view that "men and women of every race" should be considered.

The Black Student Association at Georgetown, in a petition signed by more than nine hundred people, condemned Shapiro's comments and called for the university to rescind his employment offer. The dean of Georgetown Law issued a statement in response to the outcry: "The tweets' suggestion that the best Supreme Court nominee could not be a Black woman and their use of demeaning language are appalling. The tweets are at odds with everything we stand for at Georgetown Law and are damaging to the culture of equity and inclusion that Georgetown Law is building every day."[37] The university placed Shapiro on administrative leave pending an investigation into whether he violated policies and expectations of professional conduct, nondiscrimination, and anti-harassment. He maintained that his tweets could not be grounds for disciplinary action. "My tweet was inartful and undermined my antidiscrimination message, which is why I apologized. It was not, however, a violation of any university rule or policy, and indeed is protected by Georgetown policies on free expression," which declare that "it is not the proper role of a University to insulate individuals from ideas and opinions they find unwelcome, disagreeable, or even deeply offensive" and "it is for the individual members of the University community, not for the University as an institution, to judge the value of ideas, and to act on those judgments not by seeking to suppress speech, but by openly and vigorously contesting those arguments and ideas that they oppose."[38]

Many free speech advocates agreed with Shapiro. The Foundation for Individual Rights and Expression said the investigation was "antithetical to the tenets of liberal education and cannot be squared with [the university's] promise to provide 'all members' of its community 'the broadest possible latitude to speak, write, listen, challenge, and learn' even if others find it 'offensive, unwise, immoral, or ill conceived.'" Its statement concluded, "There is nothing to investigate."[39] A nationwide letter to the dean of Georgetown Law, signed by more than two hundred law professors, said that "subjecting Shapiro to disciplinary action of any kind based on his tweet" would be contrary to basic academic freedom principles, and "debate about the President's nomination, and about whether race and sex play a proper role in such nominations more generally, would be impoverished—at Georgetown and elsewhere—if this view could not be safely expressed in universities. . . . More broadly, firing Shapiro for expressing his views will send a message to others in Georgetown . . . that debate about matters having to do with race and sex is no longer free; that the promises of academic freedom are empty; and that dissent from the majority views within the law school is not tolerated."[40] Progressive *New York Times* columnist Michelle Goldberg urged Georgetown to show restraint, saying that the law school "overreacted" since "however offensive Shapiro's words were, they're also the sort of political speech that should be protected by basic notions of academic freedom." She quoted a comment by the *Atlantic*'s Adam Serwer that "it's impossible for academic institutions to fulfill their missions if they fire or punish people under circumstances like these."[41]

Georgetown's investigators found that Shapiro's tweet would have violated university policy against discriminatory harassment if he had been employed by the university at the time, but because he had not yet started his job, the tweet was not a violation. We disagree strongly with this conclusion. The claim that one or two tweets on a social media platform could possibly constitute discriminatory harassment at the law school is unsupported by the law, which limits findings of harassment to targeted expression or expression that is so severe or persistent as to deny a person in a protected class the ability to enjoy the benefits of the educational environment on an equal footing with others. It has never been interpreted to forbid discrete public statements that offend some people. That would require colleges and universities to proactively shield their affiliates from any disagreeable or offensive idea that a faculty member might express on social media—clearly an impossible and undesirable standard.

When given the opportunity to join the Georgetown Law community in the wake of these findings and statements, Shapiro refused. He wrote in a *Wall Street Journal* editorial that "academia has become an intolerant place for anyone, not just conservatives but anyone who seeks the truth," and "one of the most pernicious parts of recent developments" is that "in the name of diversity, equity and inclusion, bureaucrats enforce an orthodoxy that stifles intellectual diversity."[42]

Although we disagree with the suggestion that Shapiro's tweet rose to the level of discriminatory harassment, the saga is complicated by the fact that he had been hired for a senior administrative position, as the executive director of the law school's Center for the Constitution. In his note to the community, the dean indicated that "I expect him, as a staff member at the Law Center, to communicate in a professional manner."[43] This is a reasonable expectation for any law school faculty member with a social media account. But as we noted earlier, the public utterances of university administrators may be held to a higher standard. Georgetown should not use anti-harassment policies against free speech. But it does not have to tolerate senior administrators who express themselves publicly in ways that undermine the university's reputation or create disruptive controversies. If the mistake about the meaning of discriminatory harassment had been resolved, Shapiro would still have faced a choice between accepting the new administrative position, understanding that he must be more careful in his public utterances, or declining the offer because he more deeply valued his right to express himself unfettered from those expectations.

The professor who suggested murder as an alternative to disruptive protests. After Wayne State English professor Steven Shaviro read the criticism of Stanford law students who disrupted a federal judge's speech at the school (discussed in chapter 1), he published a Facebook post explaining why he thought the students did not go far enough. "Although I do not advocate violating federal and state criminal codes, I think it is far more admirable to kill a racist, homophobic or transphobic speaker than it is to shout them down. . . . The exemplary historical figure in this regard is Sholem Schwarzbard, who assassinated the anti-Semitic butcher Symon Petliura, rather than trying to shout him down. Remember that Schwarzbard was acquitted by a jury, which found his action justified." Shaviro argued that disrupting right-wing speakers actually strengthens them by giving "more publicity and validation to these reprehensible views than they could otherwise attain" and by allowing the speakers to cast themselves as victims.

Wayne State's president responded with a message to the campus community. "We have on many occasions defended the right of free speech guaranteed by the First Amendment to the U.S. Constitution, but we feel this post far exceeds the bounds of reasonable or protected speech. It is, at best, morally reprehensible and, at worst, criminal." The president announced that the campus had "referred this to law enforcement agencies for further review and investigation," and pending that review, "we have suspended the professor with pay, effective immediately."[44]

Universities must take threats of violence seriously. But the president was wrong in saying that Shaviro's post exceeded the bounds of protected speech. According to the relevant Supreme Court precedents at the time, for a threat of violence to be considered an unprotected "true threat," the speaker must intend "to communicate a serious expression of an intent to commit an act of unlawful violence to a particular individual or group of individuals."[45] This does not include rhetorical hyperbole or the hypothetical endorsement of violence. Speech does not become unprotected "incitement" unless it is "directed to inciting or producing imminent lawless action and . . . likely to incite or produce such action."[46] Shaviro also explicitly stated that he was not advocating the violation of criminal law, although the post would have been protected speech under the First Amendment even without that sentence.

The best that might be said about the university's response is that it did not sanction Shaviro for violating university rules; instead, it suspended him with pay pending a review by law enforcement about whether a crime had been committed. The implication was that there would be no further action against Shaviro if the law enforcement investigation led to nothing, which is what happened. Still, the university could have decided on its own that the Facebook post could not reasonably be considered criminal. Conversely, given the rise in political violence in the United States and other democracies, it would be fully justifiable to condemn Shaviro's casual armchair admiration for people who commit assassination, especially in a context where the presumed target was a sitting federal judge.

The professor who thought cops should be killed. In February 2019, UC Davis student Nick Irvin published an investigation in the student newspaper of tweets posted in 2014 by English professor Joshua Clover in which Clover said that police officers should be killed. One tweet read, "I am thankful that every living cop will one day be dead, some by their own hand, some by others, too many of old age." Another read, "I mean, it's easier to shoot cops when their backs are turned, no?" In a 2016 interview, Clover also said, "People think that cops need to be reformed. They need to be killed." Even though the tweets and statements were years old when they were uncovered, they were especially painful to many in the community because of the recent killing of Natalie Corona, a young police officer in the city of Davis.

The university responded to the student's report by condemning Clover's statements, mourning the loss of Natalie Corona, and expressing gratitude to law enforcement. The provost told the reporter that "the basis for academic freedom is to make sure that the university is a place where unpopular and different views are heard," and he insisted that Clover be protected from sanctions because "our practice has not been to discipline people for things that they say outside the university." The reporter wasn't satisfied, noting that the university's statement of support for law enforcement "rings even more hollow when viewed against the moral fabric of our local Principles of Community," which committed the campus "to non-violent exchange and the highest standards of conduct and decency toward all." He believed the campus should "more forcefully deny speech that harkens to barbarism and bloodshed. . . . It doesn't matter that his comments came years ago; there can be no statute of limitations on violent speech when the offender in question refuses to apologize or make amends. When professors advocate murder, we all lose."[47]

Many local and state officials agreed with the student and demanded that Clover be fired. A former Sacramento sheriff said, "You're actually calling for the death of human beings. They [the university] have a right to say, 'That's not consistent with our values.'"[48] California Republicans introduced legislation calling for the university to fire Clover and delivered a petition with more than ten thousand signatures.[49] In a press conference on the UC Davis campus where he was joined by the president of the California Police Chiefs Association and the widow of a slain officer, California assemblyman James Gallagher demanded Clover's termination and claimed that rhetoric that advocated violence is not protected under the First Amendment. "We can't have free speech," Gallagher said, "when we have professors calling for the deaths of people they disagree with." The Davis College Republicans and a former student body president organized a rally: "Fire Josh Clover: A Rally Against Violence."[50] In response to a reporter's request for a statement, Clover emailed, "On the day that police have as much to fear from literature professors as Black kids do from police, I will definitely have a statement. Until then, I have nothing further to add."[51]

Despite the enormous political pressure, Chancellor Gary S. May took no action against the professor, but asked the campus legal team to review the issue. The provost noted, "We have not received a complaint of conduct that may be in violation of the Faculty Code of Conduct. If we received such a complaint, it would be reviewed in accordance with our policies. . . . Public statements like those made by Professor Clover are accorded a high level of protection under the First Amendment."[52] The campus also clarified that it was not permissible for leadership simply to fire a tenured professor. "Only the UC Board of Regents can dismiss a tenured faculty member. This must be done by a vote of the board upon recommendation by the University of California president, following consultation with the chancellor."[53]

Assemblyman Gallagher was wrong when he said that Clover's statements are not protected speech under the First Amendment. And while the student reporter was correct that the campus's principles of community explicitly denounce violence and threats of violence, those principles cannot be the basis for imposing sanctions on a professor who is exercising his rights of free speech. It is extremely difficult to stand for the principles of free speech and academic freedom amid such widespread community outrage and pressure campaigns from state officials, but the campus met the test by denouncing the statements and refusing to launch an investigation or impose sanctions.

A professor fired for antisemitic social media posts. In 2014 and 2015, Joy Karega, an assistant professor of rhetoric and composition at Oberlin College, wrote on her Facebook page that ISIS was really U.S. and Israeli intelligence personnel and that those intelligence agencies had planned the horrendous terrorist attacks on the Paris offices of *Charlie Hebdo*. She also said that Israel had shot down Malaysian Airlines flight No. 17 over Ukraine, expressed support for Nation of Islam leader Louis Farrakhan's declaration that Zionists and Israeli Jews were behind the September 11 attacks, and shared antisemitic images such as a picture of Jewish banking heir Jacob Rothschild with the words, "We own your news, the media, your oil and your government."

The college denounced her statements but defended Karega's rights to express controversial opinions. Oberlin's president wrote, "Cultivating academic freedom can be difficult and at times painful for any college community. The principles of academic freedom and freedom of speech are not just principles to which we turn to face these challenges, but also the very practices that ensure we can develop meaningful responses to prejudice." Before long, however, the college's board of trustees requested that the college investigate whether Karega's statements called her professional fitness into question.[54]

If campuses are going to take steps against faculty members, they must ask not whether extramural statements are controversial but whether they cause one to question (in the words of the AAUP) a faculty member's fitness for continuing service. If there are such concerns, then rather than take unilateral action, boards or college leaders should put that question to the faculty for assessment, just as the faculty ordinarily assesses aspects of professional competence such as teaching excellence or the quality of scholarship.

In response to the board's request, the deans of Oberlin's College of Arts and Sciences announced that "conversations have begun within the governing bodies" and that while academic freedom was nonnegotiable, "there are professional standards, expectations and responsibilities that must be recognized and upheld." Karega was suspended pending the investigation.

After what was described as "extensive consideration and a comprehensive review of recommendations from multiple faculty committees" and from the president, the board announced that it had voted to dismiss Karega for "failing to meet the academic standards that Oberlin requires of its faculty and failing to demonstrate intellectual honesty." The announcement emphasized that "the central issues are Dr. Karega's professional integrity and fitness" rather than whether her remarks were controversial. Karega, the board said, "was represented by counsel; she presented witness testimony, documents, and statements to support her position; and she had the opportunity to cross-examine witnesses testifying against her." The criteria used as part of the faculty review process was whether Karega adhered to the "Statement of Professional Ethics" of the AAUP, which required faculty members to "accept the obligation to exercise critical self-discipline and judgment in using, extending and transmitting knowledge" and to "practice intellectual honesty." The General Faculty Council concluded that her statements "irreparably impaired [her] ability to perform her duties as a scholar, a teacher, and a member of the community" and that she had demonstrated no willingness to remedy her misconduct.[55]

Since the principles of academic freedom were first articulated, it was always contemplated that as members of a prestigious profession, faculty members have a "special obligation" to be mindful of public utterances that might call into question their professional competence and ethics. As noted in the original 1915 *Declaration on Academic Freedom and Tenure*, "There may, undoubtedly, arise occasional cases in which the aberrations of individuals may require to be checked by definite disciplinary action. What this report chiefly maintains is that such action cannot with safety be taken by bodies not composed of members of the academic profession."

Oberlin's focus on professional expectations and responsibilities, rather than the mere expression of controversial opinions, is consistent with this concept of academic freedom, and the reliance on faculty bodies and peer assessment was correct. If faculty members' extramural utterances can lead to their dismissal, the process should proceed as Oberlin's did in this case. It also must be remembered that because Oberlin is a private institution, the First Amendment did not protect the professor's statements or limit the college's sanctions.

The "race realist" professor who belittled her non-white students. For years, University of Pennsylvania Law School professor Amy Wax, a self-proclaimed "race realist," made public statements reflecting beliefs in white supremacy and European cultural supremacy. Many people considered the statements racist. She said, for instance, that "on average, Blacks have lower cognitive ability than whites," that the country would be "better off with fewer Asians" as long as they tended to vote for Democrats, and that "Blacks" and other "non-Western" people harbor "resentment shame, and envy" against Western people for their "outsized achievements and contributions" even though, "on some level, their country is a shithole." She said in a podcast, "I often chuckle at the ads on TV which show a Black man married to a white woman in an upper-class picket-fence house," but "they never show Blacks the way they really are: a bunch of single moms with a bunch of guys who float in and out." She invited a white supremacist to speak to her class. A Black law student at Penn who got her undergraduate degree from Yale said that Wax told her she was admitted to those Ivy League schools "because of affirmative action." In 2018, after she publicly commented on the academic performance and grade distributions of the Black students in her required first-year course—either speaking falsely (as some said) or revealing confidential information about student grades—she was removed from teaching required courses.

Wax has contended for years that she is the target of censorship because of her conservative views, and that the pressure campaigns against her violate principles of free speech and academic freedom. She said in a podcast interview that universities want to "banish and punish" anyone "who dares to dissent, who dares to expose students to different ideas. That is a really dangerous and pernicious trend."

In 2022, the law school's dean asked the chair of the Faculty Senate to convene a hearing board to review whether Wax's conduct violated Faculty Handbook standards, especially the university's non-discrimination policies and "standards of professional competence." He claimed that "Wax has shown a callous and flagrant disregard for our University community . . . who have been repeatedly subjected to Wax's intentional and incessant racist, sexist, xenophobic, and homo-phobic actions and statements."[56] Wax had made these statements, he said, "in the classroom and on campus, in other academic settings, and in public forums in which she was identified as a University of Penn-sylvania professor," and they had led many faculty and students to "reasonably believe they will be subjected to discriminatory animus if they come into contact with her." The dean also charged her with having "exploited access to students' confidential grade information and mischaracterized Law School policies in ostensible support of derogatory and inaccurate statements made about the characteristics, attitudes, and abilities of her students."

The dean's twelve-page document included references to very dis-turbing public statements that "disparage immigrants, people of color, and women," that lacked the requisite "respect for the opinions of oth-ers," and might lead students to worry that they would not be treated fairly in Wax's classes. This alone might not be sufficient to demon-strate a lack of professional competence or ethics. But the document also detailed allegedly discriminatory statements made directly to stu-dents as well as Wax's use of derogatory and hateful stereotypes that "breached fundamental ethical and research standards of rigor and at-tribution," including, for example, improper citation of a decades-old study that did not support (as she claimed) her view that "women are less thoughtful than men." She claimed that no science was being conducted in places like Malaysia, which is false, violating the expectation that faculty members will always strive to be accurate. She made disparaging comments to faculty colleagues in apparent disregard of the professional obligation to show respect to others. Collectively these actions led African American and Asian students to avoid her courses and avoid applying for clerkships when Wax was on the relevant committee, and led her colleagues "to report that her conduct is harassing and her presence on-campus is demoralizing and disruptive."[57]

Because the dean's report seemed to mix negative reactions to what would be constitutionally protected public expressions with more specific charges about direct harassment and professional incompetence, several free speech groups criticized his request for an official hearing.[58] The Academic Freedom Alliance wrote to the university's president that the dean's request was a "a grave violation of her academic freedom" and that Wax's expression of her personal opinions did not exhibit the "flagrant disregard of the standards, rules, or mission of the University or the customs of scholarly communities" that would lead to a conclusion of unfitness.[59] The Foundation for Individual Rights and Expression called her situation a test case for academic freedom "right up on the line" but added that "we have not seen any evidence that it crosses the line. . . . Academic freedom has to protect the Amy Waxes of the academic world, so that it can be there for the Galileos of the academic world." An official at PEN America said the idea that off-campus comments can lead to an investigation "is concerning."[60]

A published version of the closing argument made before the Faculty Senate hearing board by Wax's lawyer drew attention to the question of whether Wax viewed her media commentary as an extension of her teaching at Penn and whether her statements were supported by facts and research. Presumably, if these statements were merely expressions of personal opinions about a range of topics, they might not shed light on her professional competence, but if they were an extension of her scholarly work, they might be assessed for quality and accuracy as any scholarly work might be. Her attorney's closing argument emphasized that most of the complaints concerned minority students' disapproval of things she said in the media, rather than credible stories of personal racial animus. "Statements made outside the classroom do not create a hostile environment in the classroom. . . . Academic freedom doesn't end with the tears of a student."[61]

We should disclose that one of us (Chemerinsky) was asked to be a witness in the matter and submitted a written statement. In a fifteen-page letter that reviewed Wax's statements, he concluded:

> A school's actions need not *just* be a public condemnation or an open letter. Actions can be in the form of disciplinary action taken against a professor when the professor's conduct (1) negatively impacts the learning environment; (2) violates the professional norms and rules of an institution; and (3) violates Title VI, Title VII, or Title IX. Indeed, there are times when schools have the obligation to take action so as to not be deliberately indifferent in a manner that violates the law.
>
> To be clear, I have spent my career as a staunch advocate for freedom of speech. I am very reluctant to believe that a professor should be disciplined for his or her expression. But speech is not absolute and there is a point at which a professor's speech crosses the line and can be a basis for disciplinary action. If such a line exists—and few would take the position that there is no line and that speech is absolute—then I am firmly convinced that Professor Wax's speech crosses that line and is a basis for discipline. This is not about one or two isolated statements. It is not about pedagogical choices or scholarly writing. It is about the repeated expression of racism, sexism, and homophobia, in conversations with students

and in classrooms and other settings. Disciplinary action against Professor Wax on this record would violate neither the First Amendment nor academic freedom.

Wax's statements to the media are protected by the First Amendment (which Penn, a private institution, chooses to follow), and her statements in class were generally protected by academic freedom even though some seemed to violate acceptable professional norms. But her statements to individual students that were hurtful and discriminatory are protected by neither.

Although the university has a policy of not releasing information about personnel actions, a leaked copy of the hearing board's report shows that the board recommended that Penn sanction Wax. "We regard this to be a case not of free speech, which is broadly protected by University policy . . ., but rather of flagrant unprofessional conduct by a faculty member" that "has had a detrimental impact on equal access to educational opportunities" at the law school. "For this reason, we focus in this report on widely acknowledged standards of our profession, which recognize a difference between professional conduct and protected free speech." To support a finding that Wax violated professional standards, the report references "her *uncritical* use of data and unfounded *declarative* claims in some of her courses, campus events, and elsewhere as a representative of the University of Pennsylvania." It concluded that Wax relied on "misleading and partial information" to "make unsubstantiated statements and to draw sweeping and unreliable conclusions. . . . By conveying these positions with reckless disregard for scholarly and professional norms, she has failed to effectively teach all our students, majority and minority students alike."

The board also found that Wax "has on numerous occasions, both inside the classroom and in public, flagrantly violated University norms to treat all students with equitable due respect," with the result that she "created a hostile campus environment and a hostile learning atmosphere." Many of the "examples of inequitably targeted disrespect" in appendix 1 of the report refer to public utterances.[62]

The recommended sanctions included a one-year suspension at half pay, the removal of her named chair and summer pay, and a requirement that Wax make it clear in public appearances that she was not speaking on behalf of the law school. It did not recommend that she be fired or stripped of tenure.

The Foundation for Individual Rights and Expression criticized the report for not distinguishing between claims of actual discrimination and "claims about her protected classroom and extramural speech." By emphasizing "misleading and partial information" to present "controversial views," the process had sidestepped "academic freedom protections. . . . If scholars with controversial views can lose their academic freedom merely for unspecified 'unprofessionalism' concerns, all faculty who hold minority, dissenting, or simply unpopular views are at risk." FIRE noted that "even if the conduct-related concerns are legitimate, lumping them together with Wax's speech in one process dispatches with academic freedom entirely, casting aside the special right of faculty to introduce and discuss controversial or upsetting material in class." It recommended that on appeal, Penn should hear the speech and non-speech charges against Wax separately, adhere to clear and objective standards for each charge, and recognize the importance of protecting both academic freedom and free speech in any decision.[63]

Wax called the hearing board report "brazen and absurd" and appealed the ruling.[64]

In September 2024, the university formally accepted the board's recommendations and suspended Wax for a year at half pay, removed her from her named chair, and required her to note in public appearances that she was not speaking for or as a member of the Penn Carey Law School or the University of Pennsylvania. She was not fired; nor did she lose her tenure. She also received a public reprimand from the provost, which stated that while academic freedom is very broad, teachers "must conduct themselves in a manner that conveys a willingness to assess all students fairly" and they may "not engage in unprofessional conduct that creates an unequal educational environment." The board's decision, he told Wax, reflected the view that her conduct left "many students understandably concerned that you cannot and would not be an impartial judge of their academic performance." In the future it would be "imperative" that she refrain "from flagrantly unprofessional and targeted disparagement of any individual or group in the University community." The chair of the Faculty Senate, law professor Eric Feldman, stated, "This has been a faculty driven process and . . . the decision in the case was reached after a significant amount of faculty time and thought, and is in accordance with the process set forth in the Faculty Handbook."[65]

The Amy Wax saga, which played out over many years, illustrates some of the most important yet vexing questions about when campuses can sanction professors for extramural speech. The accusations that led to the creation of a Faculty Senate hearing board reflected a mixture of distress about controversial public utterances and concerns about more in-person, on-campus statements and interactions. But we can make a few general observations about how campuses should respond to these challenges.

Student disagreement or outrage over extramural speech cannot alone be the basis for concluding that a faculty member lacks professional competence or ethics or that they are creating a hostile learning environment, even if the utterances lead one to suspect that the faculty member may be prejudiced or hostile to certain groups of students. In our current media environment, almost anything a faculty member might say about a matter of public interest could become the basis for claiming that they are not fair-minded in the classroom.

Absent actual evidence of classroom misbehavior, those public statements cannot demonstrate unfitness. On the other hand, discriminatory statements in public might supplement evidence of unequal treatment of students in learning environments.

If a faculty member publicly expresses views on topics in which they claim a scholarly expertise—such as an astronomer sharing views on an upcoming eclipse, an American historian discussing controversies over historical events, or law professors criticizing the latest court opinions—then public statements that demonstrate a lack of knowledge or expertise would be relevant to an assessment of their professional competence. Otherwise, in almost all cases, they should be considered the free speech of a citizen rather than the performance of scholarly duties. If campuses consider using public statements as a basis for assessing fitness as an expert, the nexus between the statement and the peer review should be made explicit, and it would be best if that assessment were part of the ordinary processes for reviewing scholarly contributions.

Attempts to sanction faculty on the grounds that they make unfounded declarative claims in courses or elsewhere, or that they rely on misleading and partial information to draw unreliable conclusions, require very clear and consistent specifications of when such claims might get a faculty member in trouble. Also, importantly, those standards would need to be applied evenhandedly across the entire campus. Otherwise, controversial faculty members would be put under a microscope that is never used for their colleagues. Might many faculty members sometimes make unfounded declarative claims in classrooms or in public? Or occasionally rely on partial information? What would distinguish the faculty members who are sanctioned for doing so from those who are not?

Finally, just because a faculty member claims that their controversial opinions make them a target for ideologically driven pressure campaigns, this does not mean they are not also violating norms of professional competency and ethics. We recommend that when proceeding on these grounds, investigating boards should maintain a rigorous separation between conclusions based on extramural speech and those based on other evidence, as well as a clear statement of whether the professor is being held accountable for extramural speech on the grounds that their public utterances demonstrate a lack of scholarly competence.

When Can Students Be Sanctioned for Extramural Speech?

Controversies regarding faculty extramural speech are complicated by their "special obligations" as professionals and (relatedly) by the fact that there are times when their public speech falls squarely within their free speech rights as citizens, and other times when their views are extensions of their scholarly work and thus governed by academic freedom.

The issue of student extramural speech is less complicated, even if it can cause similar amounts of disruption, outcry, and political pressure. Because students are not members of a profession whose reputation might be judged by how they present themselves, their speech on social media and in other off-campus environments is entirely governed by free speech principles. If a person in general cannot get in trouble for saying something controversial, colleges and universities should not be able to sanction students for saying it. Conversely, if the expression is not protected because (for example) it meets the legal standards for harassment, true threats, incitement, and other types of unprotected speech, then institutions can respond appropriately under the circumstances.

Still, university environments are held to different expectations because they have obligations under federal law to respond to complaints about harassment and "hostile environments" in educational settings. When members of the university community express outrage at what a student has said on a social media platform, it is risky for campuses to shrug their shoulders and call it none of their business. This is especially true because (as we discussed in chapter 1) the Department of Education's Office of Civil Rights has instructed colleges and universities that they can be held in violation of federal civil rights laws if they do not respond appropriately, even when the cause of the complaint is constitutionally protected speech. Even though students have a constitutional right to express views, a university might still be required (under federal guidance) to investigate the matter and possibly respond in some way that does not punish the student for the speech. The directives from the Office of Civil Rights also make clear that it does not call for a prohibition or punishment of speech that is protected by the First Amendment.

This federal guidance puts campuses in a difficult position, one that (for example) municipalities do not face when some resident doesn't like what another resident said on their X account. Municipalities can shrug off the complaint, but campuses cannot, at least not always. Title VI and Title IX obligate schools not to be deliberately indifferent to speech that creates a hostile environment.

Student investigated for reading historical book. One example of this challenge arose in January 2023, when a Stanford student posted an image of another student posing at a dormitory party reading Adolf Hitler's manifesto *Mein Kampf.* It was reported that the woman held the book just below her eyes and held her forefinger to her lips, as if to "convey an exaggeratedly thoughtful expression." After the image was circulated, another student submitted a "Protected Identity Harm" incident report—essentially a complaint of discrimination— through the university's reporting process, which exists to ensure that students and other community members can inform the university of situations in which they feel attacked by virtue of their protected identities.

The next day, an associate dean and the executive director of Hillel responded to students' complaints: "It can be upsetting to hear about incidents like this. If you, either as a member of that residence or a member of our broader community are feeling impacted in any way, please reach out to us."[66] Stanford rabbis informed Jewish students, "Swift action was taken by the leadership in the residential community where both the individuals who posted and the one pictured are members, and where these actions are causing the most direct damage to relationships and feelings of safety and belonging."[67] They said they were working with student affairs staff and had spoken to the individuals involved.

In response, the Foundation for Individual Rights and Expression wrote to Stanford. Any response to a student reading a book, FIRE wrote, is "unacceptably punitive and chills expressive activity. . . . Being 'invited' by administrators with institutional disciplinary authority to engage in a formal reconciliation process to atone for reading a book—one that has been previously assigned as required reading for a Stanford class and is available to check out at Stanford's library—is not conducive to the campus free speech culture." The campus's response suggests that there was something problematic about the student's actions and "they may accordingly self-censor." If this harm reporting system were to continue, the campus should "undertake a cursory review of PIH complaints and first determine whether the conduct alleged constitutes protected expression." If it did, the campus should not contact the student exercising her rights.[68]

In response, the university said that a Protected Identity Harm report is "not a judicial or investigative process" and participation is voluntary. "At the request of the student organization, we have been engaged in conversation with a number of students, seeking to provide support and foster communication. However, there has been no requirement that any student meet with or report to a university official to discuss the matter. No one is being punished or investigated by the university for reading a book."

In fact, however, many people thought an "investigation" or at least formal "process" had been set in motion simply because a student appeared to be reading a particular book. This did not sit well with a Jewish Stanford student who wrote in the *Stanford Review:*

> No matter what the context of the photo was, the community's reaction stands in opposition to the liberal values of the university. . . . We should not chastise students for reading controversial books, and we *certainly* should not spread an institutional message that "feelings of safety and belonging" should be prioritized above academic freedom to read controversial books or the personal freedom to make an off-kilter joke. . . . Any education that prioritizes student comfort over the pursuit of knowledge and full understanding is one that underestimates students' ability to grapple with complex and perhaps sensitive topics.[69]

In response to nationwide mocking of a bias report based on "Student reads historical book," a group of Stanford faculty called for an end to the system of anonymous Protected Identity Harm reporting. Although the procedure was intended to "build and maintain a better, safer, and more respectful campus community," faculty members claimed, "it reminds me of McCarthyism" and "you're basically going to be reporting people who you find offensive, right?" Though the process was not explicitly "punitive," any process that involves complaints about protected speech that leads campus officials to contact students who are merely engaging in ordinary student or expressive activities raises concerns that the climate of free expression and viewpoint diversity might be chilled.[70]

On the other hand, the Department of Education's Office for Civil Rights has instructed campuses that they must have some process by which individuals can report claims of bias against protected classes. If there are concerns that certain activities are creating a discriminatory learning environment in potential violation of Title VI, then campuses must take steps to mitigate the concern. Campuses are also directed to take meaningful steps if people believe certain activities are creating a discriminatory learning environment. If they don't, they risk a violation of Title VI of the federal Civil Rights Act. We agree with FIRE's recommendation that campuses should make an initial determination about whether the complained-about activity is protected speech, and if so, that they develop a response that does not require contact with individuals.

Investigation of a student's viral antisemitic diatribe. It is not always easy for campuses to refrain from "investigating" students whose external comments are legally protected but still inflame the campus community. Tulane University student Sarah Ma published an article titled "Ye Did Nothing Wrong" on the right-wing news platform The College Dissident, in which she promoted stereotypes about Jews and defended the antisemitic rants of the rap artist formerly known as Kanye West. After widespread demands that the campus investigate and punish her, the associate vice president and dean of students sent a campus-wide email that denounced Ma's article, pointed traumatized students to a phone line for emotional support, restated the university's free speech policy, and said that the campus would review student complaints. "Tulane strongly condemns antisemitism, anti-Blackness, and all forms of bias and discrimination," the statement read. "While the importance of free expression on a university campus cannot be overstated, words that run counter to our core values impact our community."[71]

Some free speech activists criticized the message on the grounds that it violated Tulane's own free speech policy. FIRE said that any investigation should be "both brief and entirely private." "The university should be able to read the article and say, 'OK, this is protected under our free-speech promises.' And that's it."[72] FIRE said, "Tulane could have expressed its disagreement with Ma's speech while reaffirming its commitment to free expression."

Although universities should not initiate proceedings or investigations into "student conduct" against students for exercising their rights, they have both a legal and an ethical responsibility to respond to complaints about discriminatory activity or hostile environments on their campuses. In this case, the campus merely said that the matter was being reviewed and offered concerned students access to resources; it did not say that Ma would face any sanctions for her protected speech. Campus officials even offered Ma a security detail and walked her through the process of filing harassment complaints or reporting threats.

It is, of course, a judgment call whether or when campus officials should make public statements regarding a student's controversial speech. They cannot react to every controversial utterance, and commenting risks exposing more students to messages that would otherwise be overlooked. But it does not violate anyone's rights for a campus to articulate or reiterate its values or its principles of community when campus members express hateful or discriminatory ideas that give rise to widespread concerns on the campus. It is an example of addressing an issue with "more speech" rather than censorship.

After dropping out of her sorority and resigning from the Women in Politics club, Ma took a leave of absence from Tulane. She apparently had not expected anyone there to find her piece, and she insisted that her detractors misread her article. "The only thing I did wrong," she said in a statement to *College Dissident*, "was overestimating the intelligence of most of the Tulane population."[73]

Punishing a student for a "crude" social media post. Kimberly Diei, a pharmacy graduate student at the University of Tennessee, posted images of herself (under a pseudonym) in which she was wearing a tight dress with cleavage exposed and was sticking out her tongue. In homage to the rapper Cardi B, one of her idols, she made up some raunchy rap lyrics. She thought it was all good fun but also wanted to celebrate music for people like her, "strong Black women who embrace our sexuality." An anonymous source reported her to campus officials, and a disciplinary panel declared her posts "vulgar," "crude," and not in keeping with the mores of the pharmacy profession. It ordered her expelled.

A distinctive dimension of this case was that the disciplinary panel focused on the more specific question of whether the social media posts violated the "Standards of the Health Professions," rather than on the general question of whether Diei's posts were inconsistent with expectations of students in general. The particular standards include prohibitions against "conduct which would bring disrepute and disgrace upon both student and profession and which would tend to substantially reduce or eliminate the student's ability to effectively practice the profession in which discipline he or she is enrolled." Federal courts have allowed some health professionals at public colleges to sanction and even expel students whose public statements indicate a lack of professionalism, including a nursing student whose Facebook posts joked about "giving someone a hemopneumothorax" and called a female student "a stupid bitch."[74] Yet the same document that refers to unethical and unprofessional conduct also promises that "nothing in this chapter is intended or shall be interpreted to restrict students' constitutional rights, including, but not limited to, rights of freedom of speech and assembly."[75]

If students in the health disciplines were told that their general free speech rights were limited by some "special obligation" to be careful about public utterances, then perhaps the action against Diei would have been more understandable (although still possibly wrong). But the campus said explicitly that this was not the case.

Diei was reinstated at the college three weeks after she appealed her expulsion and initiated a lawsuit against the university "to ensure that other people, especially minorities, are allowed to have their voice and are allowed to live." She specifically wanted to draw attention to how vague "professionalism" norms might improperly allow established, traditional experts to impose outdated expectations on new generations of students who come from more diverse backgrounds. It was especially problematic that the health sciences center was not able to tell her exactly what it defines as appropriate or inappropriate off-campus speech.[76] It would be troubling for professional norms to be defined so broadly as to justify a student's expulsion for a post like Diei's.

If professional schools at universities want to consider enforcing standards of professional conduct that limit what would otherwise be constitutionally protected extramural speech, they should not publish documents that promise otherwise; they should consider incidents that call for the enforcement of such restrictions to be, like violations of academic freedom obligations, incredibly rare events; and they should provide much clearer criteria for the kinds of statements that might demonstrate "unfitness" for the profession. Such actions as publishing patient details in a blog or using one's status to promote clearly unsafe treatments might qualify. Sassy or risqué social media posts, by themselves, should not.

Rescinding admission offers based on racist social media posts. After the video-recorded murder of George Floyd, several colleges and universities revoked undergraduate offers of admission after discovering racist social media posts by students who had not yet enrolled. Cornell rescinded an offer to a star high school athlete after a Snapchat video of him using a racial slur went viral. Marquette revoked an incoming freshman's admission offer because of a mocking Snapchat post about Floyd's death. An honors student bound for the University of Florida had to change plans when the university learned of an Instagram post in which the student declared she was "most definitely" a racist.[77]

We believe that campuses can consider many factors when they decide which applicants to admit, including not only a student's academic achievements but evidence of their values and whether they would make a welcome addition to the campus community. Many applicants go to great lengths to show themselves in an admirable light. Campuses must not screen for allegiance to a particular partisan ideology, but if, during the admissions process, they find evidence of racism, dishonesty, or a lack of respect for others, then it is expected that that would count against an application, given the norms and "principles of community" necessary to sustain an academic environment. At the same time, as we have repeatedly emphasized, once a student becomes a member of the university community, they should not be sanctioned for constitutionally protected extramural utterances.

The interesting question is when free speech protections for prospective students take effect. Is it when they are given offers of admission, when they arrive on campus, or when they are formally enrolled?

This is not a matter of deep principle. It would be perfectly understandable if a campus were to extend free speech rights to students as soon as they were offered admission. But it is generally understood that initial offers of admission are conditional, since there are many final steps in the admissions process (for example, submitting a final high school transcript). During the period of conditional approval, if new information arises that would have been disqualifying at the admissions stage (including matters of character or the level of academic achievement during the final high school term), then campuses can act on that. Harvard, for example, warned admitted students that the college "reserves the right to withdraw an offer of admission under various conditions including if an admitted student engages in behavior that brings into question his or her honesty, maturity, or moral character."[78]

But if campuses are going to disqualify conditionally admitted applicants at the last minute based on their public utterances, they should also take into account whether the distressing statements were made years before, when they were young teenagers, and whether it is appropriate to make such consequential decisions about their life opportunities on the basis of youthful indiscretions. In 2020 Kyle Kashuv, a survivor of the school shooting in Parkland, Florida, who became an outspoken defender of the Second Amendment, was accepted to Harvard University. But Harvard then rescinded its offer over some derogatory posts he had written as a sixteen-year-old. Maybe an applicant's frame of mind when they are sixteen is reason enough to prevent their enrollment, but maybe not, especially if subsequent life experiences may be considered transformative.

We can offer no rule of thumb, except that campuses should not rescind admission offers out of a concern about bad publicity or because of pressure campaigns. If a prospective student's record has qualified them for admission, then the admissions offer should not be withdrawn unless the new information supports a conclusion that the person is not as well qualified to join the academic community as was previously thought. Campuses should keep in mind that for every "bad apple" they believe they are belatedly tossing from the barrel, there are others who want to become better people than they were when they were younger. As Missouri State University president Clif Smart wrote in explaining why he would not rescind offers of admission to students whose racist social media posts had come to light, "We cannot expect or require that students come to us fully formed, possessing all of the skills and characteristics that exemplify Citizen Scholars. It is our job and our duty to help them develop these traits through education and exposure."[79]

This seems especially true if students acknowledge who they used to be and express the hope that their college experiences will expose them to new and better ways of thinking. Students who previously expressed intolerant or disrespectful views may get the most benefit from spending time in a setting where they are introduced to classmates who have very different worldviews and experiences, in an environment that requires them—and their classmates—to confront new ideas and reevaluate their existing ways of thinking. Northwest Missouri State University president John Jasinski put it this way, quoting Harlan Hodge, the husband of the campus's Black Alumni Chapter president: "Education is a daily confrontation with ignorance."[80]

Going Forward

Except for the McCarthy era's obsession with ridding campuses of Communists, American colleges and universities historically have seldom had to worry about controversies associated with off-campus utterances of faculty members and students. How would anyone even know what most people said to their friends and acquaintances? But social media has changed that dramatically. Over the past decade, it has become routine for campuses to have to respond to pressure campaigns triggered by members of their communities who say things that outrage people. There are now enough examples of such situations that we can draw some lessons from them.

The basic principles of free speech and academic freedom require us all to accept that some members of our community hold beliefs and express views that we object to. Institutions of higher education cannot be in the business of excommunicating heretics. This means that students should face no formal sanctions or expulsions merely because of an objectionable social media post. They should not be immune from criticism, even by university officials, who have a duty to uphold university values when a campus member speaks in ways that are inconsistent with the institution's principles of community. But it is a best practice, when criticizing someone's speech, to emphasize that the institution also protects their free speech rights and will impose no sanctions. In some cases, it is appropriate, even necessary, for institutions to have processes whereby people can report acts of bias or hostile environments, but if the complained-about activity is constitutionally protected speech, campuses should take pains to avoid involving the speaker directly in official processes.

The same applies to faculty members, with the important but rare exception of extramural utterances that might call into question their fitness as scholars and teachers. In those cases, assessments about fitness should follow the same peer-review process that characterizes all assessments of faculty quality.

We understand that this may be easier said than done. Enormous pressures can be placed on campuses by social media, the local community, and even government officials. That is why it is so important for campus leaders to have a clear understanding of the principles involved. Campuses that have managed these controversies most successfully have been the ones that, during the crisis, did not meekly shy away from these core commitments but instead articulated their fundamental principles with clarity and determination.

4

Government Control over Campus Speech

Until recently, the debates and public controversies surrounding campus speech since 2015 mostly concerned how well or poorly campuses addressed expressive activity by students, faculty, invited speakers, and protesters. Did the campuses show a clear enough commitment to free speech, even when members of the campus community demanded censorship or tried to disrupt talks or other events? Were they sufficiently committed to principles of academic freedom, even when a professor's pedagogical choices or public statements caused a firestorm? Should campuses themselves, because of their educational mission, be given more latitude to silence discriminatory or hateful speech? Should they have adopted stronger statements of principle about the importance of free speech to their mission of creating and transmitting knowledge?

For years, these debates were predominantly framed by conservatives, who criticized what they saw as an intolerant or coddled generation of progressive students and weak-kneed or unprepared administrators. This is not so surprising, considering that most of the highly publicized examples of student demands for censorship and of disruptions of events targeted conservative or right-wing speakers and programs. High-profile examples include Milo Yiannopoulos's clown show of trolling and provocation that led to an out-of-control demonstration at Berkeley in 2017, the mob at Middlebury that shut down a program featuring Charles Murray and attacked Professor

Allison Stanger, Yale Law students' attempt to stop an event that included a representative of the Alliance Defending Freedom, and the Stanford law students who disrupted a program organized by the student chapter of the Federalist Society featuring a conservative federal judge.[1]

The conservative commentator Ben Shapiro captured the attitude of critics toward students who believed their feelings of outrage permitted them to silence certain voices when he titled one of his books *Facts Don't Care about Your Feelings.*[2] His point was that campuses needed to let people have their say even if some found those views very upsetting. Conservatives in Congress signaled their concerns by introducing the Free Speech on Campus Act, intended "to return to a culture of respect and tolerance towards diversity of thought in higher education."[3]

For many years, we have argued that attempts to disrupt events because of the participants' viewpoints should be resisted and denounced. But we have also argued that the occasional heckling of speakers by students is nowhere near as threatening to campus free speech as official state censorship of the teaching and learning environment.[4]

In this chapter we turn away from controversies about the speech of students and faculty members to address what we consider the biggest threat to campus free speech and academic freedom since the McCarthy era: the efforts of many conservative state legislatures and some federal officials to exercise more control over what professors may teach and discuss in their university classrooms.

Many of the same conservatives who for years insisted that campuses must allow the expression of all viewpoints are now leading the effort to prevent teaching and advocacy of ideas they find objectionable, usually having to do with "divisive" topics relating to race, racism, sex discrimination, and gender identity. Conversely, many campus progressives who previously doubted the importance of free speech protections for hateful speech find themselves invoking these protections as defenses.

We begin by reviewing the conservative assault against Critical Race Theory and how this aspect of the culture wars eventually led many state legislatures to target state universities. We will discuss the extraordinary sweep of these attempted restrictions, which could limit professors' ability to teach basic theories and long-standing debates in a wide range of disciplines, including history, sociology, psychology, and ethnic studies. We will review some of the litigation that has resulted, especially relating to Florida's so-called Stop WOKE Act, and discuss the legal issues in play. Because many of the restrictions are premised on the claim that, as government employees, public university professors do not have free speech rights in their workplace, we will examine whether the law governing workplace speech by public employees should apply to them. We will also look at legislative efforts to restrict the use of public funds for diversity, equity, and inclusion programs to see whether free speech or academic freedom arguments apply to these efforts.

And it must be remembered that all of this preceded the Trump administration's aggressive criticism of universities and efforts to control the content of programs, and even faculty hiring and student admissions. Although at the federal rather than the state level, the basic issues of free speech and academic freedom that we discuss are the same.

The Attack on Teaching Critical Race Theory

On September 4, 2020, in the midst of the COVID pandemic, President Trump ordered Russell Vought, the director of the White House Office Management and Budget, to ban any training within the federal government related to Critical Race Theory. Vought issued a memorandum saying that Critical Race Theory is "un-American propaganda" and "contrary to all we stand for as Americans and should have no place in the federal government." He instructed the heads of federal agencies to dramatically alter racial sensitivity training programs for employees.[5]

Two days later, on September 6, President Trump issued a tweet saying that the United States Department of Education would investigate whether California schools were using the *New York Times's* "1619 Project" in the public school curriculum. "Department of Education is looking at this," he wrote. "If so, they will not be funded!"[6] The 1619 Project was an effort by the *New York Times* to look at American history through the lens of race, from the time the first enslaved individuals were brought to this country to the present.

On September 22, Trump issued the "Executive Order on Combating Race and Sex Stereotyping," attacking what he called a "destructive ideology . . . rooted in the pernicious and false belief that America is an irredeemably racist and sexist country; that some people, simply on account of their race or sex, are oppressors; and that racial and sexual identities are more important than our common status as human beings and Americans. . . . This malign ideology is now migrating from the fringes of American society and threatens to infect core institutions of our country."[7] The order set out in detail what he found objectionable:

> the concepts that (1) one race or sex is inherently superior to another race or sex; (2) the United States is fundamentally racist or sexist; (3) an individual, by virtue of his or her race or sex, is inherently racist, sexist, or oppressive, whether consciously or unconsciously; (4) an individual should be discriminated against or receive adverse treatment solely or partly because of his or her race or sex; (5) members of one race or sex cannot and should not

attempt to treat others without respect to race or sex; (6) an individual's moral character is necessarily determined by his or her race or sex; (7) an individual, by virtue of his or her race or sex, bears responsibility for actions committed in the past by other members of the same race or sex; (8) any individual should feel discomfort, guilt, anguish, or any other form of psychological distress on account of his or her race or sex; or (9) meritocracy or traits such as a hard work ethic are racist or sexist, or were created by a particular race to oppress another race.

The order prohibited federal government contractors from engaging in training programs that conveyed any of these messages. Noncompliance would mean that the "contract may be canceled, terminated, or suspended in whole or in part and the contractor may be declared ineligible for further Government contracts." Every federal agency was directed to implement this order.

At the time, few people had heard of Critical Race Theory or the 1619 Project. Critical Race Theory began in law schools in the 1980s and then became part of other social science disciplines.[8] It focuses on the way white supremacy and racial power are maintained over time, especially by the legal system, and on how race and racial oppression shape law and society. It seeks to end anti-Blackness and racism in society.

The 1619 Project is a collection of materials prepared by the *New York Times* that reframes American history around the date when the first slave ship arrived on America's shores—August 1619.[9] Its powerful presentation of the role of slavery and race in American history earned it a Pulitzer Prize, even though several prominent American historians objected to factual errors that they considered inconsistent with honest scholarship and journalism.[10]

Trump's executive order originated with Christopher Rufo, a fellow at the Manhattan Institute, a conservative think tank, who claimed that "profiteering race theorists" were teaching white federal employees that they contributed to racism. Rufo called on conservatives to "brace for a long war against the diversity-industrial complex and its enablers." He attributed their ideas to Critical Race Theory, which he described as "academic discourse centered on the concepts of 'whiteness,' 'white fragility,' and 'white privilege,'" which had as its goal "a new, racial political consciousness."[11]

Whatever its origin story, the executive order had immediate effects. Universities, which depend on federal funds, immediately began changing their policies. The University of Iowa, fearing a loss of federal research grants, ended training programs for university employees about race or sex discrimination.[12] A spokeswoman said the university's general counsel thought the executive order might apply to all employees, not just those who receive money from the federal government. Stanford University prohibited diversity training discussing whether the United States is fundamentally racist or sexist or whether meritocracy is racist, sexist, or made by one race to oppress another.[13] Other universities acted similarly to comply with the order.

All of this occurred in the final months of President Trump's first term. On January 20, 2021, on his first day in office, President Joe Biden rescinded Trump's executive order. His own executive order expressly declared: "Executive Order 13950 of September 22, 2020 (Combating Race and Sex Stereotyping), is hereby revoked."[14] The new order, "Advancing Racial Equity and Support for Underserved Communities through the Federal Government," not only rescinded the diversity training restrictions but required all agencies to prioritize and create opportunities for communities that have been historically underserved

Biden's executive order began with a dramatically different premise from Trump's: "Equal opportunity is the bedrock of American democracy, and our diversity is one of our country's greatest strengths.

But for too many, the American Dream remains out of reach. Entrenched disparities in our laws and public policies, and in our public and private institutions, have often denied that equal opportunity to individuals and communities. . . . It is therefore the policy of my Administration that the Federal Government should pursue a comprehensive approach to advancing equity for all, including people of color and others who have been historically underserved, marginalized, and adversely affected by persistent poverty and inequality. Affirmatively advancing equity, civil rights, racial justice, and equal opportunity is the responsibility of the whole of our Government."

Despite being ended at the federal level during the Biden administration, the Trump order inspired conservative state legislatures to adopt state laws that are almost identical in content to the Trump executive order. Over the next few years eighteen states adopted bans on teaching Critical Race Theory and similar concepts.[15] Most simply copied the language of Trump's order.

For example, in May 2021, Tennessee adopted a law that forbids teachers to instruct that "an individual, by virtue of the individual's race or sex, is inherently privileged, racist, sexist, or oppressive, whether consciously or subconsciously."[16] The Tennessee law also includes the prohibitions found in the Trump executive order.

In November 2021, North Dakota governor Doug Burgum signed into law a bill that bans instruction in Critical Race Theory, defined in the legislation as "the theory that racism is not merely the product of individual bias or prejudice, but that racism is systemically embedded in American society and the American legal system to facilitate racial inequality."[17] This law, too, uses language identical to that in Trump's order.

In June 2021, the Florida state board of education approved a rule that prohibits schools from teaching Critical Race Theory and the 1619 Project.[18] The following April, Republican governor Ron

DeSantis signed the Stop WOKE Act, which prohibits training or lessons teaching that individuals are inherently racist or sexist because of their race or sex, that people are privileged or oppressed due to their race or sex, and related concepts.[19] Also that spring, DeSantis signed into law HB 1557, referred to as the "Don't Say Gay" bill, which took effect on July 1, 2022. The law stated that its purpose was to "prohibit . . . classroom discussion about sexual orientation or gender identity in certain grade levels or in a specified manner."[20]

In April 2022, Georgia governor Brian Kemp, also a Republican, signed HB 1084, which prohibits schools from teaching "divisive concepts," including that "one race is inherently superior to another race" and that "the United States of America is fundamentally racist."[21] This law, too, mirrored the Trump executive order.

All of these laws apply to elementary and secondary schools, but about 40 percent of them apply to colleges and universities as well. Idaho's law, for example, clearly applies to teachers at all levels.[22] Other laws are directed just at higher education. In February 2024, Indiana enacted a law declaring public colleges and universities must deny tenure to professors who are "unlikely to foster . . . intellectual diversity."[23] For tenured professors, who undergo post-tenure reviews every five years, the law requires that these reviews include whether they fostered intellectual diversity and whether they "introduced students to scholarly works from a variety of political or ideological frameworks." Failure to do so could mean loss of tenure or firing.

These are not the first efforts by state legislatures to regulate speech at colleges and universities. In the late 1940s and early 1950s, the McCarthy era, there were widespread efforts to fire and silence suspected Communists.[24] In California, for example, the Levering Act (1950) required state employees to sign a loyalty oath that specifically disavowed radical beliefs; it was aimed in particular at employees of the University of California.[25] In the early 1990s, over

350 U.S. colleges adopted speech codes meant to prohibit hateful expression.[26]

While the hate speech codes were focused on student speech, the current laws, like the McCarthy-era restrictions, are primarily directed at faculty speech. But the current laws restricting university teaching and learning are having a dramatically greater reach than those of the 1950s. McCarthyism was directed against individuals who had certain political affiliations or viewpoints, but it did not attempt otherwise to regulate what was taught or discussed. The assumption was that if the university got rid of the bad professors, direct control of the curriculum would not be necessary. But the recent bans on "divisive" concepts restrict every professor's and student's ability to explore basic ideas in any discipline that addresses questions of race, racism, sex discrimination, or gender identity.

The laws prohibit professors from—in the words of the Stop WOKE Act—instructing students to believe that a person's status is either privileged or oppressed as a result of their race or sex, or that a person should receive adverse treatment to achieve diversity goals. Under these laws, students could hear arguments against affirmative action or reparations for slavery, but not arguments on the other side. Much of the history of political thought could not be taught or fairly debated. The position of women in most societies throughout history could not be criticized. Even modern conservative arguments for traditional gender roles—for example, claims that the military erred in giving women combat roles—could not be presented.

The Stop WOKE Act permits classroom discussion of divisive concepts so long as "instruction is given in an objective manner without endorsement of the concepts." But as we have seen, faculty members in higher education are not required or expected to be neutral or "objective" about debates within their areas of expertise, although they are required to adequately present the legitimate range of opinion and fairly evaluate the work of students even if the students arrive at different conclusions. No matter how hard a professor tries, it is often impossible to be neutral. One's views unavoidably influence what is taught and how. As professors ourselves, we often make pedagogical choices suggesting that certain arguments are stronger than others. If a class is too easily embracing one side of a controversial debate, we may advocate the other side of the debate in order to make students take those arguments more seriously. If they feared that such choices could be seen as an "endorsement" of a divisive view, faculty members facing punishment would reasonably avoid such topics. Much of what is routinely explored in history, philosophy, sociology, political science, classics, psychology, art, or many other areas (not to mention ethnic studies and gender studies) would be altered or even omitted for fear of liability.

Needless to say, from the perspective of academic freedom, especially as applied in colleges and universities, these laws are deeply troubling. The Association of American Law Schools put it this way: "The laws proposed or passed in states to ban the teaching of Critical Race Theory are designed to stifle a full exploration of the role of race and racism in United States history and, in so doing, they also erase some people from the very classrooms in which they have a right to be full participants as students and as educators. These legislative enactments also substitute political ideology for the considered judgment of professional educators, who have a duty to impart knowledge to their students and facilitate students' opportunities to learn from each other. Academic freedom means that educators—not politicians— should make decisions about teaching and learning. The efforts to restrict teaching and learning about ideas derived from Critical Race Theory are inimical to the most basic notions of academic freedom."[27]

Not even the sponsors of these laws, governors and state legislators, disagree that they are assaults on academic freedom. They argue that because liberal faculty members have politicized the curriculum rather than act as professional scholars, they are no longer entitled to the rights and privileges of academic freedom. Furthermore, defenders of the laws argue that as government employees, public university professors have no legally enforceable rights to academic freedom because the government may direct what employees can and cannot say on the job. As lawyers for the State of Florida argued in their brief for the United States Court of Appeals for the Eleventh Circuit, the question "boils down to this: who decides what is, and is not, to be taught in Florida's college classrooms—individual professors or their employer, the State, in prescribing by law the content requirements and standards that govern public universities in setting their course curricula?"[28] Since the very concept of academic freedom presupposes that professors should be treated as highly trained professionals whose judgment about transmitting higher knowledge deserves deference, there could not be a clearer statement against academic freedom than the position Florida's lawyers have taken.

We will turn to the legal issues surrounding these laws in a moment. But if courts do not find that these laws are illegal under either state or federal law, the country will confront a fundamental question about the future of higher education in the United States: are we better served by anchoring our public universities in principles of free speech and academic freedom or by treating scholars more like K-12 teachers, whose curricular choices and lesson plans are directed by politicians?

As we discussed in chapter 2, academic freedom and tenure were proposed in the early twentieth century as ways of ensuring that society would benefit from the expertise of highly trained researchers and teachers of advanced knowledge. Unlike primary and secondary school teachers, experts were assumed to know better what research questions were most appropriate and how best to teach advanced concepts. For well over a century, the ideas that were acceptable to teach or debate at colleges and universities had been controlled by politicians, boards, and administrators, and by the end of the nineteenth century it was increasingly clear that the country suffered under this tradition. If religious leaders or politicians did not want Darwin to be taught, then faculty members acquiesced to this command or risked being fired. If politicians insisted that the world was only a few thousand years old, then professors did not teach Charles Lyell's *Principles of Geology*. If the antebellum South considered abolitionism threatening to public order, that idea could not be fairly discussed. If men were considered the superior sex and women were ordained by God to perform their natural social role as wives and mothers, then no one dared explore arguments about the social equality of the sexes.

The major American universities created at the end of the nineteenth century embraced the so-called German model of intellectual freedom because it was seen as generating important new knowledge and better educational outcomes for college students. Few doubt that in the twentieth century, America's colleges and universities became the envy of the world—precisely because academic freedom and tenure were the foundations of American higher education.

If there truly are no legal barriers to state governments ending their commitments to academic freedom, and if they choose to direct what is taught or debated in public universities, then the United States could enter a period in which there will be two distinct practices of public higher education. Some states will retain the dominant model of the twentieth century, while other states will go back to political control of the faculty. We believe this would be a tragic loss for much of the country, and especially for those students who rely on public colleges as their best opportunity to access higher education.

Curricular battles would be bitter, intense, and never-ending as state officials worked to advance their personal political and religious views. Faculty members in politically controlled settings would know that any false step or demonstration of independent thought would be risky, making it rational for them to transform the classroom into sterile territory where only the dominant opinion is acceptable. Professors who said controversial things would have no protections against demands that they be sanctioned or fired—especially since many of the states that are rejecting academic freedom are also working to weaken or even eliminate tenure.[29] At many public universities, the driving force behind the generation of new ideas—the ability to challenge accepted wisdom, stand against public opinion, imagine how the world could be better—would be seriously eroded, and the social progress we have come to expect from universities would be diminished.

For many conservative politicians, the arguments for academic freedom have been eroded by their sense that faculty members and campus cultures are hostile to conservative values. They feel that professors are requiring fidelity to views about white privilege, structural racism, and gender identity that the politicians find unacceptable or even abhorrent. As they see it, academic freedom is justified only if professors act in accordance with scholarly values, and if professors or campuses substitute political advocacy for neutral scholarship and teaching, then state politicians might as well take over. As stated in the AAUP's original resolution on academic freedom, "The liberty of the scholar to set forth his conclusions, be they what they may, is conditioned by their being conclusions gained by a scholar's method and held in a scholar's spirit; that is to say, they must be the fruits of competent and patient and sincere inquiry."[30] Conservative complaints about higher education are certainly not new: William F. Buckley Jr. first gained fame in the 1950s through a screed against his alma mater, Yale; Dinesh D'Souza earned his stripes at the *Dartmouth Review* in the early 1980s; and "political correctness" at colleges has been a topic of debate since at least the 1990s. But in recent years the conservative case against higher education has reached a fever pitch.[31] According to a Pew poll, by 2019 a majority of Republicans thought universities have a "negative effect on the way things are going in the country."[32] (On the other hand, when asked who should have greater influence on what is taught in college, both Democrats and Republicans say it should be professors rather than state government.)[33]

We agree that when faculty members are in their professional environments, academic freedom imposes an expectation of scholarly temperament on them. This is one of the reasons we argued in chapter 2 against academic departments or associations making official declarations on controversial political and social matters, and one of the reasons we recommended against a policy of having all prospective faculty members, regardless of discipline, submit a statement regarding their contributions to diversity, equity, and inclusion. It is also one of the reasons we have constantly tried to ensure that all viewpoints can be expressed on our own campuses, without fear of sanction or disruption.

We agree that in the long run, support for public higher education depends on public confidence in the quality and importance of the work being done by faculty members, including the embrace of diverse viewpoints as a necessary feature of a working culture of inquiry, deliberation, and debate. A recent report on diversity of thought at the University of Michigan argued that campuses should be viewed as places that support the airing of multiple perspectives on controversial or unsettled issues, as well as constructive disagreement with a range of ideas and arguments, without personal attack or other inappropriate pressures. After extensive consultation with the University of Michigan community, the report's authors found that "both conservatives and liberals worried that the climate of opinion at UM was overwhelmingly liberal or progressive" and that many people "presumed that left-wing views were correct, that everyone agreed with them, that there was nothing to be said in favor of conservative views." The authors also found a lack of constructive disagreement on the campus, arising "from either the lack of representation of disagreement in the curriculum and campus more generally, or barriers to freedom of expression experienced by people who disagree with prevailing views."[34]

Universities cannot perform their distinctive mission unless their leaders and most of the campus community understand the value of diversity of thought and are eager to practice constructive disagreement. But no administrative order can be issued that will result in a greater tolerance of opposing viewpoints, especially given our highly polarized political system. Academic freedom means that faculty cannot simply be required to construct their syllabi in ways that are inconsistent with their professional judgment, either about the content or about the legitimate range of debate within their fields. We, of course, favor ideological diversity among faculty and students, but universities cannot use ideology as a basis for hiring or admissions decisions. It would be wrong for a school to hire one person over another because they were conservative or liberal. Ideally, ideological diversity would be present on every campus, but it is very difficult for schools to engineer their decisions to achieve it.

We have advocated strongly for a robust free speech culture on campuses precisely to encourage the university community to be more willing to embrace viewpoint diversity as foundational to the enterprise. As the Michigan report notes, "Students, faculty, and staff must recognize the importance of free speech and diversity of thought, and then play their own part and meet their own responsibility for fostering such a culture and engage in constructive dialog in the quest for knowledge and solutions."

Even acknowledging the importance of this issue, we also believe the complaints that campuses have been transformed into engines of liberal or Marxist political indoctrination are overblown. They are fueled by media and social media ecosystems that traffic in exaggerated impressions designed to generate manufactured outrage. Relentless political indoctrination is not the experience of most of the students who attend college and have positive life-transforming experiences. With so many students and so many independent faculty members, some students will undoubtedly be exposed to ideas that make them uncomfortable or that challenge their dearly held views. But that is a feature, not a bug, of the culture of higher education. We are also confident that some universities' legitimate concerns about the extent of viewpoint diversity or toleration in a few disciplines can and should be addressed without destroying the foundational principles of modern American higher education.

Likewise, our commitment to academic freedom and our opposition to political control of faculty also applies if, rather than prohibit the discussion of certain divisive concepts, officials require faculty to incorporate particular views about race or racism into their teaching and research. This is why we oppose the 2022 effort by the board of governors of California's community college system to require faculty to demonstrate that they employ diversity, equity, inclusion, accessibility, and anti-racist principles in their work. Faculty were instructed to "demonstrate an ongoing awareness and recognition of racial, social, and cultural identities with fluency regarding their relevance in creating structures of oppression and marginalization," "develop and implement a pedagogy and/or curriculum that promotes a race-conscious and inter-sectional lens," and "participate in a continuous cycle of self-assessment of one's growth and commitment to DEI and acknowledgement of any internalized personal biases and racial superiority or inferiority."[35] For the same reason that they prohibit *restricting* what faculty members can say about structural racism and similar issues, academic freedom and free speech principles prohibit *compelling* them to associate themselves with particular viewpoints.

Still, if there are no legal barriers to these state efforts, we could see the most important change to American higher education in over a century. These efforts to control teaching have been adopted in many states and could spread to others. Even in the first few months of the Trump administration there are efforts to adopt them at the federal level, including as conditions on federal education funds. The question is: are these laws legal?

Do State Educational Gag Orders
Violate the Constitution?

Following passage of Florida's Stop WOKE Act, a group of students and educators filed a lawsuit arguing that the act violated both the First Amendment and the equal protection clause.[36] We believe there is great merit to this suit. We recognize, of course, that schools at all levels of instruction have broad discretion to define the content of their curricula.[37] But there are still constitutional limits on how legislatures, or even universities, can regulate the teaching.

First, many aspects of the state laws restricting the teaching of Critical Race Theory are unconstitutionally vague and overbroad. A law is unconstitutionally vague if a reasonable person cannot tell what speech is prohibited and what is permitted.[38] Courts have been particularly troubled by vague laws restricting speech because they may also chill constitutionally protected speech. The Supreme Court has called freedom of speech "delicate and vulnerable, as well as supremely precious in our society," and noted that "the threat of sanctions may deter their exercise almost as potently as the actual application of sanctions."[39] Further, in *NAACP v. Button,* the Court said that "standards of permissible statutory vagueness are strict in the area of free expression. . . . Because First Amendment freedoms need breathing space to survive, government may regulate in the area only with narrow specificity."[40] Closely related, a law is unconstitutionally overbroad if it regulates substantially more speech than the Constitution allows to be regulated, and a person to whom the law constitutionally can be applied can argue that it would be unconstitutional if applied to others.[41]

Teachers face sanctions, including dismissal, for violating these state laws. Matthew Hawn, a high school teacher in Tennessee, was fired for teaching about "white privilege" in violation of that state's law.[42] A hearing officer upheld Hawn's firing, saying that he failed to provide students "varying viewpoints" on the existence of white privilege during a lesson on police brutality against Black men.[43]

The Indiana law says explicitly that failure to teach "diverse viewpoints" is a basis for firing. But the law is unclear as to what "diverse viewpoints" means or what would be sufficient to meet the requirements of the law. Does it mean that a calculus teacher has to teach diverse viewpoints about the value of π? Does someone teaching about the Holocaust have to include the Holocaust-denial viewpoint? The Indiana law leaves it to the university's trustees, many of whom are appointed by the governor, to determine what intellectual diversity actually means for faculty members and whether they have provided it.[44] It provides no guidance to individual faculty members as to what they can and can't teach.

The laws throughout the country also commonly prohibit teaching that "any individual should feel discomfort, guilt, anguish, or any other form of psychological distress on account of his or her race or sex." It is impossible to know how to avoid teaching in a way that provokes emotions. We hope that our students will feel discomfort and anguish as they read about slavery and study the Supreme Court decisions that protected the rights of owners of enslaved individuals. How would we, as teachers, know when inspiring those emotions violates the law?

A federal district court found that President Trump's anti-DEI executive order was "so vague that it is impossible for Plaintiffs to determine what conduct is prohibited" and that "the line between teaching or implying (prohibited) and informing (not prohibited) 'is so murky, enforcement of the ordinance poses a danger of arbitrary and discriminatory application.'"[45] The same is true of the many state laws based on that executive order.

Second, these laws restrict the speech of teachers in a way that violates the First Amendment in public schools.[46] The laws are obviously viewpoint discrimination: teachers are not allowed to express specific views with regard to race and sex. The state laws that have been adopted in recent years commonly prohibit teaching that "the United States is fundamentally racist or sexist." How is a teacher to know when instruction about racism or sexism crosses this line? Does a teacher really have to be impartial in discussing topics like slavery or the Jim Crow laws that mandated segregation of the races? An Arizona law prohibits "instruction that presents any form of blame or judgment on the basis of race, ethnicity, or sex."[47] In other words, a teacher would violate the law by talking about how white slave owners oppressed Black enslaved individuals.

The Supreme Court has made clear that viewpoint restrictions of speech are virtually never allowed.[48] "Viewpoint discrimination is . . . an egregious form of content discrimination," it wrote in *Rosenberger v. Rector & Visitors of Univ. of Virginia,* and even schools "must abstain from regulating speech when the specific motivating ideology or the opinion or perspective of the speaker is the rationale for the restriction."[49] The entire point of the Stop WOKE Act is to suppress a "motivating ideology": to prevent "woke"-associated messages from being expressed in classrooms. This is the very definition of viewpoint discrimination. As the district court noted in granting its preliminary injunction against Florida's law, "Defendants argue that, under this Act, professors enjoy 'academic freedom' so long as they express only those viewpoints of which the State approves. This is positively dystopian." The court continued:

The State has chosen affirmative action as one of its eight concepts because the State has deemed it to be repugnant and "noxious to the people of Florida." . . . Stated otherwise, you can discuss affirmative action as a historical fact, and you can certainly condemn it as a failed policy, but because the idea of affirmative action is so odious, so repugnant, so vile, and so dangerous that it offends the basic principles of common decency, you cannot have a guest speaker submit their views in favor of affirmative action, even to a class of law students.[50]

Third, the laws prohibiting the teaching of Critical Race Theory and other material can be challenged as denying the right of students to receive information.[51] This right is less clearly developed than the requirement that government regulations of speech avoid vagueness and overbreadth, and that they be viewpoint-neutral. But in *Board of Education, Island Trees Union Free School District No. 26 v. Pico,* the Supreme Court considered the constitutionality of removing books from school libraries on account of their being deemed objectionable.[52] The plurality spoke of the government's broad authority to set the curriculum, but it also said school boards must comport with the "transcendent imperatives of the First Amendment."[53] "The Constitution protects the right to receive information and ideas," the Court wrote, noting that this right is an essential corollary to the rights of free speech and the press.[54]

Federal courts of appeals have also found a right of students to receive information. The Eighth Circuit Court of Appeals concluded that a school "board must establish that a substantial and reasonable governmental interest exists for interfering with the students' right to receive information."[55] The Fifth Circuit, while expressing more deference to schools, found that there was a First Amendment violation if the range of choices made available to students was "motivated by 'narrowly partisan or political' considerations."[56] The laws prohibiting teaching of divisive concepts seem clearly all about political considerations.

Again, there is difficult line-drawing. *Pico* and other cases recognize the latitude schools have in setting their curriculums. But broadly setting the curriculum is very different from prohibiting instructors' expression of certain ideas. There is a strong argument that laws like the Stop WOKE Act and those prohibiting the teaching of Critical Race Theory are intended to stop students from receiving information and particular viewpoints about race. They thus cannot be reconciled with a constitutional right to receive information.

Fourth, these laws raise an equal protection issue. The decision of the United States Court of Appeals for the Ninth Circuit in *Arce v. Douglas* is on point.[57] In 2010, the Arizona legislature passed H.B. 2281, outlawing ethnic studies classes in the state.[58] The statute prohibited a school district or charter school from offering any courses or classes that: (1) "Promote the overthrow of the United States government," (2) "Promote resentment toward a race or class of people," (3) "Are designed primarily for pupils of a particular ethnic group," or (4) "Advocate ethnic solidarity instead of the treatment of pupils as individuals."

Although not the same as laws prohibiting teaching of Critical Race Theory, this law certainly was a precursor to those statutes. Its effect was to stop all Mexican American studies classes in Tucson schools. The Ninth Circuit found that the Arizona law was race neutral on its face, but that there was sufficient evidence of both a discriminatory purpose and discriminatory effect to state a claim for an equal protection violation. The court remanded the case, and on remand, the district court concluded that the law violated the equal protection clause of the Fourteenth Amendment.

Like the Arizona law, the purpose of the anti–Critical Race Theory laws is to prevent the teaching of a certain perspective on race. In the lawsuit challenging Florida's law, the plaintiffs argued that in addition to various First Amendment violations, the law violated equal protection because it was intended to discriminate against Black educators and students. One of the plaintiffs, Johana Dauphin, a Black student at Florida State University, stated, "I fear that this law will cause my professors to avoid discussing race and gender altogether, which will result in my perspective and lived experience as a Black, female student being effectively minimized and erased in the classroom."[59]

Even if a state has some latitude to control curriculum, as well as the kinds of books available at public libraries, it cannot make these decisions in ways that have a discriminatory purpose and effect. A state may be able to limit all preschool books from a library, but not all books by Black authors. A state may require colleges to teach basic civics or government, but it cannot prohibit the presentation of materials that support the civil rights of gays and lesbians, women, or transgender persons.

Given the vagueness of many of these laws, it may be less straightforward to determine whether they represent efforts to create a discriminatory environment for protected classes of people. But the focus on issues of race, sex, and gender as "divisive" and therefore unworthy subjects for discussion and debate raises serious concerns. Just imagine how conservative lawmakers or judges would respond to a state that prohibited faculty from arguing that religious practitioners should be able to have their sectarian religious views embodied in law and represented in government-sponsored memorials, on the grounds that such views are inconsistent with the Constitution's establishment clause and thus are "divisive." If you predict, as we do, that these laws would be denounced as discriminatory against religious practitioners, then you understand why the current wave of laws is unconstitutional.

All of these constitutional concerns call into question the legality of these educational gag orders. But underlying these debates is the question of whether the academic freedom of professors at public universities is also protected by the Constitution. This is a more challenging question, given what courts have said about government's authority to regulate its employees' speech.[60] Indeed, the attorneys general of Florida and Indiana have argued that their states' restriction of faculty speech raises no First Amendment issues because professors are government employees and have no constitutional protection for their on-the-job expression.

The argument against First Amendment protections for academic freedom at public universities is based on the Supreme Court's 2006 decision in *Garcetti v. Ceballos*.[61] The case involved Richard Ceballos, a supervising district attorney in Los Angeles County, who concluded that a witness in one of his cases, a deputy sheriff, was not telling the truth. He wrote a memo to this effect and felt he was required by the Constitution to inform the defense. After he was transferred to a less desirable position and denied a promotion, Ceballos alleged that his employers were retaliating against him for this speech.

The issue before the Supreme Court was whether Ceballos's speech was protected by the First Amendment. Although the Court has long held that the speech of government employees is constitutionally protected, it ruled against Ceballos.[62] It drew a distinction between speech "as a citizen" as opposed to "as a public employee" and said that only the former is protected. Justice Kennedy wrote: "When public employees make statements pursuant to their official duties, the employees are not speaking as citizens for First Amendment purposes, and the Constitution does not insulate their communications from employer discipline."[63]

The Court acknowledged that distinct issues of academic freedom may arise when the government employee works as an instructor, but left this for future cases to address: "There is some argument that expression related to academic scholarship or classroom instruction implicates additional constitutional interests that are not fully accounted for by this Court's customary employee-speech jurisprudence. We need not, and for that reason do not, decide whether the analysis we conduct today would apply in the same manner to a case involving speech related to scholarship or teaching."[64] Justice Souter wrote in a dissent: "I have to hope that today's majority does not mean to imperil First Amendment protection of academic freedom in public colleges and universities, whose teachers necessarily speak and write 'pursuant to . . . official duties.'"[65]

The United States Court of Appeals for the Ninth Circuit, directly addressing this question in *Demers v. Austin,* held that the First Amendment protects the speech of university professors and that *Garcetti v. Ceballos* does not apply in this context.[66] David Demers was a tenured associate professor at Washington State University who alleged that after he distributed a short pamphlet and drafts from an in-progress book, university administrators retaliated by giving him negative performance evaluations, in violation of the First Amendment. The federal district court dismissed the case based on *Garcetti v. Ceballos,* concluding that since the pamphlet and drafts were based on Demers's professional work as a scholar, they qualified as speech on the job in the scope of his duties, for which there was no First Amendment protection.

The Ninth Circuit reversed the district court.[67] It stressed the Supreme Court's protection of academic freedom under the First Amendment and stated: "*Garcetti* does not—indeed, consistent with the First Amendment, cannot—apply to teaching and academic writing that are performed 'pursuant to the official duties' of a teacher and professor. We hold that academic employee speech not covered by *Garcetti* is protected under the First Amendment."[68]

There are good reasons to think that the Ninth Circuit is correct and the *Garcetti* government speech doctrine should not apply to professors. To the extent that *Garcetti* is premised on the assumption that the state must be able to control its employees' speech in order for government programs to function, then that rationale does not apply to higher education. The core of the modern university is that it can work only if the government defers to the judgment of highly trained experts. Or, to put it another way, it is hard to see how advanced research and teaching can function if politicians are controlling how expert knowledge is pursued or taught.

To the extent that *Garcetti*'s presumption of government control over employee speech is rooted in the belief that ordinary government employees (such as district attorneys) are understood by the public as speaking for the government, this also would be a reason to differentiate the speech of professors, since no one believes professors are speaking for state government when they are teaching or publishing scholarly research. Unless, of course, the government is allowed to assert that nothing can be taught at public universities without approval by the government, which is an assertion that begs the question under discussion.

In the 1960s, when the Supreme Court finally addressed efforts by a state government (New York's) to require faculty in its state university system to certify that they had never been Communists, the justices struck down the requirement. They explained that "our Nation is deeply committed to safeguarding academic freedom, which is of transcendent value to all of us. . . . [The First Amendment] does not tolerate laws that cast a pall of orthodoxy over the classroom."[69] That language echoed the twentieth-century consensus that American higher education was the envy of the world precisely because of its commitment to open inquiry. "Teachers and students must always remain free to inquire, to study and to evaluate, to gain new maturity and understanding," the Court wrote; otherwise, "our civilization will stagnate and die."[70]

If courts decide that state educational gag orders for higher education are not governed by the *Garcetti* rule, it will be because they have embraced arguments about the distinctive nature of higher education and the premise that colleges and universities cannot make their important contributions to society without a commitment to free speech, academic freedom, and the value of free inquiry.

At the same time, the possibility that federal judges may incorporate professors' academic freedom into their First Amendment jurisprudence raises important complications. As we have made clear, the concept of free speech is fundamentally different from the concept of academic freedom. Modern free speech jurisprudence is anchored in the proposition that the government cannot engage in "viewpoint" discrimination. If a member of the public believes the moon is made of green cheese, that's their business; the government cannot punish them for having incorrect views. Academic freedom, however, is not premised on viewpoint neutrality but on requirements of professional competency and peer review. This is why a budding astronomer can be denied tenure for advancing the Green Cheese Theory. The boundary conditions for justifiable viewpoints or defensible pedagogical choices are established and assessed by other experts as part of a system of peer review, not by people who know very little about the topic under discussion.

But perhaps we cannot incorporate academic freedom protections into First Amendment jurisprudence without assuming that life-tenured federal judges have the qualifications necessary to assess which classroom comments or research projects deserve protection and which do not. The danger is that politically appointed judges will replace faculty experts as the main advisers for academic freedom protections, and will improperly incorporate general free speech principles into an arena that should be governed by more professional considerations. To be clear, and as we explained in chapter 2, in many instances academic freedom and the First Amendment would give faculty members the same protection. But our concern here is where they don't: where academic freedom would deny protection because the professor is not meeting accepted professional norms, but the courts nonetheless would accord First Amendment protection.

We have reasons to worry, given that one federal court has already determined that academic freedom is protected by the First Amendment and that this protection includes the right of professors to disregard university policies and "misgender" their students if their personal or religious beliefs are inconsistent with the campus requirements.[71] As we previously discussed, we are strongly critical of this conclusion. A university can prohibit faculty from making sexist or racist or antisemitic comments in class. Refusing to refer to students by their chosen pronouns can be regarded by the university as similarly unacceptable and inappropriate in the classroom.

If judges recognize a First Amendment right to academic freedom, we would hope that their understanding of the scope of that right would be informed by testimony from scholars with the relevant disciplinary expertise. The analysis would resemble judicial determinations of what constitutes "standard of care" by physicians, in the sense that the determination should flow from the judgment of professional peers rather than the nonexpert opinions of judges.

If judges do not recognize a First Amendment right to academic freedom, there are still many legal bases available for striking down the worst elements of state educational gag orders. More fundamentally, however, we would urge politicians who are concerned about aspects of higher education to address those concerns in ways that do not undermine the foundational role that free speech and academic freedom play in the American system of higher education—which, to repeat, remains the envy of the world.

We endorse the views expressed by a federal district court in the 2022 case of *Pernell v. Florida Board of Governors of the State University System,* which struck down a Florida statute identical to those described above.[72] The court said that the case "squarely presents the tension . . . between university professors' and students' First Amendment rights and the State of Florida's claim that it has an unfettered right to prohibit professors from expressing viewpoints with which it disagrees."[73] The court's opinion drew a distinction between the government's ability to prescribe curriculum and its authority to proscribe expression of particular views. "It should go without saying," the judge explained, "that enacting a prophylactic ban on protected expression of certain viewpoints—in the interest of suppressing those viewpoints because the State of Florida finds them 'repugnant'—is neither sufficiently weighty nor reasonable. If that were the case, the State of Florida could declare *any* idea repugnant and prohibit its professors from expressing approval of that idea while in the classroom."[74] The court also found, as we argued above, that the Florida statute is unconstitutionally vague.

The opinion concluded:

> One thing is crystal clear—both robust intellectual inquiry and democracy require light to thrive. Our professors are critical to a healthy democracy, and the State of Florida's decision to choose which viewpoints are worthy of illumination and which must remain in the shadows has implications for us all. If our "priests of democracy" are not allowed to shed light on challenging ideas, then democracy will die in darkness. But the First Amendment does not permit the State of Florida to muzzle its university professors, impose its own orthodoxy of viewpoints, and cast us all into the dark.[75]

Government Prohibitions on University DEI Efforts

In their efforts to reshape the culture and practices of public universities, conservative state legislatures have enacted other laws besides the educational gag orders. A particular sore point is university programs that focus on diversity, equity, and inclusion, or DEI.

Many campuses have argued—and we agree—that DEI efforts are an effective strategy for overcoming long-standing historic practices that systematically excluded women, people of color, and other historically marginalized or oppressed communities from the benefits of higher education, with devastating consequences for their social standing and for the principle of equal opportunity. Conservative critics respond that in practice, DEI unconstitutionally compels speech by enforcing a view of America as inherently racist and oppressive, and unconstitutionally encourages race-conscious decision-making in hiring.[76] This has led many legislatures to prohibit colleges from having DEI offices or staff; ban mandatory diversity training; forbid institutions to use diversity statements in hiring and promotion; or bar colleges from considering race, sex, ethnicity, or national origin in admissions or employment.[77]

When Florida governor Ron DeSantis signed his anti-DEI legislation, he declared, "This bill says the whole experiment with DEI is coming to an end in the state of Florida. . . . We are eliminating DEI programs." The bill prohibited public colleges and universities from expending state or federal funds on any program or campus activity that advocates for diversity, equity, and inclusion, and required governing boards to review programs that are "based on theories that systemic racism, sexism, oppression, or privilege are inherent in the institutions of the United States and were created to maintain social, political, or economic inequities."[78] As of August 2024, eighty-six similar bills had been introduced in twenty-eight states, and fourteen were passed.[79]

To the extent that these bills prevent members of the university community from devising their own mission statements and strategic plans, they raise many of the same issues about the autonomy of the scholarly community that arise with more straightforward educational gag orders. Clearly universities should be able to acknowledge the history of exclusionary practices in higher education and commit to a more inclusive future. Some of these bills may also put their universities in a challenging position with higher education accreditors, which often insist on robust protections for academic freedom and admissions outreach efforts. The Florida bill declared that accrediting agencies "may not compel any public postsecondary institution to violate state law" or take any "adverse action" against a university for complying with state law. Downgrading a postsecondary institution's accreditation would greatly harm its ability to pursue its academic mission.[80] Some outreach efforts might also be required as a condition of receiving certain federal grants and contracts, which would put a campus's research mission at risk. And needless to say, to the extent that any of these anti-DEI efforts are intended to prevent members of the university community from expressing views about systemic racism and similar topics, they would violate the First Amendment.

The Trump administration in its first months took aggressive actions to try to end DEI. A "Dear Colleague" letter from the interim head of the Office of Civil Rights indicated that all diversity efforts were illegal. Universities faced funds being cut off, in part for having DEI programs.

But are there legal or constitutional barriers to state laws that prohibit the use of state funds to support DEI offices or staff?

Here we can see how the special protections for faculty speech may not prevent other restrictions on campus activities. Educational gag orders violate the academic freedom rights of faculty members in making decisions about their teaching and research. But academic freedom principles do not always apply when legislatures put conditions on the allocation of public funds.

Campuses, and especially public universities, cannot be insulated from all government efforts to shape their activities. While legislatures cannot directly censor or punish the expression of ideas, they can influence curricular choices or areas of research focus by dedicating funds to preferred areas of study. The California legislature provides line-item funding for research areas it supports, including "labor centers" on UC campuses, telecommunications and information technology research, immunology and immunotherapy research, and stem cell research. States may also require certain courses of study as graduation requirements: California required in 2020 that all undergraduates in the California State University system take ethnic studies. All public university leaders know that state officials will sometimes threaten campus funding because of activities they do not like. When the government funds something, it will exercise some control.

We oppose efforts by the government to prohibit campuses from creating staff offices and hiring officeholders dedicated to advancing DEI. But we do not believe that such prohibitions, narrowly construed, violate academic freedom (since they do not apply to faculty members' professional activities) or free speech principles. This conclusion also applies to legislative prohibitions on mandatory employee training programs that are premised on assertions about structural racism and sexism, or on certain ideas about sex and gender identity. The government is not required to fund offices or administrative programs that convey messages or support activities that public officials oppose, so long as the restrictions do not otherwise affect the academic freedom of professors or the individual free speech rights of faculty, students, and staff; are not phrased so vaguely as to be impossible to implement without fear of arbitrary sanctions; and do not prevent campuses from informing employees of their federal legal obligations to maintain nondiscriminatory education and workplace environments.

What about legislative prohibitions against requiring and using diversity statements in hiring and promotion? Between October 2023 and September 2024, six states adopted legislation curtailing the use of DEI statements in academic hiring and admissions: Idaho, Indiana, Iowa, Utah, Alabama, and Kansas.[81]

The Idaho law, adopted in 2024, is typical. Idaho's Senate Bill 1274 "prohibit[s] public colleges from requiring diversity statements as part of the hiring or admissions process." The law says: "No public postsecondary educational institution in the state of Idaho shall require or solicit a diversity statement as part of an admissions process, employment application process, hiring process, contract renewal process, or promotion process or as a condition of participation in any administrative or decision-making function of the institution."[82] Idaho's law prohibits "public colleges from requiring diversity statements and giving preferential treatment to anyone based on such statements."[83]

As we discussed in chapter 2, we believe that it is possible to use DEI statements in a way that does not raise First Amendment concerns about viewpoint discrimination in hiring. But if they are used to impose an ideological litmus test for faculty positions or admission, then they are objectionable and unconstitutional. If they are used as a subterfuge for racial preferences, they also run afoul of the Constitution.[84] These concerns, along with persistent disagreements among faculty members about the utility of such statements, lead us to recommend that they not be required of all applicants but rather be tied to debates within particular disciplines or research topics. Ability to teach a diverse population of students can be addressed in the more traditional teaching statements. In the limited cases where DEI statements may be justified on scholarly grounds, they should be accompanied by a clear statement of what they are and are not used for. The university should make clear that these statements are not used to give any preference based on race, sex, or ideology in hiring or admissions.

Still, are state laws prohibiting DEI statements constitutional? Unlike laws prohibiting teaching of Critical Race Theory, we do not see a constitutional problem if state legislatures prohibit DEI statements. We do not agree with such legislation. We think it should be for the schools to decide their admission and hiring criteria (so long as they comply with the Constitution and other laws). To be clear, as a matter of policy preference, we think there is a proper place for DEI statements in faculty recruitment and student admissions, if they are used appropriately. But that does not make their prohibition unconstitutional.

We have expressed our very strong objections to the educational gag orders that have arisen in many conservative states. They represent much more serious threats to campus free speech and academic freedom than the more familiar controversies surrounding provocative speakers, protests, social media posts, and pedagogical choices. We also believe the assault on DEI programs is an overreaction to a social media ecosystem that feeds on generating outrage based on invented stories or outlier events. There are approximately five thousand colleges and universities in the United States. A dedicated group of cultural warriors can always find a campus program or campus official somewhere that improperly seems to insist that faculty, staff, and students adopt some controversial viewpoint.

But we agree with conservative critics of higher education on one point: we oppose any effort to establish a "pall of orthodoxy" on college campuses, whereby professors or administrators require campus affiliates to profess particular beliefs about race, racism, sex discrimination, gender identity, or any other topic. This is why we advocate so strongly that campuses defend free speech and academic freedom, especially the principle that no one on a campus be censored or punished merely because they hold or express a viewpoint that others object to. It is also why we urge campus leaders, faculty members, and students to take seriously the question of whether there is sufficient viewpoint diversity and constructive disagreement on their own campuses, and consider appropriate ways to expand the range of legitimate debate.

No commitment to diversity, equity, and inclusion—that is, to eradicating long-standing traditions of exclusion from higher education to disfavored groups—can justify violations of, or deviations from, a commitment to open inquiry and independent thought. Conservative officials who are concerned about alleged political indoctrination should join us in supporting free speech and academic freedom rather than trying to eviscerate these protections in favor of political controls on what professors can say or teach.

These censorious efforts also offer a cautionary tale to those professors and students on the left who have criticized the free speech tradition as being too accommodating of so-called hate speech. In an earlier book we addressed this topic directly and explained why, despite the well-known harms of being exposed to hateful, racist, sexist, antisemitic, Islamophobic, transphobic speech, allowing such views to be expressed without censorship or punishment is still preferable to empowering government officials to censor speech that they consider hateful or inappropriate.[85] History has shown time and again that the power of the censor will always be used against marginalized and historically oppressed communities who are advocating for progressive change. Progress always comes not from silencing reactionary forces or opponents of change but by ensuring that those calling for a better future cannot be silenced.

We still encounter students who claim that free speech is racist because it protects white supremacists at the expense of people of color. We understand why they feel this way. They believe it is possible to create a world where they can say whatever they please while silencing the speech they abhor. But that is not how censorship works.

To abandon free speech principles is to give *existing structures of power* the authority to censor or punish speech they do not like. Some on the campus left insist that people in positions of authority should censor hate speech. The examples we reviewed in this chapter demonstrate that when you advocate for that policy, you should not be surprised if the officials you are empowering conclude that the speech that deserves to be censored is your own; that the speech they consider divisive is the speech that promotes diversity, equity, and inclusion; that the biggest danger to society comes from those who consider themselves vehemently anti-racist. If those on the left are on record as dismissing the importance of protecting free speech and academic freedom, on what basis can they oppose those who seek to silence them?

Principles, Practices, Precautions

In previous chapters we discussed in great detail how to apply principles of free speech and academic freedom to a wide range of circumstances. In many cases we recognize that situations can be complicated and require the exercise of judgment. Not every challenging situation can be resolved with a simple set of rules about what and what not to do. But acknowledging the inevitability of nuance should not prevent us from attempting to provide clear guidance about some basic matters.

Our earlier book, *Free Speech on Campus,* included a chapter of concrete suggestions for what campuses can and can't do in dealing with free speech challenges, and we continue that practice here by offering a digestible and practical set of recommendations based on the events discussed in earlier chapters. These recommendations take the form of paired sets of "Do's" and "Don't's." We offer these suggestions not in a rigid or pedantic spirit, but rather in the hope that they will be helpful to those who confront these issues.

Again, we realize that First Amendment restrictions apply only to government action, and private colleges and universities have more latitude in dealing with speech issues. But academic freedom principles are the same at both public and private schools, and we believe all institutions of higher education should have the same basic commitments to freedom of expression.

We will begin by briefly repeating some of the suggestions from *Free Speech on Campus.* They are still relevant, and omitting them would leave this chapter incomplete. Although they address issues that were most discussed several years ago, they lay the foundation for dealing with the more challenging issues that have arisen since. In some cases we elaborate a bit on our suggestions from 2017. Here is the list from our earlier treatment of campus speech issues.

A campus can't censor or punish speech merely because a person or group considers it offensive or harmful.

A campus can censor or punish speech that meets the legal criteria for incitement harassment, true threats, or other speech unprotected by the First Amendment.

A campus can't prevent protesters from having a meaningful opportunity to get their views across in an effective way.

A campus can impose time, place, and manner restrictions on protests for the purpose of preventing protesters from disrupting the normal work of the campus, including the educational environment and administrative operations.

A campus can't engage in content-based discrimination against faculty, students, or other speakers or writers who seek to express themselves outside the professional context.

A campus can engage in content-based evaluation of faculty and students who are operating within the professional educational context, as long as this evaluation is based on professional standards or peer assessments of the quality of scholarship or teaching.

A campus can't deny recognition to a student organization or impose sanctions against it for the views or ideas expressed by the organization, its members, or its speakers.

A campus can ensure that all student organizations, as a condition for recognition and receipt of funding, be open to all students, and it can impose sanctions on student organizations for conduct that is not protected by principles of freedom of speech.

Based on our discussion in this book, we also suggest the following.

Articulating Basic Principles of Free Speech and Academic Freedom

DO have clear, prominently available statements about freedom of speech and academic freedom, and incorporate them into orientation and regular programming.

DON'T assume people have a natural instinct to protect offensive speech or an understanding of relevant history or civics.

In our experience, people often have a strong desire to stop and even punish speech that they find objectionable or harmful. Often this desire to restrict speech is based on good intentions and phrased in terms of noble objectives.

It thus is important that every institution have a clear statement of its commitment to freedom of speech and academic freedom, as well as a statement of the relationship between these concepts and the institution's core mission. The Chicago Principles are one example, but they are neither the only nor the best way for an institution to articulate these values.[1] Moreover, it is better for each campus to do the work of formulating and conveying these commitments in the language most appropriate to it—as the University of Michigan did, for example, with its Principles on Diversity of Thought and Freedom of Expression.[2]

Having a statement of values, however nuanced and well done, is not sufficient. These values must be communicated to everyone on campus and be easily accessible on websites and in other materials. Orientations for new students, staff, and faculty are obvious opportunities to do this. But a one-and-done approach isn't sufficient; members of the campus community must have regular opportunities to discuss, apply, and debate these principles in public settings. Campuses should find opportunities for programs to discuss their free speech principles, including the hard questions that arise in implementing them. And they should provide additional resources to those on campus who are dealing with and debating issues regarding freedom of speech and academic freedom.

At the same time, we advise against conveying these principles in ways that overlook or minimize people's concerns about hateful speech or violent rhetoric. Freedom of speech is protected as a fundamental right precisely because speech is powerful, but its impact can be harmful as well as beneficial. Recent generations of students have grown up in an educational system that encourages them to value diversity, demonstrate mutual respect, and condemn bullying behavior. Before reaching college their educational environments had very little tolerance for hateful speech or conduct. They don't think it's right for people to belittle or harass others.

It is for the better that these students bring these values to higher education, just as it is for the better that today's student bodies are more diverse and inclusive than those in the past. When students object to hateful speech, it is a reflection of their concerns about the harms of such expression—and their objections are also protected speech. The problem arises when objection becomes an attempt at suppression. Almost no one has an instinct to protect speech they find offensive or harmful. The arguments for protecting bad speech require careful elaboration as well as a knowledge of history and an understanding of the risks of creating a censorship regime. Statements of free speech principles that condescend to students, take a finger-wagging tone, or fail to acknowledge legitimate concerns about bad speech will not win any converts. Education is what campuses are built for, and ongoing education is necessary to maintaining a robust culture of free expression.

Establishing and Enforcing "Principles of Community"

DO pair statements about free expression with the principles of community that campus affiliates should embrace in order to act as a scholarly community of people with different backgrounds and viewpoints.

DON'T leave the impression that the aspirational norms of the principles of community can be the basis for sanctioning protected speech by professors or students.

Campuses can and should express their values as educational institutions, but those commitments may be superseded by the First Amendment or principles of academic freedom. We often remind our students that just because there is a right to say something, that doesn't mean it should be said. We hope our students will always treat one another with mutual respect and toleration, and hopefully kindness, but these aspirations should be advanced through advocacy about the culture necessary to engage in higher education rather than enforced through punitive sanctions. The very idea of a scholarly community presupposes a level of mutual respect and toleration for diversity, including diverse points of view. Although universities are obligated to protect free speech rights, no university could do its important work if it only valued the free-wheeling norms of unrestrained speech.

Principles of community are a way for schools to express their values and aspirations. Again, there is no best set of such principles. And while they are largely similar across most schools, there may be differences among institutions, especially as to how they are expressed. UC Berkeley, for example, states as its principles of community:

We are committed to ensuring freedom of expression and dialogue that elicits the full spectrum of views held by our varied communities.

We embrace open and equitable access to opportunities for learning and development as our obligation and goal.

We believe that active participation and leadership in addressing the most pressing issues facing our local and global communities are central to our educational mission.

We place honesty and integrity in our teaching, learning, research and administration at the highest level.

We recognize the intrinsic relationship between diversity and excellence in all our endeavors.

We affirm the dignity of all individuals and strive to uphold a just community in which discrimination and hate are not tolerated.

We respect the differences as well as the commonalities that bring us together and call for civility and respect in our personal interactions.[3]

We began this book with the congressional hearing in which three university presidents were asked about speech that advocated genocide of Jews. If we were asked such a question, we would stress how such speech violates our principles of community. We too, like the presidents who were pilloried for it, would have said that whether the speech can be punished depends on context. Campuses cannot ban expression of even deeply objectionable ideas. But we can and must express our values, even when they cannot be a basis for sanctions. It is important to make clear that principles of community are aspirational, not enforceable in disciplinary proceedings.

Balancing Free Expression with Nondiscriminatory Learning Environments

DO articulate the campus's ethical and legal obligations to maintain nondiscriminatory learning environments, especially for people with protected identities.

DON'T implement these obligations in ways that interfere with protected speech.

Schools have a legal as well as a moral duty to create a nondiscriminatory learning environment for all students. Title VI imposes this requirement with regard to race and national origin, and Title IX does it with regard to sex. Campuses face sanctions, including loss of federal funding, if they fail in these obligations. State laws also create these obligations.

As we discussed in chapter 1, Catherine Lhamon, the assistant secretary of education for civil rights in the Biden administration, was emphatic that speech that is protected by the First Amendment can be a basis for finding that there was a hostile environment. Although schools cannot punish protected speech, that does not mean they can do nothing. As the Office of Civil Rights fact sheet states, "A school has a legal duty to take prompt and effective steps that are reasonably calculated to: (1) end the harassment, (2) eliminate any hostile environment and its effects, and (3) prevent the harassment from recurring. OCR evaluates the appropriateness of the school's responsive action by assessing whether it was reasonable, timely, and effective."

Although it is clear that schools cannot exhibit "deliberate indifference," what action is sufficient to meet a school's legal duties under Title VI and Title XI remains unclear. Lhamon's "Dear Colleague" letter of May 2024 said that "to meet its obligation, a university can, among other steps, communicate its opposition to stereotypical, derogatory opinions; provide counseling and support for students affected by harassment; or take steps to establish a welcoming and respectful school campus, which could include making clear that the school values, and is determined to fully include in the campus community, students of all races, colors, and national origins."[4] This is another reason principles of community are essential to both free speech and anti-discrimination commitments: they are nonpunitive ways for an institution to take steps to comply with its Title VI and Title XI requirements.

It will take some time before it is clear what universities' obligations are when constitutionally protected speech risks creating a discriminatory learning environment. "Speaking out" and "reaching out" are the most obvious steps, although it is unreasonable to expect campus leaders to make public statements every time a professor or student expresses an opinion considered discriminatory. But one step that should be avoided, irrespective of OCR's expectations, is to launch "investigations" against students and faculty members when the expression subject to complaint is clearly constitutionally protected. OCR does not seem to require them, and they would be inconsistent with the campus's commitment to protecting free speech rights.

Ultimately, the question that will be asked in any situation is whether the school responded reasonably and has made adequate efforts to create an inclusive learning environment. While there cannot be a litmus test for this, it is clear that doing nothing (or almost nothing) is deliberate indifference. Campuses should also ensure that their responses to the concerns of students in protected categories are consistent and that there is no double standard in responding to different groups' complaints.

Addressing Nonprotected Speech

DO respond quickly to unprotected speech that harasses or threatens campus affiliates or incites imminent lawlessness.

DON'T assume that the campus has no responsibilities when the unprotected speech occurs in social media rather than physically on campus.

As we have made clear both in *Free Speech on Campus* and here, freedom of speech is not absolute. Some types of speech are unprotected by the First Amendment, including incitement of illegal activity, true threats, and harassment, and campuses have the moral and often the legal duty to respond to such expression.[5] Even public universities may impose punishment for unprotected speech.

As we have discussed, there is a debate among university officials about when to speak out about national issues. But even for those who profess to adhere to institutional neutrality, which limits when campus officials make statements, it is inherently different when there is an event on one's own campus. University officials have a moral obligation and often a legal duty to respond to what occurs on their campus.

There is an important distinction between speech or other activities that violate the law and those that infringe campus rules but don't break the law. Violations of the law—and incitement and true threats violate the criminal law, as do vandalism and destruction of property—are handled by the criminal justice system. Violations of campus rules are handled through campus disciplinary proceedings. Of course, conduct that violates the law generally also violates campus rules. A challenge for campus administrators is that there often is a demand to punish those who transgress campus rules, but disciplinary proceedings for students, and often for faculty, are confidential, making it very difficult for campus officials to reassure the community that actions have been taken or respond to questions about what has been done.

There used to be a clear delineation between speech that occurred on campus and that taking place elsewhere. Berkeley's famous Free Speech Movement of the mid-1960s was about students' ability to speak on campus about matters that interested them. But social media has obliterated that line. Speech by students or faculty over

Facebook or Instagram or X is easily circulated and can cause great harms. Yet a public university, or a private one committed to free speech principles, confronts the question of whether and when it can punish off-campus speech over social media. The simple answer is that the medium is unlikely to matter. If the speech causes a hostile learning environment, the campus must respond.

There has been one Supreme Court case dealing with schools and speech over social media. Although *Mahanoy Area School District v. B.L.* arose at the high school level, the protections and limits it places on speech apply in colleges and universities as well.[6] Brandi Levy made the Mahanoy Area High School junior varsity cheerleading team as a freshman. She tried out for the varsity team as a sophomore but was again assigned to the junior varsity squad. She was especially upset because an incoming freshman made varsity. On Saturday, from off campus, Levy posted two messages on her Snapchat "Story." They were visible on Snapchat for twenty-four hours. Her first message consisted of a photo in which she and a classmate raised their middle fingers at the camera; the caption read: "Fuck school fuck softball fuck cheer fuck everything."[7] The second message, posted shortly thereafter, was a complaint that Levy and another student were on junior varsity again, but it did not contain any profanities.

The coaches determined that the posts "could impact students in the school" and had violated team rules that Levy had agreed to follow, including that cheerleaders should "have respect for [their] school, coaches, teachers, [and] other cheerleaders" and avoid "foul language and inappropriate gestures."[8] They removed Levy from the cheer team for the school year but told her she could try out again as a rising junior. No other disciplinary action was taken.

Levy and her parents sued in federal district court, which granted a preliminary injunction reinstating her to the team and then summary judgment in her favor. The United States Court of Appeals for the Third Circuit affirmed, stressing that schools cannot punish off-campus speech.

The Supreme Court, in an 8-1 decision, (with only Justice Thomas dissenting), also ruled in favor of the student and against the school. Justice Breyer, in his opinion for the Court, made clear that this student's speech was protected, but he did not go as far as the Third Circuit, which ruled that schools can never punish off-campus speech. The Court left open the ability of schools to punish off-campus expression that involves bullying, harassment, or cheating.

Justice Breyer stressed that Levy's speech was critical of a school official, and that the core of the First Amendment has long been seen as safeguarding expression about the government and its officers. He rejected the school's claimed interest in teaching good manners or in upholding team morale, and also stressed that there was no evidence that Levy's speech was significantly disruptive of school activities.

Justice Breyer observed that "it might be tempting to dismiss B. L.'s words as unworthy of the robust First Amendment protections discussed herein. But sometimes it is necessary to protect the superfluous in order to preserve the necessary."[9] Levy's speech was sophomoric, but she was a sophomore.

Importantly, the Court did not hold that schools can never punish off-campus speech. Justice Breyer's opinion was explicit in rejecting the Third Circuit's approach: "The school's regulatory interests remain significant in some off-campus circumstances. . . . These include serious or severe bullying or harassment targeting particular individuals; threats aimed at teachers or other students; the failure to follow rules concerning lessons, the writing of papers, the use of computers, or participation in other online school activities; and breaches of school security devices, including material maintained within school computers."[10]

The same principles would apply for colleges and universities. Such speech, even over social media, could be a basis for campus disciplinary proceedings.

Creating and Implementing Time, Place, and Manner Regulations

DO have clear and transparent policies regulating the time, place, and manner of speech that are clearly connected to legitimate campus interests such as protecting the learning and research environment.
DON'T implement these policies differently depending on the viewpoint of the speaker or group.

The events of 2024 have made even clearer how important it is that campuses have clear time, place, and manner rules with regard to speech. The Supreme Court has classified government property into different types of forums, with distinct rules for each. In *Minnesota Voters Alliance v. Mansky*, the Court stated:

> Our cases recognize three types of government-controlled spaces: traditional public forums, designated public forums, and nonpublic forums.[11] In a traditional public forum—parks, streets, sidewalks, and the like—the government may impose reasonable time, place, and manner restrictions on private speech, but restrictions based on content must satisfy strict scrutiny, and those based on viewpoint are prohibited. The same standards apply in designated public forums—spaces that have "not traditionally been regarded as a public forum" but which the government has "intentionally opened up for that purpose." In a nonpublic forum, on the other hand—a space that "is not by tradition or designation a forum for public communication"—the government has much more flexibil-

ity to craft rules limiting speech. The government may reserve such a forum "for its intended purposes, communicative or otherwise, as long as the regulation on speech is reasonable and not an effort to suppress expression merely because public officials oppose the speaker's view."[12]

The Court has recognized the category of "limited public forums" in other cases as well. In *Christian Legal Society v. Martinez*, it said government entities establish such forums by opening property "limited to use by certain groups or dedicated solely to the discussion of certain subjects. In such a forum, a governmental entity may impose restrictions on speech that are reasonable and viewpoint-neutral."[13]

There is a strong argument that many places on campuses, and certainly the venues of campus events, constitute limited public forums. This means their use can be restricted to members of the campus community and to the discussion to specific subjects. But even in areas that are deemed public forums, campuses can regulate speech if certain requirements are met.[14] First, the regulation must be content-neutral unless the content restriction is justified by strict scrutiny (that is, it is necessary to achieve a compelling purpose). Second, time, place, or manner restrictions must be reasonable, serve an important government interest, and leave open adequate alternative places for speech. Third, a licensing or permit system for the use of public forums must serve an important purpose, give clear criteria to the licensing authority that leaves it almost no discretion, and provide procedural safeguards such as a requirement for prompt decisions of license requests and judicial review of denials. Finally, the Court has ruled that regulation of speech in public forums need not use the least restrictive alternative, but it must be narrowly tailored to achieve the government's purpose.

In *Heffron v. International Society for Krishna Consciousness, Inc.*, the Court said that it had often approved time, place, and manner restrictions, "provided that they are justified without reference to the content of the regulated speech, that they serve a significant governmental interest, and that in doing so they leave open ample alternative channels for communication of the information."[15]

Campuses may have time, place, and manner restrictions that meet these requirements. But in both their rules and how they are administered, campuses cannot discriminate among speech or speakers based on message. Permissible time, place, and manner restrictions might involve limiting protests or demonstrations near classroom buildings while classes are in session. Schools can limit noise in or near dormitories at night, prohibit the use of sound amplification equipment on campus to prevent disruptions, prohibit encampments (which many now have done). These examples have in common that they would apply to all speech, whatever its viewpoint or subject matter. All would be constitutional.

Preparing for Planned "Major Events"

DO prepare comprehensive viewpoint-neutral policies that allow for an assessment of logistics, including security considerations.
DON'T tie these policies to "controversial" events or charge organizers more for security merely because of anticipated protest activity.

Every campus needs a set of policies that anticipates the issues that arise when activities are planned for campus spaces, either by members of the campus community or outside groups. Unlike freestanding time, place, and manner regulations that apply to everyday campus activity, the policies governing planned events require active coordination between campus administrators and event sponsors, on everything from facility reservation deadlines to insurance requirements to appropriate staffing levels. Most of these events are managed without drama by facility staff.

Occasionally, however, an event will be planned that, because of its scope and complexity, requires engagement by a broader team of campus officials and approvers. In these circumstances it is important to have a regular process for bringing in a larger team and making viewpoint-neutral decisions on the full range of issues, including (when appropriate) working with organizers to adjust proposed plans to ensure that the event can be held successfully.

The challenges that arise without such a policy became evident in 2017, when a conservative group at UC Berkeley planned to sponsor a talk by the provocative conservative commentator Ben Shapiro. Just months earlier, an event featuring hatemonger Milo Yiannopoulos had been canceled after 150 "black bloc" community anarchists streamed into a large group of peaceful student protesters and caused a violent riot that included window breaking, arson, and attacks on police with rocks and firecrackers. To ensure that the Shapiro event would be more successful, the campus tried to work with the sponsoring group, Young America's Foundation, to find a date and time that would permit an appropriately large venue or, alternatively, to hold it at the sponsor's preferred time in a smaller venue, or else in a space for which the group would have to pay a higher rental fee and a special security fee.[16]

The Shapiro event went off successfully despite the presence of hundreds of protesters, a few arrests, and security costs estimated at $600,000.[17] But afterward, the event organizers sued the campus, arguing that its "unconstitutionally vague" policies for handling "major events" resulted in conservative speakers being treated differently from others. For example, the security fee charged for Shapiro's talk was well above a fee at the same venue for Supreme Court justice Sonia Sotomayor. A federal judge rejected the campus's bid to dismiss the lawsuit.[18] The university eventually settled the lawsuit by agreeing to consider what it described as "non-substantive changes" to its policies, including eliminating "complexity" as a criterion for what constitutes a major event, refining which "authorized campus officials" were responsible for decision making, and reemphasizing the prohibitions against viewpoint discrimination.[19]

Mindful of these controversies, when UC Irvine updated its "major events" policies, we started with a preamble that underscored that the goal was to "facilitate free speech and expression and to ensure safe and successful events." Rather than define a "major event" with reference to viewpoint judgments such as "controversial speakers," the campus focused on whether (1) "300 or more people are expected to participate or attend"; (2) "authorized campus officials determine that the event is likely to significantly affect campus safety, security and/or campus services" based on ten specified conditions; or (3) officials determined that "the event is likely to significantly interfere with other campus functions or activities" based on similarly specified conditions. Organizers are required to fill out a "Campus Events Risk Grid" that may trigger a more thorough security assessment based on "objective and credible evidence of specific risks, and not on assessment of the viewpoints, opinions or anticipated expression of event speakers." Recommended security measures may include "adjusting the venue, date and/or time of the event; providing additional law enforcement; imposing controls or security checkpoints; and creating buffer zones around the venue."

Importantly, under UC Irvine's policy, organizers are expected to pay "Basic Event Security" costs based on the elements of the event that the organizers control (such as the number of participants) "in the absence of any expected disturbance." But they do not have to pay for "Extraordinary Event Security" costs associated with the need to address anticipated protests. A distinction such as this is necessary to avoid a situation where those who sponsor more controversial events are always expected to pay more than those whose events do not trigger protests.[20] The security cost is a serious challenge. When Berkeley worked in 2017 to ensure that conservative campus groups could successfully hold events despite student and community efforts at disruption, it spent almost $4 million in one month—an amount that is certainly not sustainable.[21] UC Irvine hoped to avoid such a situation, but that is not a reasonable expectation for every campus. When UCLA developed its major events policy, it took a different approach: it limits total spending per year on security costs associated with planned "Public Expression Activities" and then, once the budget is exhausted, allows no other events. In the words of their policy:

> To properly balance UCLA's interest in making its venues available with the need for fiscal responsibility and other important educational and public service priorities of the University, UCLA will not spend more than . . . $500,000 in total per academic year on security costs incurred to respond to Public Expression Activities in connection with Major Events. . . . Once an applicable cap has been reached, no new Major Event subject to that cap will be scheduled for the remainder of the academic year.[22]

This policy keeps the university from drowning in security costs from an endless series of controversial planned events, but at the price of limiting opportunities for campus members or outside groups to host events. It is unclear whether UCLA's approach is constitutional. And if this approach is permissible, it is uncertain how courts will draw the line as to what amount of money is too restrictive of speech under the First Amendment.

Different campuses will find different ways to balance these competing considerations, and as long as their policies are viewpoint-neutral, they likely will satisfy the requirements for protecting expressive

PRINCIPLES, PRACTICES, PRECAUTIONS

activity. The important point is that campuses should anticipate these issues and develop policies in advance, rather than be forced to make ad hoc decisions after controversial speakers have already been invited.

Anticipating Disruptions of Campus Activities

DO make it clear that free speech does not include the right to disrupt authorized campus activities, including invited speakers.
DON'T treat all disruptions the same or adopt exclusively punitive approaches to disruptions.

If campuses are to be places where all ideas can be expressed, they must resist calls to impose censorship or punishment merely for the expression of an idea, and they must prevent others from using a "heckler's veto" to stop a program or silence a speaker. Freedom of speech and academic freedom become meaningless if protesters and dissenters have a recognized right to disrupt events or shout down speakers they disapprove of. If a heckler's veto is allowed, the only speech that occurs will be that which no one cares enough about to shout down. Eventually, no one would be able to hold an event worth attending. For people who find certain programs or speakers offensive, the proper response is to protest peacefully or bring in their own speakers.

Yet creating an adequate policy on "disruption" of authorized campus events is more complicated than it might seem. When UC Irvine first began developing such a policy, one of us (Gillman) believed it would be a good summer project; in fact, working through all the issues with the wide range of campus stakeholders took over a year. Care needed to be taken to appropriately define what does and does not count as a disruption and specify how to distinguish serious violations of the policy from less serious ones.

The UC Irvine policy begins by situating the issue within the larger context of free speech, noting that "just as UCI does not deny speakers access to UCI venues because of their views, UCI does not tolerate Disruptions of University Activities."[23] With respect to activities involving a speaker or presenter, a disruption "means undue interference with the ability of the speaker to deliver, or the audience to receive, the speaker's message." At the same time, "because no view or message is beyond criticism, UCI will always ensure that members of the UCI community can peacefully protest and express condemnation of views with which they disagree."

The factors weighing in favor of a finding of disruption include whether the conduct was violent or involved a threat of violence, whether it incited an immediate breach of the peace, whether it lasted long enough to unduly interfere with the activity, whether it stopped when a request to stop was addressed to the disruptor(s), whether it was intentionally aimed at interfering with the event, and whether it interfered with ingress or egress of pedestrian or vehicle traffic. Among the factors considered in determining appropriate discipline are whether the individual or group engaging in the conduct had been previously counseled or disciplined regarding disruption, whether the conduct had a serious adverse effect on participants (as shown, for example, by submission of complaints), and whether the individual or group took steps to mitigate or compensate for the consequences of their actions. These factors would distinguish someone who spontaneously interrupts an event with a brief outburst but sits quietly afterward from someone who enters the venue intending to make the event impossible to sustain.

The policy also made it clear that "this definition is not meant to eliminate the usual range of human reactions commonly displayed by an audience during heated discussions of controversial topics" and should not prohibit expressions of protest that do not prevent the speaker from delivering a message or the audience from receiving it. Examples of such nondisruptive conduct include holding an eight-and-a-half-by-eleven-inch piece of paper in front of one's body, engaging with the speaker if the speaker chooses to engage, wearing clothing with (constitutionally protected) words or images on it, or silently kneeling. Disruptive conduct would include deliberately blocking the audience's view of the speaker, producing noise that prevents the speaker from being heard, using laser pointers, turning off lights, setting off fire alarms, and displaying real or facsimile weapons.

It is important to help event organizers prevent disruptions and respond properly when one is happening. When there are concerns about possible disruptive activity, the organizers are asked to confer with campus officials about additional staffing by people with expertise in "constructive engagement." They are also highly encouraged to make an announcement at the beginning of the event saying that the campus supports the freedom to protest "so long as it does not unduly interfere with the ability of the speaker to deliver the message or the ability of the audience to receive" it. They are asked to say that a "protester whose actions interfere in this manner will be warned," and if the interference continues, they will be escorted out and held accountable under relevant policies. A short-term disruption that allows the program to continue is generally not a violation of policy, especially if it was spontaneous and not preplanned. If a protest continues, organizers are asked to follow UCI's constructive engagement model, which favors resolution through the initial engagement by administrators and other officials, not campus security or officers, unless there is a threat to public safety.[24] The overriding goal should be "to reestablish with deliberate speed an atmosphere conducive to communication between the speaker and audience" while respecting the rights of all parties.

There may be unfortunate instances in which safety requires moving an event to Zoom (or other similar medium) or canceling it entirely. Clear policies and careful planning, ideally, will lessen the need for this, but the reality is that safety must be paramount and sometimes there is no other way to protect those present.

Controversies Surrounding Extramural Speech by Students

DO make it clear that protected speech by students in public or online settings will not be the basis for campus sanctions.

DON'T confuse improper campus sanctions with proper university statements condemning outrageous speech or with outreach efforts to support upset students.

Throughout most of the history of higher education, few people ever knew what individual students said in off-campus settings. Today, many students live highly expressive lives online, and if they post something disagreeable or hateful, the entire world may potentially discover it. Campuses can be quickly embroiled in social media firestorms with demands to remove the perceived evil speakers from the community.

Managing these controversies may pose challenges for leadership, but free speech principles make one thing very clear: campuses cannot censor or punish a student merely because they express a view that others object to, assuming the expression is constitutionally protected speech. Protecting speech that others may hate is the foundational principle of free speech. This means that campuses should not take steps like launching formal "investigations" of students when it is clear that the speech in question is constitutionally protected and therefore not even potentially in violation of a university's anti-harassment policies.

Rather than be tempted to act as censors, campuses should anticipate social media firestorms and have a support structure and a set of resources available to students who are their targets. These resources might include advice on how to prioritize their physical safety, collect and preserve evidence of potential lawbreaking by third parties, quiet the noise by "muting" certain channels of communication, report harassment, access mental health services, and (if possible) make different short-term housing accommodations.[25] Preparing these kinds of responses in advance is especially important given the culture of "doxxing"—revealing private information about people over social media—and the practice of some national political or advocacy organizations to target and harass students who take certain political positions.

But committing in advance to protecting students whose public statements may cause outrage does not mean the campus cannot publicly defend its own values. There are those who say that publicly denouncing statements by students violates their free speech rights, but we disagree. Campus officials have expressive rights, and there are times when speaking out is warranted. While campuses cannot use their principles of community as a basis for punishing students, they can urge members of the campus community to aspire to create an environment of mutual respect, exploration, discovery, and the transmission of advanced knowledge.

Administrators should also be prepared to provide outreach and support to students and other campus affiliates who might be affected by outrageous or hateful expression. As we have mentioned, the Department of Education has instructed campuses that this kind of outreach is sometimes required by the federal law (Title VI) that obligates institutions to create and maintain nondiscriminatory learning environments. In highly distressing cases, deliberate indifference to the impact of hateful speech is not permitted.

We should emphasize again that this advice applies to students' extramural speech. It does not apply when students are in the university's professional settings, such as in classrooms, where the expectations of appropriate speech and conduct are subject to the institution's legitimate interest in fostering appropriate learning environments.

Extramural Speech by Professors

DO make it clear that extramural speech by faculty members is, in almost every circumstance, protected and will not lead to sanctions.

DON'T overlook the possibility that extramural speech by a faculty member may be evidence of a lack of competence in their scholarly field.

Most of the advice we have given about student extramural speech also applies to controversial statements by faculty members. Like anyone else, they will sometimes say things on social media or in other nonprofessional settings that people consider beyond the pale. In recent years, professors have caused firestorms by expressing hateful views against certain groups of people, supporting violence against police officers, and celebrating the death of beloved monarchs. But professors have the same free speech rights as everyone, and if their remarks are constitutionally protected, universities cannot sanction them for holding or expressing outrageous or even false views that are unrelated to their scholarly expertise.

At a public university, the First Amendment protects the speech of faculty and staff if it involves a matter of public concern and if the speech interests outweigh the university's interests. This is the test articulated in *Pickering v. Board of Education,* a key case in holding that other speech by government employees is protected by the First Amendment.[26] A teacher was fired for sending a letter to a local newspaper that was critical of the way school officials had raised money for the schools. The Supreme Court held that the firing violated the teacher's First Amendment rights. Justice Marshall, writing for the majority, said the Court's task was to balance the free speech rights of government employees against the government's need for efficient operation. He wrote: "The State has interests as an employer in regulating the speech of its employees that differ significantly from those it possesses in connection with regulation of the speech of the citizenry in general. The problem . . . is to arrive at a balance between the interests of the teacher, as a citizen, in commenting upon matters of public concern and the interest of the State, as an employer, in promoting the efficiency of the public services it performs through its employees."[27] In other words, the First Amendment does not automatically protect all speech by government employees. Under well-established law, speech is protected by the First Amendment only if involves a matter of public concern, and only if its protection is on balance desirable.[28]

As with student speech, the obligation to protect faculty members' free speech rights does not mean that administrators must be silent in the face of outrage over remarks that apparently violate the campus's principles of community. So long as it is made clear that professors will not be formally punished by the institution, it does not violate their rights if campus leaders denounce outrageous speech. Again, freedom of speech does not mean freedom from criticism.

If a faculty member expresses views that are widely despised, campus leaders may need to consider reassigning some of their teaching responsibilities, perhaps by having them teach elective rather than required courses to give students the option of avoiding the professor.

Or they may choose to offer alternative sections of required courses. Individual faculty members do not generally have a right to teach whatever courses they want. Course assignments are typically managed by deans and department chairs, who consider a variety of factors in constructing teaching schedules, including putting the most highly regarded professors in larger required courses.

This discretion is uncontroversial so long as changes in the faculty member's teaching responsibilities do not deny them the ability to teach within their areas of expertise. Still, options such as these should be used very rarely, since professors inevitably hold some views that some students will find disagreeable, and it would be unwise if not impossible to create an expectation that students never have to take courses from faculty members whose views they do not like. If faculty members are acting competently and ethically in the classroom, their opinions on other matters should not be relevant.

There is one important way in which the rules governing faculty extramural speech differ from those governing student speech. That is when the speech calls into question their fitness to serve as professional scholars.

The AAUP's 1940 *Statement of Principles on Academic Freedom and Tenure* declares that when faculty members "speak or write as citizens, they should be free from institutional censorship or discipline." But it goes on to say that when representing their profession, they have "special obligations" to "remember the public may judge their profession and their institution by their utterances," and hence "they should at all times be accurate, should exercise appropriate restraint, should show respect for the opinions of others, and should make every effort to indicate that they are not speaking for the institution."[29] In 1964, the AAUP's Committee on Academic Freedom elaborated that the "controlling principle is that a faculty member's expression of opinion as a citizen cannot constitute grounds for dismissal unless it clearly demonstrates the faculty member's unfitness to serve. Extramural utterances rarely bear upon the faculty member's fitness for continuing service."[30] If an engineering professor is a Holocaust denier in public statements, there should be no professional repercussions, but the issue would be different if the Holocaust denier were a modern European historian.[31]

In cases where a professor's extramural statements raise questions about their fitness to serve in their profession, the process for considering sanctions should resemble the ordinary process of peer review. It should arise from the same kind of process that is used to assess a scholar's competence in ordinary circumstances. University administrators should not base a decision about sanctions on their unilateral assessment.

Assessing Controversies Involving Classroom Speech by Professors

DO make it clear that academic freedom protects virtually all pedagogical decisions made by faculty members even when students or community members find them objectionable.

DON'T relieve professors of the obligation to demonstrate professional competency and ethical behavior in the classroom.

It is vital to distinguish general free speech protections from the protections of academic freedom. Faculty members have free speech rights when they act outside their professional environments and responsibilities, including most social media posts and political activity, but when they are engaging in their professional activities, they do not have an unlimited right to express any view without consequence. In classroom settings, for example, faculty members are governed by principles of academic freedom, which guarantee them wide discretion in making decisions as highly trained experts about how best to teach advanced knowledge but also impose obligations of professional competence and ethical behavior. Classrooms are not private playpens where a professor may indulge their personal or political views.

The protections of academic freedom, which are vital to the functioning of modern universities, give competent and ethical faculty extraordinary leeway in deciding what and how to teach within their fields of expertise. Faculty members may introduce material into the classroom that students find objectionable if it is not gratuitous and is germane to the topics under discussion. This includes material that might be religiously objectionable (such as medieval paintings depicting the Prophet Muhammad) or contain language that today would be unacceptable (such as nineteenth-century American novels discussing race) or reflect artistic choices now considered wildly insensitive (such as movies where actors appear in blackface). Professors may advance disagreeable viewpoints into a discussion as a way of forcing students to develop better arguments against those views.

Of course, some words are so inflammatory that introducing them into the classroom may poison the learning environment, and many faculty members have changed their practices in response to the diversity of their students. Still, the educational reference to hateful words or disturbing concepts is not the same as their use as epithets, and there are settings where exposure to such words and concepts must be defended.

When approaching sensitive topics, competent and ethical faculty members should be mindful of how a provocative lesson plan might affect the learning environment, and they should properly prepare students for the experience. But it would violate faculty members' academic freedom if institutions required, for example, that professors preface exposure to provocative material with "trigger warnings." It is up to individual faculty members to determine whether such warnings or accommodations are the best way to accomplish pedagogical goals, or whether they might undermine those goals.

Nothing said here is meant to lessen the rights of students to criticize their teachers' choices. Academic freedom does not include freedom from criticism. But students' right to criticize does not include the right to disrupt the classroom work of a professor or an entitlement to options that would allow them to receive course credit without having to encounter a professor's approaches that they find objectionable. In some circumstances, institutions may provide alternative course options for students who do not want to encounter a particular professor. But campuses are not required to provide special accommodations to students who disagree with a professor's approaches or views.

While academic freedom necessarily provides broad protections to professors, their discretion is not absolute. Faculty members' choices are not always consistent with norms of competency and ethical behavior. Most of the mistakes they make are rooted in the misconception that they have "free speech" rights when doing their jobs rather than the privileges and responsibilities of academic freedom. Instructors cannot convey that students of certain political backgrounds are not welcome in their classrooms. They cannot interject non-germane material into the classroom to indulge their personal, political, or religious views. They cannot encourage or provide incentives to students to engage in the professor's preferred political activities or evaluate student performance differently based on extraneous factors such as a student's political or religious views. They cannot ignore university policies regarding the necessary elements of a syllabus (such as specifications of learning outcomes, clear grading criteria, academic integrity expectations, or resources to request disability accommodations). They are also expected to maintain a classroom culture in which no student experiences a discriminatory learning environment as defined by civil rights law.

We readily acknowledge the difficulty in drawing lines between the permissible and the impermissible under principles of academic freedom. But that does not mean that there is no line. It is one that must be administered carefully, with fair procedures and great deliberation.

Political Statements Associated with Academic Departments and Schools

DO prohibit or restrict the ability of faculty members to associate their academic departments and schools with political statements reflecting individuals' views.

DON'T prevent individual faculty or groups of faculty from making political statements.

Faculty members have the right to express themselves on issues, and they may do so individually or collectively. But it is a quite different matter when a department or a school within the university takes a position. Under First Amendment law, a distinction is often drawn between the speech of individuals and the speech of entities. Individual faculty members have First Amendment rights and are protected by academic freedom, but institutions—departments and schools—do not and are not. Moreover, the authority to speak for the institution is generally restricted to its board of directors (often called "regents") and top campus officials.

The directors delegate authority to departments and schools to set their own academic policies and procedures, but this does not include making statements about controversial issues on behalf of the university or its schools or departments. Academic freedom principles protect the rights of faculty to express views about the subjects on which they have expertise, but they also emphasize that when doing so, faculty should make it clear that they are not speaking on behalf of the institution; using department websites for such statements is a very clear violation of that ethical standard. Moreover, when "departments" make political statements (rather than collections of faculty members), it leaves the impression that students who hold different viewpoints may not be welcome to study in that department. This suggestion is as much a violation of professional ethics as making enrollment in a course conditional on whether students share the professor's political ideology. Statements made by departments could also raise Title VI concerns if the students who are made to feel unwelcome are associated with a protected category under federal civil rights laws.

Even if departments and schools are authorized to make such statements, we think it is unwise. On any controversial issue, there are often people within a school or department who disagree with the majority. The mere process of deciding whether the department should issue a statement may be very divisive. Also, it is hard enough for untenured faculty to oppose their more senior colleagues. It is much more difficult for them to disagree with an official department statement on a controversial issue.

Closely related is the authority of departments or schools to place statements on their websites reflecting their members' views. Again, although we strongly support the right of faculty members, as individuals or groups, to express themselves in the forums of their choice, we do not think official institutional websites are the appropriate place for this. We agree with the policy adopted by the University of California Board of Regents in 2024, which states:

> While individual members of the University community are free to express constitutionally protected viewpoints through all non-official channels of communication, they may not associate the official administrative units of the University with their personal viewpoints. Long-standing principles of academic freedom have recognized that when faculty members speak or write as citizens, they should make every effort to indicate that they are not speaking for the institution.
>
> The University of California establishes websites and other official channels of communication maintained by the schools, departments, centers, units, and other entities for purposes of conducting the official business of the University and these entities. Examples of an entity's official business may include delivering informational resources about the unit, such as course descriptions, and communicating personnel changes, dates of upcoming events, the release of new publications, the issuance of new policies, and similar activities. The official channels of communication, including the main landing pages of websites, of schools, departments, centers, units, and other entities should not be used for purposes of publicly expressing the personal or collective opinions of unit members or of the entity, as other means of publicly conveying such opinions are available.[32]

We recommend that universities have clear policies as to when schools and departments may (or may not) take positions and how institutional websites may be used. We also suggest that they reaffirm the right of individuals and groups to express positions. But they should discourage or forbid schools and departments from taking positions on controversial issues or using their websites to communicate such views.

Official Statements by Campus Leaders
about Social and Political Topics

DO exercise restraint in deciding when campuses should make statements about controversial social and political matters.

DON'T create unsustainable expectations that the leader will either address many issues or never speak on public matters.

Campus leaders are constantly called on to make statements about events, especially those that affect members of their community. It is difficult to know when to speak as a university administrator. One cannot respond to every event or accede to every demand for a statement. If one speaks often, it decreases the impact when a statement is most necessary.

As we discussed earlier, many campus administrators have embraced the Kalven Report from the University of Chicago and its approach of strict institutional neutrality. We think this is too categorical: there are times when there is the obligation to speak out, such as most did after the murder of George Floyd or after January 6. Those on campus rightly want their leaders to voice their pain, express compassion, and perhaps offer some moral clarity.

Some leaders have said they will issue statements only on matters that relate directly to those on campus. We share this approach, but it is not always clear what is sufficiently related to the campus. We suggest some basic considerations:

1. We speak out to express our policies about free speech. It is imperative that campuses have clear principles and policies about freedom of expression and academic freedom.

2. As we indicated, we encourage campus officials to speak out if an event on campus necessitates a response. Several years ago, for example, Harvard law professor Alan Dershowitz spoke at Berkeley

Law. Someone drew a swastika over a flyer on a bulletin board with his picture. One of us (Chemerinsky), feeling it was essential to remind the community of our values, immediately sent a message to our entire community condemning the defacement.[33] This was also an instance in which a message from the leader to that particular community, the law school, was preferable to a general campus message by a president or chancellor.

A very different example: in fall 2023, a professor at Berkeley Law wrote an op-ed in the *Wall Street Journal* encouraging employers not to hire Berkeley law students who he thought had shown themselves to be antisemitic.[34] Understandably, many students were deeply upset by this and demanded that he be disciplined or even fired. The dean does not have the authority to do that, and it could not be done without violating the First Amendment. But a message was sent to the community, which said in part:

> Each year, I write to the community to express our commitment to freedom of speech, which includes the right of people to say things that others find offensive, even deeply offensive. My guess is that in the last week most of us have heard things that offended and upset us. Some in our community were upset yesterday when a professor published an op-ed that called on employers not to hire students who expressed particular views. To be clear, that professor was speaking for himself and not for the institution. The Law School is strongly committed to helping all of our students find employment. Our Career Development Office is unflagging in this effort to work with each student to obtain employment during and after law school.[35]

To say nothing in response to his op-ed would have sent the wrong message. While some would have preferred a strongly worded condemnation, it was enough that the message expressed the most crucial point: he did not speak for the law school, and we help every student get a job as best we can.

3. Administrators should be most reluctant to speak out on national and world events in messages to the campus community. But there are times when silence will inevitably be viewed as complicity. There are certainly risks in doing this. Any message might further divide the community or alienate some supporters. The standard used by one of us (Gillman) is to speak when "the external event causes a level of disruption that raises questions about our community's ability to pursue education, research or other operations—or for members of the community to function effectively in their roles—manifesting a need to affirm our commitment to community, mission and/or values." Obviously, these are judgment calls. There is no algorithm for deciding when to make a statement.

We recognize, of course, that each campus has its own population and political situation. What makes sense at one institution might not at another.

4. Campus officials must resist creating an impression that these statements are to be expected. They should be exceptional events. Some campus leaders, including one of us (Gillman), have created a "statement on statements" to foster realistic expectations about when statements will be issued.[36]

Requiring Applicants to Submit Statements Regarding Diversity, Equity, and Inclusion

DO assert a commitment to the values of DEI as central to the success of universities.

DON'T require every job applicant for a faculty position to write a separate statement about their commitment to DEI.

Diversity, of every kind, is integral to the mission of higher education. Everyone's education is enhanced when they are exposed to diverse viewpoints and to people from different backgrounds. Research, too, benefits from a diversity of ideas.

We thus strongly disagree with those who have rejected the importance of diversity as a value in college and universities. Nothing in the Supreme Court's recent decision in *Students for Fair Admission v. President and Fellows of Harvard College* precludes schools from valuing and pursuing diversity as an objective.[37] The Court only limited the means that could be used by saying that no preference could be given on account of race in college admissions. In other words, the Court limited *how* a school could pursue the goal of diversity, not the goal itself.

We hope that colleges and universities will reaffirm their commitment to diversity of thought as well as racial, ethnic, and religious diversity in their faculty and student populations. But we are more skeptical about requiring faculty candidates or student applicants to prepare a "Diversity, Equity, and Inclusion Statement." (We also recognize that these have been prohibited in some jurisdictions.)

On one hand, it is important for schools to assess the ability of faculty to teach a diverse student body and for students to work effectively in a diverse environment. DEI statements are one way to assess this, and if properly used, they can be a component in this evaluation and present no problems under the First Amendment.[38] They also have the benefit of reminding students and faculty that diversity matters. On the other hand, if these statements are seen as an ideological litmus test for hiring, this is highly undesirable, and if they are actually used that way, it is unconstitutional. Diversity statements cannot be the twenty-first-century equivalent of loyalty oaths.

We recommend that if a school is going to require DEI statements of faculty candidates or student applicants, it should give a clear explanation of how they are and are not used. The requirement for DEI statements should be accompanied by a statement that they are not employed to give any preference in hiring or admission based on race, sex, or political views. They are used to get a better sense of how a faculty member will teach a diverse student body and how a student will function in a diverse environment.

But campuses should also consider that the appropriateness of such statements is disputed, even among faculty members who support DEI initiatives. Rather than a uniform campus-wide requirement for such statements, we suggest a more flexible approach: some programs may choose to justify them with reference to traditional scholarly criteria within particular disciplines, while others may collect the relevant information through familiar statements about research and teaching. We also urge campuses to monitor whether hiring decisions are being made on irrelevant political grounds and to create mechanisms whereby faculty members can raise concerns if they believe improper considerations played a part in recommendations or decisions.

There is an inherent discomfort in giving advice as well as a risk of sounding pedantic. Our goal in this chapter has been to take the principles discussed in earlier chapters and translate them into practical suggestions. Some pieces of advice are based on the current law, others on what we think is prudent. Most of all, we hope that these suggestions are helpful as campus administrators and others struggle with the difficult questions that constantly arise concerning free speech on campus.

Conclusion

Although we have titled this section "Conclusion," it is written with the knowledge that so long as there are colleges and universities, there will be no conclusion to the issue of free speech on campus. Freedom of speech and academic freedom are integral to the very essence of schools' essential missions of teaching and research. But at the same time, some will always wish to restrict speech that they deem inappropriate, offensive, or inimical to the purpose of higher education. Those who, in different eras, tried to stop heresy or communism, or in more recent years hate speech or the teaching of Critical Race Theory, always felt that they were acting in the best interests of students, schools, and society.

If speech had no effects, it would not be protected as a fundamental right and there would not be hard questions. It is precisely because words matter so much that enormously difficult issues arise. How should freedom of speech be balanced with preventing disruption of teaching and research? How should it be balanced with the need to create a conducive learning environment for all students, and to ensure that there is not a hostile environment based on race, national origin, sex, religion, and sexual orientation? How should it be balanced with the ability of those governing educational institutions to define their mission and their environment? How should the freedom to speak be balanced against those who do not want to hear particular messages?

Underlying our approach to all of these questions is the conviction that colleges and universities made such remarkable contributions to the well-being of our society in the twentieth century precisely because they became increasingly anchored in a commitment to free inquiry and robust debate. Earlier assumptions that colleges should be anchored in religious teachings and that they should prevent professors and students from challenging certain prevailing orthodoxies stifled the development of ideas that later became widely accepted truths about (for example) the age of the planet or the origin of species. Similar advances were stifled when it was assumed that professors and students should not hold opinions that were inconsistent with the views of politicians or trustees.

America's scholarly and scientific prowess could not have become the envy of the world in a system that sought to control what ideas could be expressed or challenged or taught. America's ongoing progress as a society dedicated to becoming an even more perfect union would not be possible if there was no room within higher education for the critic and the iconoclast to have their say free from the sanctions of existing powerholders. There is a reason, after all, why authoritarians prioritize the political control of institutions that protect independent thought and dissent, including universities.

As we have discussed, these hard-earned protections for free inquiry are nevertheless premised on the assumption that the professional work of university professors will take place within a system of rigorous peer review in order to ensure that innovative and iconoclastic opinions nevertheless conform to what is expected of highly trained and ethical experts in their disciplines. This remains the ongoing social contract that undergirds commitments to academic freedom and tenure, and no discussion of campus "free speech" should overlook the special obligations that faculty members have when they are expressing their professional views in professional settings. The

CONCLUSION

public needs confidence that those who hold positions of privilege as professionals dedicated to the creation and transmission of advanced knowledge are acting as such.

We have advocated so strongly in favor of campus free speech and academic freedom precisely because we believe that America's modern universities can rightly be considered one of the greatest forces for individual freedom and social progress ever invented—and because history has taught that there is nothing inevitable about the maintenance of the norms and practices that made these century-long contributions possible. The conditions can be eroded from the inside, by university stakeholders who demand the silencing of viewpoints they detest, and from the outside, by politicians and other powerful groups that want educational institutions to stifle views and debates that challenge their interests or agendas.

We are concerned about the present moment precisely because the threats to the foundations of modern universities seem to be relentless and coming from many sides. Yet we also believe that we can weather these stormy circumstances with a reinvigorated appreciation of how much our world has benefited because modern universities have attempted—imperfectly, to be sure—to create and maintain a culture of free inquiry, reasoned debate, tolerance of opposing views, and mutual respect for every person who voluntarily chooses to pursue higher knowledge.

Our goal in this book has been to apply the basic principles of campus free expression to the many issues that have arisen in recent years. Although the contexts and situations have often been novel, the underlying principles remain unchanged: campuses must be places where all ideas and views can be expressed; freedom of speech is not absolute, and there are types of speech that are not safeguarded by either the Constitution or academic freedom; campuses may impose time, place, and manner restrictions so long as they are content-neutral;

and there is a basic difference between speech in a professional capacity and in a nonprofessional one.

In the years to come we will undoubtedly face a whole new set of unexpected challenges, emerging both from new political contexts and from innovations in the platforms of expressive activity—not just social media but also artificial intelligence. It is hard enough today to assess what counts as discriminatory harassment requiring university action, so let us not yet speculate what we will do when the alleged harasser is an AI algorithm. Still, we hope that our review in this book of a wide range of fact-specific case studies also demonstrates the value of starting with the underlying principles that have made modern universities work.

We set forth these principles in our earlier book, *Free Speech on Campus,* and we continue to believe what we wrote there. Yet, as we reread it, we realize that it makes many issues sound simpler than the situations schools have actually faced in the years since it was published. And so we conclude this new book with the recognition that free speech on campus will continue to be contested and challenged by new circumstances. Students and faculty will find new ways to express themselves, campus officials will find new ways to regulate speech, and new controversies will arise that we are not able to foresee. Above all, we hope that our experience—as administrators and as teachers and scholars who focus on the First Amendment—will provide insights and tools for thinking to those who must deal with the controversies arising right around the corner.

Notes

Prologue

1. Annie Karni, "Questioning University Presidents on Antisemitism, Stefanik Goes Viral," *New York Times,* December 8, 2023, https://www.nytimes.com/2023/12/07/us/politics/elise-stefanik-antisemitism-congress.html.

2. Matt Egan, "UPenn President Liz Magill under Fire over Her Testimony on Antisemitism: 'An Utter Disgrace,' CNN, December 8, 2023, https://www.cnn.com/2023/12/08/business/upenn-president-liz-magill-resign/index.html.

3. Egan, "UPenn President Liz Magill under Fire."

4. Erwin Chemerinsky and Howard Gillman, *Free Speech on Campus* (New Haven: Yale University Press, 2017), 49–81.

5. Letter from the General Services Administration, U.S. Department of Health and Human Services, and U.S. Department of Education to Harvard president Alan M. Garber and Harvard Corporation Lead Member Penny Pritzker, April 11, 2025, https://www.harvard.edu/research-funding/wp-content/uploads/sites/16/2025/04/Letter-Sent-to-Harvard-2025-04-11.pdf.

6. FIRE, *Adopting the Chicago Statement,* https://www.thefire.org/research-learn/adopting-chicago-statement (last visited September 19, 2024). The Chicago Principles refer to a series of statements by faculty at the University of Chicago concerning freedom of speech. They are collected in Tony Banout and Tom Ginsburg, eds., *The Chicago Canon on Free Inquiry and Expression* (Chicago: University of Chicago Press, 2024).

7. *Brandenburg v. Ohio,* 395 U.S. 444, 447 (1969).

8. *Counterman v. Colorado,* 600 U.S. 66, 69 (2023).

9. *Davis v. Monroe Cnty. Bd. of Educ.,* 526 U.S. 629, 633 (1999).

10. Charles R. Lawrence III, "If He Hollers Let Him Go: Regulating Racist Speech on Campus," *Duke Law Journal* 431 (1990); Mari Matsuda, "Public Response to Racist Speech: Considering the Victim's Story," *Michigan Law Review* 87 (1989): 2320; Richard Delgado, "Words That Wound: A Tort Action for Racial Insults,

Epithets, and Name-Calling," *Harvard Civil Rights–Civil Liberties Law Review* 17 (1982): 133.

11. See *Christian Legal Society v. Martinez,* 551 U.S. 661, 669 (2010) (defining limited public forums).

12. Robert Post, "Theorizing Student Expression: A Constitutional Account of Student Free Speech Rights," *Stanford Law Review* 76 (2014): 1643, 1652.

13. Claire Finkelstein, Opinion, "To Fight Antisemitism on Campuses, We Must Restrict Speech," *Washington Post,* December 10, 2023.

14. Relatively few cases have arisen concerning speech in grades lower than high school, and it is quite likely that in such situations courts would give even more deference to school officials.

15. See, e.g., *Morse v. Frederick,* 551 U.S. 393 (2007) (finding no First Amendment violation in punishing a student for displaying a banner that was perceived as encouraging illegal drug use); *Hazelwood Sch. Dist. v. Kuhlmeier,* 484 U.S. 260 (1988) (finding no First Amendment violation in a principal's censorship of stories in a school newspaper); *Bethel Sch. Dist. No. 403 v. Fraser,* 478 U.S. 675 (1986) (allowing discipline for a student for a speech with sexual innuendo at a school assembly).

16. See, e.g., *Tinker v. Des Moines Indep. Cmty. Sch. Dist.,* 393 U.S. 503, 508 (1969) ("There is no indication that the work of the schools or any class was disrupted"). See also *Mahanoy Area Sch. Dist. v. B. L.,* 594 U.S. 180 (2021) (applying *Tinker* to off-campus speech over social media).

17. See, e.g., *Papish v. Bd. of Curators of the Univ. of Mo.,* 410 U.S. 667 (1973) (holding that a student could not be expelled for a political cartoon in a newspaper). See also *Healy v. James,* 408 U.S. 169 (1972) (holding that a college could not exclude a chapter of the Students for a Democratic Society because of its views, even if it expressed a philosophy of violence and destruction, and that the speech was protected unless it met the test for incitement).

18. Chemerinsky and Gillman, *Free Speech on Campus,* 82–110.

Chapter 1. Speech on Campus

1. For a description of this event, see Josh Moody, "Law Students Shout Down Controversial Speakers," *Inside Higher Ed,* March 22, 2022, https://www.insidehighered.com/news/2022/03/23/law-student-protests-stifle-speakers-yale-uc-hastings; David Lat, "Is Free Speech in American Law Schools a Lost Cause?" *Original Jurisdiction,* March 17, 2022, https://davidlat.substack.com/p/is-free-speech-in-american-law-schools.

2. Available at *UC Hastings Event Policy, Adopted October 1, 2022,* Foundation for Individual Rights and Expression, https://www.thefire.org/research-learn/uc-hastings-event-policy-adopted-october-1-2022.

3. For a description of these events, see Moody, "Law Students Shout Down Controversial Speakers"; Philip Mousavizadeh, "Moderator Denounces Law School Protests in Faculty-Wide Memo," *Yale Daily News,* April 4, 2022, https://yaledailynews.com/blog/2022/04/04/moderator-denounces-law-school-protesters-in-faculty-wide-memo/; Aaron Sibarium, "Looking to Tamp Down Controversy, Yale Law School Restricts Access to Free Speech Panel," *Washington Free Beacon,* January 24, 2023, https://freebeacon.com/campus/looking-to-tamp-down-controversy-law-school-restricts-access-free-speech-panel.

4. For a description of these events, see Jessie Appleby, "Stanford Law Hecklers Demanding 'Free Speech' Don't Know What They're Asking For," Foundation for Individual Rights and Expression, March 15, 2023, https://www.thefire.org/news/stanford-law-hecklers-demanding-free-speech-dont-know-what-theyre-asking; "Law School Dean Discusses Recent Protest, Outlines Next Steps," *Stanford Report,* March 23, 2023, https://news.stanford.edu/report/2023/03/23/law-school-dean-discusses-recent-protest-outlines-next-steps/; Seth Stern, "Stanford Law Diversity Head Is Out After Judge's Disrupted Talk," *Bloomberg Law,* July 21, 2023, https://news.bloomberglaw.com/us-law-week/stanford-law-diversity-head-is-out-after-judges-disrupted-talk.

5. Jenny S. Martinez, "Dean Martinez: Next Steps on Protests and Free Speech," *Stanford Law School,* March 22, 2023, https://law.stanford.edu/documents/dean-martinez-next-steps-on-protests-and-free-speech/.

6. For a description of these events, see Scott Jaschik, "Anti-Trans Speaker Blocked at U of North Texas," *Inside Higher Ed,* March 6, 2022, https://www.insidehighered.com/quicktakes/2022/03/07/anti-trans-speaker-blocked-u-of-north-texas;Valeria Olivares, "UNT Students Protest Jeff Younger, Conservative Speech on 'Transgender Child Abuse,' " *Dallas Morning News,* March 3, 2022, https://www.dallasnews.com/news/education/2022/03/03/unt-students-protest-conservative-speech-on-transgender-child-abuse/; Foundation for Individual Rights and Expression, *Protesters Disrupt Remarks by Jeff Younger at the University of North Texas,* YouTube, March 4, 2022, https://www.youtube.com/watch?v=HWF4RFdfQwM.

7. Josh Marcus, "Tomi Lahren Evacuated as Crowd of Protesters Pound Doors at University of New Mexico Speech," *Independent,* September 17, 2022, https://www.independent.co.uk/news/world/americas/tomi-lahren-speech-new-mexico-b2169143.html;Tamara Lopez, "Protesters Shut Down Tomi Lahren Event at UNM,"

KOB 4 Eyewitness News, September 17, 2022, https://www.kob.com/new-mexico/protesters-shut-down-tomi-lahren-event-at-unm/.

8. "UNM Statement on Tomi Lahren Event Held Sept. 15, 2022," *University of New Mexico News,* September 16, 2022, http://news.unm.edu/news/unm-statement-on-tomi-lahren-event-held-sept-15–2022.

9. For a description of these events, see Bill Chappell, "Penn State Cancels Proud Boys Founder's Speech, Citing the Threat of Violence," NPR, https://www.npr.org/2022/10/25/1131300978/penn-state-cancels-proud-boys-speech-protests&sa=D&source=docs&ust=1695943750253820&usg=AOvVaw2Fe_81FPBrMHnmwHc xyr-7 (last updated October 25, 2022); Jason Wilson, "Far-Right Student Organization Brings Extremists McInnes, Doyle to Penn State and Tennessee," *Southern Poverty Law Center,* October 20, 2022, https://www.splcenter.org/hatewatch/2022/10/20/far-right-student-organization-brings-extremists-mcinnes-doyle-penn-state-and-tennessee.

10. For a description of these events, see "Conservative Speaker Event at UC Davis Canceled After Brawl," *Associated Press,* October 26, 2022, https://apnews.com/article/education-california-university-of-701b6b4d5429305098405c7853787f5d; Aaron Corpora, "Charlie Kirk Event at UC Davis Prompts Violent Protest," Foundation for Individual Rights and Expression, March 20, 2023, https://www.thefire.org/news/charlie-kirk-event-uc-davis-prompts-violent-protest; UC Davis News and Media Relations, *UPDATED: Controversial, Student-Led Event Goes on as Planned,* https://www.ucdavis.edu/news/controversial-student-led-event-goes-planned (last updated March 14, 2023).

11. For a description of these events, see Vanessa Miller, "University of Iowa to Host Conservative Commentator Matt Walsh," *Gazette,* https://www.thegazette.com/higher-education/university-of-iowa-to-host-conservative-transgender-commentator-matt-walsh/#:~:text=IOWA%20CITY%20%E2%80%94%20Conservative%20commentator%20Matt,to%20shut%20down%20his%20lecture (last updated April 7, 2023); Liam Halawith and Emily Delgado, "Hundreds Protest, Attend Lecture of Conservative Commentator Matt Walsh at UI," *Daily Iowan,* April 20, 2023, https://dailyiowan.com/2023/04/20/hundreds-protest-attend-lecture-of-conservative-commentator-matt-walsh-at-the-university-of-iowa/; Ryan Hansen, "Protesters Block Campus Streets during Conservative Matt Walsh's Appearance in Iowa City," *Iowa City Press-Citizen,* https://www.press-citizen.com/story/news/local/2023/04/20/demonstrators-protest-anti-trans-speaker-matt-walshs-iowa-appearance/70133924007/ (last updated April 20, 2023).

12. For a description of this event, see Jacob Gurvis, "Protesters Dog Israeli Speaker at LA Holocaust Museum After UC Berkeley Event Canceled," *Times of*

Israel, March 2, 2024, https://www.timesofisrael.com/protesters-dog-israeli-speaker-at-la-holocaust-museum-after-uc-berkeley-event-canceled/#:~:text=What%20hap
pened%20at%20Berkeley%2C%20he,had%20come%20for%20the%20event..

13. 408 U.S. 92, 95–96 (1972).

14. *R.A.V. v. City of St. Paul,* 505 U.S. 377, 382 (1992); *United States v. Alvarez,* 567 U.S. 709, 717 (2012) (plurality opinion).

15. 512 U.S. 622, 640 (1994).

16. This incident is described in Louis H. Guard and Joyce P. Jacobsen, *All the Campus Lawyers: Litigation, Regulation, and the New Era of Higher Education* (Cambridge, Mass.: Harvard University Press, 2024), 63–64.

17. Guard and Jacobsen, *All the Campus Lawyers,* 64.

18. See *Seattle Mideast Awareness Campaign v. King Cnty.,* 781 F.3d 489, 497 (9th Cir. 2015) (quoting *Arkansas Educ. Television Comm'n v. Forbes,* 523 U.S. 666, 679 [1998]). School property, like a lecture hall, is generally regarded as a limited public forum. See *Hickok v. Orange Cty. Cmty. Coll.,* 472 F. Supp. 2d 469, 475 (S.D.N.Y. 2006) ("The lecture hall at the College is a limited public forum"); *Young Am.'s Found. v. Kaler,* 370 F. Supp. 3d 967, 983 (D. Minn. 2019), vacated and remanded on other grounds by *Young Am.'s Found. v. Kaler,* 14 F.4th 879 (8th Cir. 2021) ("the Supreme Court and Eighth Circuit have generally held that . . . university property (like lecture halls) . . . are 'limited public forums' ") (collecting cases); see also *Hotel Emps. & Rest. Emps. Union, Loc. 100 of New York, N.Y. & Vicinity, AFL-CIO v. City of New York Dep't of Parks & Rec.,* 311 F.3d 534, 545 (2d Cir. 2002) ("Examples of limited public fora include state university meeting facilities opened for student groups").

19. *Christian Legal Soc. v. Martinez,* 561 U.S. 661, 685 (2010).

20. *Seattle Mideast,* 781 F.3d at 499 (citing *Forsyth Cnty., Ga. v. Nationalist Movement,* 505 U.S. 123, 132–33 [1992]).

21. 14 F.4th 879 (8th Cir. 2021).

22. 2018 WL 1947766 (N.D. Cal. April 25, 2018).

23. UC Irvine Administrative Policies and Procedures, UCI Guidance concerning Disruption of University Activities, January 2019, § 900–23, https://ucipolicy.ellucid.com/documents/view/131/?security=18e5fb8561f751a87c6975d1592325f4039
8df74.

24. 312 U.S. 569 (1941).

25. 312 U.S. 569 (1941) at 574.

26. 312 U.S. 569 (1941) at 577.

27. 505 U.S. 123 (1992).

28. 505 U.S. 123 (1992) at 132.

29. 505 U.S. 123 (1992) at 133.

30. 2018 WL 804497 (W.D. Wash. February 9, 2018).

31. Erica Goldberg, "Must Universities 'Subsidize' Controversial Ideas? Allocating Security Fees When Student Groups Host Divisive Speakers," *George Mason University Civil Rights Law Journal* 21 (2011): 349. See also Rebecca Roman, Note, "When Speech Isn't Free: The Rising Costs of Hosting Controversial Speakers at Public Universities," *University of Chicago Legal Forum* (2020): 451.

32. See, e.g., *Satanic Temple, Inc. v. Saucon Valley Sch. Dist.*, No. 5:23-CV-01244-JMG, 2023 WL 3182934 (E.D. Pa. May 1, 2023).

33. *In re Kay*, 464 P.2d 142, 149 (Cal. 1970).

34. The facts are described in Faiza Majeed, "The Irvine 11 Case: Does Nonviolent Student Protest Warrant Criminal Prosecution?" *Law & Inequality* 30 (2012): 371.

35. UC Irvine Administrative Policies and Procedures, UCI Guidance concerning Disruption of University Activities.

36. Sonel Cutler, Forest Hunt, and Alecia Taylor, "How Colleges Have Responded to Student Encampments," *Chronicle of Higher Education,* May 1, 2024, https://www.chronicle.com/article/how-colleges-have-responded-to-student-encampments.

37. The events at Columbia are described in Katrina Ventura, "A Timeline of the 14-Day Gaza Solidarity Encampment in Columbia University," *Columbia Journalism School,* May 3, 2024, https://columbianewsservice.com/2024/05/03/protest/.

38. Katie Houlis and Mark Prussin, "Columbia Security Breaks Up New Encampment Before Alumni Weekend, Social Media Video Shows," *CBS News,* https://www.cbsnews.com/newyork/news/columbia-protest-encampment-alumni-weekend/ (last updated June 2, 2024).

39. Johanna Alonso, "Why Are Students Camping on University Lawns?" *Inside Higher Ed,* April 24, 2024, https://www.insidehighered.com/news/students/free-speech/2024/04/24/students-set-encampments-coast-coast; and Jessica Blake, "Protests Roil Columbia, Spread to Other Campuses," *Inside Higher Ed,* April 23, 2024, https://www.insidehighered.com/news/students/free-speech/2024/04/23/person-classes-cancelled-protests-roil-columbia-others.

40. Solcyre Burga, "Students at University of Florida Continue Encampment Despite Arrests. University Says It Is 'Not a Daycare,'" *Time,* April 30, 2024, https://time.com/6972870/university-of-florida-encampment/.

41. This is described in Lisa Kurian Philip, "Northwestern Ended Its Encampment without Cops or Violence: Why Is Congress Upset?" *Chicago Sun Times,* May 15, 2024, https://chicago.suntimes.com/education/2024/05/15/northwestern-encampment-protest-michael-schill-congress.

42. Michael Loria, " 'Reprehensible and Dangerous': Jewish Groups Slam Northwestern University for Deal with Activists," *USA Today,* May 3, 2024, https://www.usatoday.com/story/news/nation/2024/05/03/northwestern-under-fire-for-deal-with-pro-palestine-activists/73562034007/.

43. See Sharon Otterman, "At Rutgers, Holloway Has Faced Scrutiny for Several Unpopular Moves," *New York Times,* May 23, 2024, https://www.nytimes.com/2024/05/23/us/jonathan-holloway-antisemitism-hearing.html; Annie Ma and Collin Binkley, "Rutgers, Northwestern Defend Deals with Student Protesters: 'We Had to Get the Encampment Down,' " *AP,* May 23, 2024, https://apnews.com/article/congress-antisemitism-northwestern-ucla-rutgers-41cd2b843999523bccc92 7004b13d5e0.

44. For a description of these events, see "Timeline: UCLA's Night of Violence Before Police Moved In," *Los Angeles Times,* May 1, 2024, https://www.latimes.com/california/story/2024-05-07/a-ucla-timeline-from-peaceful-encampment-to-violent-attacks-aftermath; Jonathan Wolfe and Benjamin Royer, "U.C.L.A. Declares Encampment Illegal, Says Protesters Should Leave," *New York Times,* April 30, 2024, https://www.nytimes.com/2024/04/30/nyregion/ucla-encampment-protests.html.

45. Vimal Patel, "Dartmouth's Leader Called In Police Quickly. The Fallout Was Just as Swift," *New York Times,* May 13, 2024, https://www.nytimes.com/2024/05/13/us/dartmouth-campus-protests-police-beilock.html; and Stephanie Saul, "Dartmouth's President Is Censured by Faculty over Protest Actions," *New York Times,* May 20, 2024, https://www.nytimes.com/2024/05/20/us/dartmouth-president-beilock-censure.html.

46. Howard Gillman, "Update on Campus Protests and University Response," UCI Office of the Chancellor, May 3, 2024, https://chancellor.uci.edu/communications/campus/2024/240503-update-on-campus-protests.php.

47. Hannah Fry, Ruben Vives, Richard Winton, Grace Toohey, Angie Orellana Hernandez, Ashley Ahn, and Terry Castleman, "Police Arrest 47 at UC Irvine After Sweeping Protest Camp, Clearing Barricaded Building," *Los Angeles Times,* May 15, 2024, https://www.latimes.com/california/story/2024-05-15/police-converge-on-pro-palestinian-protest-at-uc-irvine-students-are-told-to-shelter-in-place.

48. Jessica Bryant and Margaret Attridge, "Where College Students Have Set Up Pro-Palestinian Protest Encampments," Best Colleges, https://www.bestcolleges.com/research/student-protests-pro-palestinian-encampments/#:~:text=During%20the%20spring%202024%20academic,by%20local%20or%20campus%20authorities (last updated September 12, 2024).

49. 468 U.S. 288 (1984).

50. Gabe Efros, "Stop Believing in a 'Right Way to Protest,' " *Michigan Daily*, May 15, 2024, https://www.michigandaily.com/opinion/columns/stop-believing-in-a-right-way-to-protest/.

51. Although it must be recognized that the definition of "peaceful" is itself difficult. For example, a federal district court found that the encampment at UCLA kept Jewish students from accessing parts of the campus and thus violated Title VI and the Jewish students' free exercise of religion. *Frankel v. Regents of the University of California*, 744 F.Supp.3d 1015, 2024 WL 3811250 (C.D. Cal. 2024).

52. John McWhorter, "I'm a Columbia Professor. The Protests on My Campus Are Not Justice," *New York Times*, April 23, 2024, https://www.nytimes.com/2024/04/23/opinion/columbia-protests-israel.html.

53. Theresa Watanabe, "UC Unveils Steep Price Tag for Handling Campus Protests: $29 Million, Most for Policing, *Los Angeles Times*, July 18, 2024, https://www.latimes.com/california/story/2024–07–18/uc-unveils-price-tag-for-this-springs-campus-unrest.

54. 530 U.S. 703 (2000).

55. 530 U.S. 703 (2000) at 720.

56. Gary Robbins, "Breaking His Silence, UCSD Chancellor Pradeep Khosla Explains His Crackdown on a Gaza Encampment," *San Diego Union Tribune*, June 14, 2024, https://www.sandiegouniontribune.com/2024/06/13/breaking-his-silence-ucsd-chancellor-pradeep-khosla-explains-his-crackdown-on-a-gaza-protest-encampment/.

57. *Frankel v. Regents of the University of California*, Case No.2:24-cv-04702-MCS-PD, Order Re: Motion for Preliminary Injunction (ECF No.48), https://becket-newsite.s3.amazonaws.com/20240813183534/injunction.pdf.

58. Abigail A. Graber, "Religious Discrimination at School: Application of Title of the Civil Rights Act of 1964," Congressional Research Service, March 22, 2024, https://crsreports.congress.gov/product/pdf/LSB/LSB11129/1.

59. The Section 1981 holdings in *Shaare Tefila Congregation v. Cobb*, 481 U.S. 615 (1987), and *Saint Francis College v. al-Khazraji*, 481 U.S. 604 (1987).

60. OCR fact sheet, https://www.ed.gov/sites/ed/files/about/offices/list/ocr/docs/ocr-factsheet-shared-ancestry-202301.pdf.

61. *Porto v. Town of Tewksbury*, 488 F.3d 67, 72–73 (1st Cir. 2007), quoting *Davis v. Monroe Cnty. Bd. of Educ.*, 526 U.S. 629, 650 (1999).

62. OCR fact sheet.

63. OCR fact sheet.

64. *Feminist Majority Found. v. Hurley*, 911 F.3d 674 (4th Cir. 2018). It should be disclosed that one of the authors, Erwin Chemerinsky, argued this case in the Fourth Circuit on behalf of the plaintiffs.

65. *Feminist Majority Found. v. Hurley* at 683.

66. *Feminist Majority Found. v. Hurley* at 688.

67. Catherine E. Lhamon, "Dear Colleague Letter: Protecting Students from Discrimination, Such as Harassment, Based on Race, Color, or National Origin, Including Shared Ancestry or Ethnic Characteristics," White House, May 7, 2024, https://www.whitehouse.gov/wp-content/uploads/2024/05/colleague-202405-shared-ancestry.pdf.

68. *Stand With Us Center for Legal Justice v. MIT,* No. CV 24-10577-RGS, 2024 WL 3596916 (D. Mass. July 30, 2024).

69. *Kestenbaum and Students against Antisemitism v. President and Fellows of Harvard College,* No. CV 24-10092-RGS, 2024 WL 3658793 (D. Mass. August 6, 2024).

70. *Loper Bright Enterprises v. Raimondo,* 144 S.Ct. 2244 (2024) (the Administrative Procedure Act requires courts to exercise their independent judgment in deciding whether an agency has acted within its statutory authority, and courts may not defer to an agency interpretation of the law simply because a statute is ambiguous; *Chevron* is overruled.). The *Chevron* doctrine was the principle that courts should defer to federal agency interpretations of ambiguous statutes. This was overruled by the Supreme Court in *Loper Bright.*

71. Guard and Jacobsen, *All the Campus Lawyers,* 59.

72. Ryan A. Miller and Four Other Scholars, "Bias Response Teams: Fact vs. Fiction," *Inside Higher Ed,* June 16, 2019, https://www.insidehighered.com/views/2019/06/17/truth-about-bias-response-teams-more-complex-often-thought-opinion.

73. 939 F.3d 756 (6th Cir. 2019).

74. *Speech First, Inc. v. Fenves,* 979 F.3d 319 (5th Cir. 2020); *Speech First, Inc. v. Killeen,* 968 F.3d 628 (7th Cir. 2020).

75. L. Rachel Lerman et al., "Civil Rights Violations at Berkeley Unified School District ('Busd')," Louis D. Brandeis Center for Human Rights Law, February 28, 2024, https://brandeiscenter.com/wp-content/uploads/2024/02/Brandeis-Center-ADL-Complaint.pdf

76. *Christian Legal Society v. Martinez,* 561 U.S. 661 (2010) *Alpha Delta Chi v. Reed,* 648 F.3d 790 (9th Cir. 2011).

77. 515 U.S. 557 (1995).

78. 515 U.S. 557 (1995) at 572.

79. 515 U.S. 557 (1995) at 575.

80. Kenneth L. Marcus, "Berkeley Develops Jewish-Free Zones," *Jewish Journal,* September 28, 2022, https://jewishjournal.com/commentary/opinion/351854/berkeley-develops-jewish-free-zones/.

81. Julia Swerdin, "Zionist Speakers Banned by Pro-Palestinian Group at UC-Berkeley Law School," Georgetown University Free Speech Project, September 6, 2023, http://freespeechproject.georgetown.edu/tracker-entries/zionist-speakers-banned-by-pro-palestine-group-at-uc-berkeley-law-school/. OCR subsequently ended its investigation of this complaint when the lawsuit about the bylaws was filed.

82. *The Louis D. Brandeis Center, et al. v. Regents of the University of California, et al.,* U.S. District Court, Northern District of California, No.23-06133. Karen D'Souza, "Lawsuit Intensifies Spotlight on Free Speech Controversies at UC Berkeley," *Edsource,* December 6, 2023, https://edsource.org/2023/lawsuit-intensifies-spotlight-on-free-speech-controversies-at-uc-berkeley/701834.

83. *The Louis D. Brandeis Center, et al. v. Regents of the University of California, et al.,* U.S. District Court, Northern District of California, No.23-06133, Motion to Dismiss Complaint and Motion to Strike Jury Demand, Filed February 5, 2024, https://fingfx.thomsonreuters.com/gfx/legaldocs/lbpgblrndvq/UC%20Berkeley%20Motion%20to%20Dismiss.pdf. Karen Sloan, "UC Berkeley Cites First Amendment in Bid to End Antisemitism Lawsuit," *Reuters,* February 6, 2024, https://www.reuters.com/legal/litigation/uc-berkeley-cites-first-amendment-bid-end-antisemitism-lawsuit-2024-02-06/. As of the end of 2024, the federal court has not ruled on the University of California's motion to dismiss the lawsuit.

Chapter 2. Speech in Professional Academic Settings

1. For an excellent discussion of the relationship of freedom of speech and academic freedom, and an elaboration of the concept of academic freedom, see David M. Rabban, *Academic Freedom: From Professional Norm to First Amendment Right* (Cambridge, Mass.: Harvard University Press, 2024).

2. This test for incitement is articulated by the Supreme Court in *Brandenburg v. Ohio,* 395 U.S. 444 (1969).

3. American Association of University Professors, *Declaration of Principles on Academic Freedom and Academic Tenure* (1915).

4. University of California, *Academic Personnel Manual,* § 010 (Academic Freedom) (rev. September 29, 2003) [hereinafter *APM 010*].

5. *Statement of Principles: Student Freedom of Scholarly Inquiry* (rev. September 14, 2009), included in *APM 010.* (Because academic freedom attaches to faculty members by virtue of their status as highly qualified experts, students do not have academic freedom rights. However, as noted in the UC document on student freedom of scholarly inquiry, "Students should be free to take civil and reasoned exception to the data or views offered in any course of study and to reserve judgment about matters of

opinion, but they are responsible for learning the content of any course of study for which they are enrolled" and "The faculty has authority for all aspects of the course, including content, structure, relevance of alternative points of view, and evaluations.").

6. Press release, Council on American-Islamic Relations, "CAIR Announces Official Position on Hamline University Controversy, Islamophobia Debate," January 13, 2023.

7. Vimal Patel, "A Lecturer Showed a Painting of the Prophet Muhammad. She Lost Her Job," *New York Times,* January 8, 2023; Statement from Hamline University, January 17, 2023, https://www.hamline.edu/news/2023/01/statements-hamline-university-january-2023-present.

8. Liz Navratil, "Hamline University Reaches Settlement with Instructor Who Showed Images of Prophet Muhammad in Class," *Star Tribune,* July 23, 2024.

9. Jennifer Schuessler, "A Blackface 'Othello' Shocks, and a Professor Steps Back from Class," *New York Times,* October 15, 2021.

10. Lucia Martinez Valdivia, "Professors Like Me Can't Stay Silent about This Extremist Moment on Campuses," *Washington Post,* October 27, 2017 ("The right to speak freely is not the same as the right to rob others of their voices").

11. Anders Anglesey, "SDSU Professor Disciplined over Racial Slurs Claims 'Merely Doing His Job,'" *Newsweek,* April 10, 2022; press release, Academic Freedom Alliance, "AFA Sends Letter to San Diego State on Professor's Suspension," March 8, 2022; FIRE, Faculty Letter in Support of J. Angelo Corlett, March 10, 2022, https://www.thefire.org/research-learn/faculty-letter-support-j-angelo-corlett-march-10-2022.

12. American Association of University Professors, *Freedom in the Classroom* (June 2007).

13. Tom Bartlett, "A Professor Has Long Used a Racial Slur in Class to Teach Free-Speech Law. No More, He Says," *Chronicle of Higher Education,* March 7, 2019.

14. Hailie Higgins, "Professor Suspended After Saying N-Word in Class," *Campus Times,* August 12, 2024); Letter from the Academic Freedom Alliance to Dean Culver, November 15, 2021.

15. Andrew Koppelman, "Yes, This Is a Witch-Hunt," *Chronicle of Higher Education,* November 17, 2021.

16. *Kilborn v. Amiridis,* 131 F.4th 550 (7th Cir. 2025).

17. Colleen Flaherty, "SUNY Fredonia Reviewing Professor's Comments on Pedophilia," *Inside Higher Ed,* February 2, 2022.

18. Jessica Blake, "SUNY Fredonia Fights to Keep Controversial Professor off Campus," *Inside Higher Ed,* August 18, 2023.

19. Colleen Flaherty, "Academic Freedom above All?" *Inside Higher Education,* February 6, 2022.

20. "AFA Sends Letter to SUNY Fredonia regarding Stephan Kershnar," February 3, 2022, https://academicfreedom.org/afa-sends-letter-to-suny-fredonia-regarding-stephen-kershnar/. See also Letter from Foundation for Individual Rights in Education (FIRE) to President Kolison, February 3, 2022.

21. Michael Wines, "Florida Bars State Professors from Testifying in Voting Rights Case," *New York Times,* October 29, 2021.

22. American Association of University Professors, *Statement of Principles on Academic Freedom and Tenure* (1940).

23. Andrew Atterbury, "University of Florida Reverses on Professors Testifying against DeSantis-Backed Voting Bill," *Politico,* November 5, 2021.

24. Susan Svrluga and Lori Rozsa, "Judge Rules for Professors in University of Florida Academic Freedom Case," *Washington Post,* January 21, 2022.

25. Divya Kumar, "UF Trustees Blast Faculty over Free Speech Controversy," *Tampa Bay Times,* December 3, 2021.

26. Chris Gaither, "Berkeley Course on Mideast Raises Concerns," *New York Times,* May 16, 2002.

27. Richard C. Atkinson, *Academic Freedom and the Research University,* UC Office of the President: Presidential Papers—Richard Atkinson (2004).

28. Snejana Farberov, "Stanford Teacher Suspended for Allegedly Separating out Jewish Students in Class as 'Colonizers,' " *New York Post,* October 13, 2023; conflicting accounts are reported in Caroline Chen, "Stanford Suspended a Lecturer to Investigate Identity-Based Targeting. Here's What Students Say Happened," *Stanford Daily,* October 18, 2023.

29. Susan Svrluga, "Professor Barred from University System for Class That Offered Course Credit to Students Who Protested Kavanaugh," *Washington Post,* October 20, 2018.

30. Matthew Impelli, "Professor Gives Pro-Palestinian Protesters Chance to Make Up Classes," *Newsweek,* April 26, 2024; Sinead Baker and Grace Eliza Goodwin, "UC Berkeley Academic Offered Her Students Extra Credit for Going to Pro-Palestinian Protests and Lobbying Congress about Gaza," *Business Insider,* October 25, 2023; Jeremiah Dobruck, "CSULB Warned Faculty Not to Cancel Classes, Give Extra Credit in Support of Protests," *Newsbreak,* May 8, 2024.

31. Provost Message, Political Advocacy, Academic Freedom, and Instruction, May 3, 2024, https://provost.uci.edu/2024/05/03/political-advocacy-academic-freedom-and-instruction-copy/; University of California Board of Regents, Regents

Policy 2301: Policy on Course Content, https://regents.universityofcalifornia.edu/governance/policies/2301.html; Faculty Code of Conduct, https://www.ucop.edu/academic-personnel-programs/_files/apm/apm-015.pdf.

32. *Meriwether v. Hartop,* 992 F.3d 492 (6th Cir. 2021).

33. Shirin Ali, "Professor Disciplined for Refusing to Use Transgender Student's Pronouns to Receive $400k in Settlement," *The Hill,* April 19, 2022.

34. *Johnson-Kurek v. Abu-Absi,* 423 F.3d 590 (6th Cir. 2005); *Hetrick v. Martin,* 480 F.2d 705 (6th Cir. 1973).

35. Nicholas Meriwether, "The Truth about My Stand against a University's Enforced Orthodoxy," *The Hill,* September 28, 2020.

36. UCLA Asian American Studies Department, *Statement of Solidarity with Palestine,* May 21, 2021.

37. Aaron Bandler, "UC Regents Members Call UCLA Asian American Studies Dept. Statement Accusing Israel of 'Yellow-Washing' 'Inappropriate,' " *Jewish Journal,* January 26, 2022.

38. Letter from Ad Hoc Faculty Committee for Academic Integrity to University of California President Michael Drake, July 20, 2021.

39. Palestinian Feminist Collective, Gender Studies Departments in Solidarity with Palestinian Feminist Collective, http://genderstudiespalestinesolidarity.weebly.com (last visited September 14, 2024); Elizabeth Redden, " 'An Unprecedented Wave' of Palestinian Solidarity Statements," *Inside Higher Ed,* June 1, 2021.

40. An Open Letter to the Leadership of USC, August 8, 2021, https://usc-faaz-2021.org.

41. University of Illinois Urbana-Champaign Senate, Committee on General University Policy, Guidelines on Departmental Statements, December 5, 2022.

42. Joint Senate-Administration Workgroup, Report on the Role of the University and Its Units in Political and Social Action, May 2022. It should be noted that as of September 2024, the administration of the Berkeley campus has taken no steps to adopt or implement the task force's recommendations.

43. American Association of University Professors, *Statement of Principles on Academic Freedom and Tenure* (1940).

44. Dear Colleague Letter from University of California Academic Senate Chair regarding Recommendations for Department Political Statements, June 2, 2022.

45. U.S. Department of Education, Office for Civil Rights, Dear Colleague Letter on Fighting Antisemitism, May 25, 2023.

46. University of California Regents, Policy on Public and Discretionary Statements by Academic Units, July 18, 2024.

47. "University of California Regents Ban Political Statements on University Homepages," *Associated Press,* July 18, 2024; University of California, Regents Policy on Public and Discretionary Statements by Academic Units, May 2024 (approved July 2024).

48. Alexandra Crosnoe, "UC Regents Votes to Pass Item J2 Following Months of Revision and Deferred Voting," *Daily Bruin,* July 17, 2024.

49. Keith Whittington, On Institutional Neutrality and the Purpose of a University, April 10, 2024, 30–31, available at SSRN: Whittington, Keith E., On Institutional Neutrality and the Purpose of a University, April 20, 2024, https://ssrn.com/abstract=4801896 or http://dx.doi.org/10.2139/ssrn.4801896.

50. "Should CEOs Comment on Politically Contentious Topics?" *Wall Street Journal,* September 30, 2023, https://www.wsj.com/business/c-suite/ceo-company-politics-public-comments-beb94d8.

51. Josh Moody, "Presidents Can't Win," *Inside Higher Ed,* October 18, 2023.

52. University of Chicago, Report on the University's Role in Political and Social Action, November 1, 1967.

53. Christopher L. Eisgruber, "Princeton's Tradition of Institutional Restraint," *Princeton Alumni Weekly,* November 7, 2022; Coco Gong and Judy Gao, "Still No Department Guidelines as Debate over Institutional Neutrality Rages," *Daily Princetonian,* December 4, 2023.

54. Wyatt King, "Beyond Political Neutrality in Higher Education: An Interview with Brian Rosenberg," *Columbia Political Review,* February 22, 2024.

55. Michael T. Nietzel, "The Kalven Report and the Limits of University Neutrality," *Forbes,* December 26, 2023; Tilly R. Robinson, "Universities Nationwide Have Embraced Institutional Neutrality. How Does Harvard's Report Stack Up?" *Harvard Crimson,* May 30, 2024.

56. Howard Gillman, On Statements, https://chancellor.uci.edu/communications/on-statements/index.php.

57. UC San Diego, Contributions to Diversity Statements, https://facultydiversity.ucsd.edu/recruitment/contributions-to-diversity.html.

58. UC Davis, Guidelines for Writing a Statement of Contributions to Diversity, Equity, and Inclusion, https://academicaffairs.ucdavis.edu/guidelines-writing-diversity-statement.

59. Sarah Brown,"More Colleges Are Asking Scholars for Diversity Statements. Here's What You Need to Know," *Chronicle of Higher Education,* January 19, 2019, https://www.chronicle.com/article/more-colleges-are-asking-scholars-for-diversity-

statements-heres-what-you-need-to-know/; Foundation for Individual Rights (FIRE), "FAQ: Diversity, Equity, and Inclusion Statements," https://www.thefire. org/research-learn/diversity-equity-and-inclusion-statements-faq; American Association of University Professors, "The 2022 AAUP Survey of Tenure Practices," May 2022, https://www.aaup.org/report/2022-aaup-survey-tenure-practices; Robert Maranto and James D. Paul, "Other Than Merit: The Prevalence of Diversity, Equity, and Inclusion Statements in University Hiring," American Enterprise Institute, November 8, 2021, https://www.aei.org/research-products/report/other-than-merit-the-prevalence-of-diversity-equity-and-inclusion-statements-in-university-hiring/.

60. University of California Office of the President, "Evaluating Contributions to Diversity for Faculty Appointments and Promotion under APM—210," February 2017, https://facultydiversity.ucsd.edu/recruitment/files-recruitmentpage/C2D%20 Guidelines_UCOP.pdf.

61. National Science Board, "New Report Shows We Must Do More to Include 'Missing Millions' in Science and Engineering," November 16, 2023, https://www. nsf.gov/nsb/news/news_summ.jsp?cntn_id=308617.

62. N. Honeycutt, S.T. Stevens, and E. Kaufmann, *The Academic Mind in 2022: What Faculty Think about Free Expression and Academic Freedom on Campus* (2023), Foundation for Individual Rights and Expression, https://www.thefire.org/research-learn/academic-mind-2022-what-faculty-think-about-free-expression-and-academic-freedom; Kate Marijolovic, "Professors Are Sharply Divided on DEI Statements in Hiring, Survey Finds," *Chronicle of Higher Education,* February 28, 2023, https://www.chronicle.com/article/professors-are-sharply-divided-on-dei-statements-in-hiring-survey-finds?sra=true.

63. "A Word from . . . Abigail Thompson, a Vice President of AMS," *Notices of the American Mathematical Society* 66, no. 11 (December 2019):, 1778–79, https://www. ams.org/journals/notices/201911/rnoti-p1778.pdf.

64. Brian Leiter, "The Legal Problem with Diversity Statements," *Chronicle of Higher Education,* March 13, 2020, https://www.chronicle.com/article/the-legal-problem-with-diversity-statements/; *Wagner v. Jones,* 664 F.3d 259 (8th Cir. 2012) (reversing summary judgment grant of qualified immunity for defendant law school dean where evidence indicated that dean was on notice that faculty's negative recommendation was based on plaintiff's political beliefs and associations).

65. Brian Soucek, "How to Protect DEI Requirements from Legal Peril," *Chronicle of Higher Education,* May 24, 2022, https://www.chronicle.com/article/the-legal-problem-with-diversity-statements/.

66. Ryan Quinn, "The Curious Rise of a Conservative—or Civic-Minded?— Center at the University of Florida," *Insider Higher Ed,* July 23, 2024, https://www. insidehighered.com/news/faculty-issues/shared-governance/2024/07/23/curious-rise-conservative-or-civic-minded-uf.

67. Robert Shibley, "UCLA Diversity Requirement Threatens Academic Freedom, Trust in Academia," Foundation for Individual Rights and Expression, November 9, 2018, https://www.thefire.org/news/ucla-diversity-requirement-threatens-academic-freedom-trust-academia.

68. Musbah Shaheen, "Stop Requiring DEI Statements from Faculty Applicants," *Forbes,* June 5, 2024, https://www.forbes.com/sites/musbahshaheen/2024/06/05/ stop-requiring-dei-statements-from-faculty-applicants/.

69. Steven Pinker, "A Five-Point Plan to Save Harvard from Itself," *Boston Globe,* December 11, 2023, https://www.bostonglobe.com/2023/12/11/opinion/steven-pinker-how-to-save-universities-harvard-claudine-gay/.

70. Randall L. Kennedy, "Mandatory DEI Statements Are Ideological Pledges of Allegiance. Time to Abandon Them," *Harvard Crimson,* April 2, 2024, https://www. thecrimson.com/column/council-on-academic-freedom-at-harvard/article/2024 /4/2/kennedy-abandon-dei-statements/.

71. FIRE Statement on the Use of Diversity, Equity, and Inclusion Criteria in Faculty Hiring and Evaluation, Foundation for Individual Rights and Expression, https://www.thefire.org/research-learn/fire-statement-use-diversity-equity-and-inclusion-criteria-faculty-hiring-and.

72. Academic Freedom Alliance, "AFA Calls for an End to Required Diversity Statements," August 22, 2022, https://academicfreedom.org/afa-calls-for-an-end-to-required-diversity-statements/.

73. Jeremy W. Peters, "Is This the End for Mandatory D.E.I. Statements?" *New York Times,* June 6, 2024, https://www.nytimes.com/2024/06/06/us/politics/dei-statements-harvard-massachusetts-institute-of-technology.html.

74. Ryan Quinn, "MIT Will Stop Asking Faculty Applicants for Diversity Statements," *Inside Higher Ed,* May 8, 2024, https://www.insidehighered.com/news/ quick-takes/2024/05/08/mit-stops-asking-faculty-applicants-diversity-statements; Editorial Board, "The Problem with Diversity Statements—and What to Do about Them," *Washington Post,* May 19, 2024, https://www.washingtonpost.com/opinions/ 2024/05/19/universities-dei-academic-freedom/.

75. Laura Spitalniak, "Georgia Public Colleges Put End to Required DEI Statements in Hiring," *Higher Ed Dive,* August 31, 2023, https://www.highereddive.com/ news/georgia-public-colleges-ban-required-dei-statements-hiring/692318/.

Chapter 3. "Extramural" Speech

1. Ligaya Mishan, "The Long and Tortured History of Cancel Culture," *New York Times Style Magazine,* December 3, 2020, https://www.nytimes.com/2020/12/03/t-magazine/cancel-culture-history.html; Aja Romano, "Why We Can't Stop Fighting about Cancel Culture," *Vox,* August 25, 2020, https://www.vox.com/culture/2019/12/30/20879720/what-is-cancel-culture-explained-history-debate.

2. John McWhorter, "Academics Are Really, Really Worried about Their Freedom," *Atlantic,* September 1, 2020, https://www.theatlantic.com/ideas/archive/2020/09/academics-are-really-really-worried-about-their-freedom/615724/.

3. 911 F.3d 674 (4th Cir. 2018).

4. See Keith E. Whittington, "What Can Professors Say in Public? Extramural Speech and the First Amendment," *Case Western Reserve Law Review* 73 (2023): 1121, 1126–27.

5. American Association of University Professors, *Declaration of Principles on Academic Freedom and Academic Tenure* (1915). For an excellent discussion of the history behind this declaration, see David M. Rabban, *Academic Freedom: From Professional Norm to First Amendment Right* (Cambridge, Mass.: Harvard University Press, 2024), 52.

6. American Association of University Professors, *History of the AAUP,* https://www.aaup.org/about/history-aaup.

7. American Association of University Professors, *Statement of Principles on Academic Freedom and Tenure* (1940).

8. Keith E. Whittington, "Academic Freedom and the Scope of Protections for Extramural Speech," *Academe* (Winter 2019).

9. Whittington, "Academic Freedom."

10. A. Lawrence Lowell, "President's Report," *Office of the Registrar Harvard University* 15 (1918): 5, 20.

11. American Association of University Professors, *Statement of Principles on Academic Freedom and Tenure* (1940), n.6.

12. Stacy Weiner, "Is Spreading Medical Misinformation a Physician's Free Speech Right? It's Complicated," *AAMC News,* December 26, 2023; Kathleen M. Sullivan, "The Intersection of Free Speech and the Legal Profession: Constraints on Lawyers' First Amendment Rights," *Fordham Law Review* 67 (1998): 569; Renee Knake Jefferson, "Lawyer Lies and Political Speech," *Yale Law Journal* 131 (October 24, 2021): 114.

13. Heather Knight, "In San Francisco, Doctors Feud over 'Do No Harm' When It Comes to War Protests," *New York Times,* June 24, 2024.

14. For a discussion of the academic freedom of students, see Rabban, *Academic Freedom: From Professional Norm to First Amendment Right*, 282–97.

15. University of California, *Principles of Community*, https://ucnet.universityof california.edu/career-community/building-community/community-values/princi ples-of-community/.

16. UC Santa Cruz, *Principles of Community and the First Amendment*, https:// freespeech.ucsc.edu/learn/principles-community-first-amendment.html.

17. Scott Jaschik, "Must Deans Be Silent?" *Inside Higher Ed*, May 18, 2014.

18. See *Jeffries v. Harleston*, 52 F.3d 9 (2d Cir. 1994) (upholding the removal of CUNY professor Leonard Jeffries from the position as chair of the Black studies department after he advocated the view that Jews financed the slave trade and used the movie industry to hurt Black people).

19. Steven Salaita (@stevesalaita), Twitter (July 2014).

20. Steven Salaita, "Why I Was Fired," *Chronicle of Higher Education*, October 5, 2015; Eric Owens, "America 2014: University of Illinois Professor Blames Jews for Anti-Semitism," *Daily Caller*, July 21, 2014.

21. Scott Jaschik, "The Emails on Salaita," *Inside Higher Ed*, August 24, 2014.

22. Colleen Flaherty, "Officially Out of a Job," *Inside Higher Ed*, September 11, 2014.

23. Robert Mackey, "Professor's Angry Tweets on Gaza Cost Him a Job," *New York Times*, September 12, 2014.

24. Colleen Flaherty, "Settling with Salaita," *Inside Higher Ed*, November 12, 2015.

25. Sabrina Conza, "FIRE Demands University of Texas at Dallas End Investigation of Professor for Tweet Asking for a 'Cure for Homosexuality,'" Foundation for Individual Rights and Expression, July 22, 2022.

26. Kate McGee, "UT-Dallas Is Investigating a Professor's Homophobic Tweet with Misinformation about Monkeypox," *Texas Tribune*, July 20, 2022.

27. "Farage Apologizes After Backlash from UTD Community," *Mercury*, July 25, 2022, https://utdmercury.com/farage-apologizes-after-backlash-from-utd-community/.

28. Andrew Lawrence, "Uju Anya on the Queen, Jeff Bezos and the Family History behind Her Tweet," *Guardian*, September 14, 2022; Emma Folts, "CMU's Answer to Prof's Tweet, Wishing 'Excruciating' Pain for Queen, Stirs Campus Backlash," *PublicSource*, September 12, 2022; Marcela Rodrigues, "Jeff Bezos Criticized a Professor's Tweet about the Queen. Then the University Condemned Her Comments," *Chronicle of Higher Education*, September 9, 2022.

29. Michael Levenson, "University to Investigate Professor Who Tweeted about 'Black Privilege,'" *New York Times*, June 5, 2020.

30. Jack Stripling, "The Professor Is Canceled. Now What?" *Washington Post,* June 21, 2022.

31. Michael Levenson, "University Must Reinstate Professor Who Tweeted about 'Black Privilege,' " *New York Times,* May 19, 2022.

32. Nicholas Bogel-Burroughs, "Our Professor's Views Are Vile, University Says. But We Can't Fire Him," *New York Times,* November 22, 2019.

33. Hank Reichman, "On Indiana University's Response to Professor Rasmusen," *Academe Blog,* November 22, 2019.

34. Stripling, "The Professor Is Canceled."

35. President Biden, Remarks on the Retirement of Supreme Court Justice Stephen Breyer, January 27, 2022.

36. Lauren Lumpkin, "Incoming Georgetown Law Official Placed on Administrative Leave for Tweets about Supreme Court Pick," *Washington Post,* January 31, 2022.

37. Lumpkin, "Incoming Georgetown Law Official Placed on Administrative Leave."

38. Neil Vigdor, "Georgetown Suspends Lecturer Who Criticized Vow to Put Black Woman on Court," *New York Times,* January 31, 2022.

39. FIRE, Statement on Georgetown's Suspension and Investigation of Ilya Shapiro, January 31, 2022, https://www.thefire.org/news/fire-statement-georgetowns-suspension-and-investigation-ilya-shapiro.

40. Faculty Letter in Support of Ilya Shapiro, January 31, 2022, https://www.thefire.org/research-learn/faculty-letter-support-ilya-shapiro-january-31-2022.

41. Michelle Goldberg, "Georgetown Law, Don't Punish Your New Hire over His 'Lesser Black Woman' Tweet," *New York Times,* February 4, 2022.

42. Anemona Hartocollis, "A Conservative Quits Georgetown's Law School amid Free Speech Fight," *New York Times,* June 6, 2022.

43. William M. Treanor, Dean's Statement on Ilya Shapiro, June 2, 2022, https://www.law.georgetown.edu/deans-statement-re-ilya-shapiro/.

44. Sylvia Goodman, "A Professor Is Suspended for Suggesting It's Better to 'Kill' Racist or Homo4hobic Speakers Than Shout Them Down," *Chronicle of Higher Education,* March 28, 2023; David Jesse, "Wayne State Suspends Professor over Social Media Post Allegedly Advocating Violence," *Detroit Free Press,* March 27, 2023.

45. *Virginia v. Black,* 538 U.S. 343, 359 (2003); see also *Watts v. United States,* 394 U.S. 705, 708 (1969). Subsequently, in *Counterman v. Colorado,* 143 S.Ct. 2106 (2023), the Court said that a true threat requires that there be a conscious disregard by the speaker that the speech would be regarded as a serious threat of imminent physical danger.

46. *Brandenburg v. Ohio,* 395 U.S. 444, 447 (1969).

47. Nick Irvin, "A UC Davis Professor Thinks Cops 'Need to Be Killed,' " *The Aggie,* February 2019.

48. "University Professor Condemned for Previous Comments Saying Cops 'Need to Be Killed,' " *CBS News,* February 26, 2019.

49. Benjamin Fearnow, "California Republicans Propose Firing UC Davis Professor over Anti-Police Remarks," *Newsweek,* March 21, 2019.

50. Ally Russell, "California Assemblyman Calls for Termination of UC Davis Professor Who Said Cops 'Need to Be Killed,' " *The Aggie,* March 2019.

51. Chelsea Shannon, "Why UC Davis Hasn't Fired English Professor over Tweets That Cops Should Be Killed," *ABC 10,* March 5, 2019.

52. Tanya Perez, "UCD Professor Won't Retract Anti-Cop Statements," *Davis Enterprise,* February 26, 2019.

53. Letter from Gary S. May, Chancellor, UC Davis, to James Gallagher, Assemblymember, Calif. State Assembly, March 28, 2019, https://www.ucdavis.edu/news/statements-regarding-public-comments-made-by-tenured-member-faculty.

54. Colleen Flaherty, "Suspended for Anti-Semitism," *Inside Higher Ed,* August 3, 2016.

55. Valerie Strauss, "Oberlin College Dismisses Professor Who Posted Anti-Semitic Messages on Social Media," *Washington Post,* November 15, 2016; Oberlin College Board of Trustees, Statement on Assistant Professor Joy Karega, November 15, 2016, https://www.oberlin.edu/news/board-trustees-statement-assistant-professor-joy-karega.

56. Chanel Hill, "Penn Law Professor Faces Evaluation by Peers for 'Racist Speech,' " *Philadelphia Tribune,* July 18, 2022.

57. Hill, "Penn Law Professor Faces Evaluation."

58. The University of Pennsylvania is a private university so the First Amendment does not directly apply. But it chooses to follow First Amendment principles.

59. Letter from Academic Freedom Alliance to President Magill, July 18, 2022, http://academicfreedom.org/wp-content/uploads/2022/07/Rev-Amy-Wax-Letter-7_14_2022.pdf.

60. Vimal Patel, "UPenn Accuses a Law Professor of Racist Statements. Should She Be Fired?" *New York Times,* March 13, 2023.

61. David J. Shapiro, Respondent's Closing Statement, May 5, 2023, https://www.nas.org/storage/app/media/New%20Documents/20230505-respondents-closing-statementredacted.pdf.

62. University of Pennsylvania Office of the Faculty Senate, Report in the Just Cause Matter regarding Professor Amy Wax, June 21, 2023, https://drive.google.com/file/d/1X811rWaORjWqJ5FWGenHc2zpxdKztAUk/view.

63. Graham Piro, "Amy Wax Hearing Report Confirms Fears over Erosion of Academic Freedom at Penn," FIRE, March 4, 2024.

64. Elea Castiglione, "Penn Hearing Board Recommended Sanctions against Amy Wax, Prompting Ongoing Appeal," *Daily Pennsylvanian*, February 20, 2024; Ethan Young, " 'Brazen and Absurd': Penn Professor Amy Wax Criticizes Recommended Sanctions in New Interview," *Daily Pennsylvanian*, April 1, 2024.

65. Susan Snyder, "Penn Will Sanction Amy Wax, the Law Prof Who Invited a White Nationalist to Speak to Her Class," *Philadelphia Inquirer*, September 23, 2024; "Final Determination of Complaint against Professor Amy Wax," *University of Pennsylvania Almanac*, September 24, 2024.

66. Lexi Nelson, "Uproar at Stanford After Photo of Student Reading "Mein Kampf" Spreads on Social Media," Free Speech Project, February 17, 2023.

67. Jaime Adame, "A Photo Prompts Complaints and Controversy," *Inside Higher Ed*, January 29, 2023.

68. Patrick Reilly, "Free Speech Org Blasts Stanford After Student Reported for Reading *Mein Kampf*," *New York Post*, January 26, 2023; Letter from FIRE to Marc Tessier-Lavigne, President, Stanford University, January 25, 2023, https://www.thefire.org/research-learn/fire-letter-stanford-university-january-25–2023.

69. Julia Steinberg, "Nazis Banned Books. We Shouldn't," *Stanford Review*, January 23, 2023.

70. Douglas Belkin, "Stanford Faculty Say Anonymous Student Bias Reports Threaten Free Speech," *Wall Street Journal*, February 23, 2023.

71. Email from Erica Woodley, Dean of Students, Tulane U. to Students, January 12, 2023, https://www.thefire.org/news/no-dissidents-allowed-tulane-investigating-student-after-op-ed-supporting-kanye-west.

72. Sylvia Goodman, "By Announcing an Investigation, Did Tulane Censor Her?" *Chronicle of Higher Education*, February 23, 2023.

73. Goodman, "By Announcing an Investigation, Did Tulane Censor Her?"

74. *Keefe v. Adams*, 840 F.3d 523 (8th Cir. 2016).

75. University of Tennessee Health Science Center, "Standards of the Health Professions," https://catalog.uthsc.edu/content.php?catoid=33&navoid=3383#Maintenance_of_Ethical%20and_Professional_Standards_of_the_Health_Professions.

76. Greta Anderson, "Personal or Professional?" *Inside Higher Ed*, February 14, 2021; Anemona Hartocollis, "Students Punished for 'Vulgar' Social Media Posts Are Fighting Back," *New York Times*, February 5, 2021.

77. Dan Levin, "Colleges Rescinding Admissions Offers as Racist Social Media Posts Emerge," *New York Times,* July 2, 2020; Rachel Paula Abrahamson, "Colleges Are Revoking Admissions Offers Due to Racist Posts," *Today,* July 31, 2020.

78. Will Creeley, "The Problem with Rescinding Admission," Foundation for Individual Rights and Expression, June 23, 2020.

79. Clif Smart, "Balancing Rights and Responsibilities When Our Values Are Offended," Missouri State Presidential Updates, June 2, 2020, https://blogs. missouristate.edu/president/2020/06/02/balancing-rights-and-responsibilities-when-our-values-are-offended/.

80. John Jasinski, "Northwest Responding to Video Depicting Prospective Student," Northwest Missouri State University, June 1, 2020, https://www.nwmissouri. edu/media/news/2020/06/01Jasinskistatement.htm.

Chapter 4. Government Control over Campus Speech

1. Josh Moody, "Law Students Shout Down Controversial Speakers, " *Inside Higher Ed,* March 22, 2022; Allison Stanger, "Understanding the Angry Mob at Middlebury That Gave Me a Concussion," *New York Times,* March 13, 2017; Madison Park and Kyung Lah, "Berkeley Protests of Yiannopoulos Caused $100,000 in Damage," CNN.com, February 2, 2017.

2. Ben Shapiro, *Facts Don't Care about Your Feelings* (Hermosa Beach, Calif.: Creators, 2019).

3. Kevin Kiley, "Kiley Introduces Landmark Free Speech Legislation," Press Release, May 18, 2023.

4. Howard Gillman and Erwin Chemerinsky, "Yale Heckling Is Bad. State Censorship? Worse," CtPost.com, March 26, 2022.

5. Memorandum from Russell Vought, Dir. Off. Mgmt. & Budget, to Heads of Exec. Dep'ts & Agencies, September 4, 2020.

6. Kevin Liptak, "Trump Says Department of Education Will Investigate Use of 1619 Project in Schools," CNN, September 6, 2020.

7. Exec. Order No. 13950, 85 Fed. Reg. 60683, September 28, 2020, Combating Race and Sex Stereotyping.

8. See, e.g., Richard Delgado et al., *Critical Race Theory: An Introduction,* 3rd ed. (New York: New York University Press, 2017).

9. Nikole Hannah-Jones, *The 1619 Project: A New American Origin Story* (London: W. H. Allen, 2019).

10. Jake Silverstein, "We Respond to the Historians Who Critiqued the 1619 Project," *New York Times Magazine,* December 20, 2019.

11. See Keith Whittington, *You Can't Teach That! The Battle over University Classrooms* (Cambridge: Polity, 2024).

12. Hailey Fuchs, "Trump Attack on Diversity Training Has a Quick and Chilling Effect," *New York Times,* October 13, 2020.

13. Khari Johnson, "Stanford Rushes to Comply with Trump Executive Order Limiting Diversity Training," VentureBeat, November 17, 2020.

14. Exec. Order No. 13985, 86 Fed. Reg. 7009, January 25, 2021, Advancing Racial Equity and Support for Underserved Communities through the Federal Government.

15. Sarah Schwartz, "Map: Where Critical Race Theory Is under Attack," *Education Week* (updated June 13, 2023).

16. Tenn. Code § 49-7-1902 (2022).

17. N.D. Cent. Code § 15.1-21-05.1 (2021).

18. Schwartz, "Map."

19. Stop WOKE Act, 2022 Fla. Laws 72 (amending Fla. Stat. §§ 760.10, 1000.05, 1003.42, 1006.31, 1012.98, 1002.20, 1006.40).

20. Parental Rights in Education Act, 2022 Fla. Laws 22 (amending Fla. Stat § 1001.42).

21. Protect Students First Act, 2022 Ga. Laws 136 (codified at O.C.G.A. § 20-1-11 [2022]).

22. 2021 Idaho Sess. Laws 293 (codified at Idaho Code § 1-33-138).

23. Ryan Quinn, "Indiana Governor Signs Bill Tying Tenure to 'Intellectual Diversity,' " *Inside Higher Ed,* March 14, 2024.

24. We describe this in Erwin Chemerinsky and Howard Gillman, *Free Speech on Campus* (New Haven: Yale University Press, 2017), 41–42.

25. Marc Stickgold, " 'The Hysteria of Our Times': Loyalty Oaths in California" (2010), *Publications,* Paper 174. In *Shelton v. Tucker* (1960) the Supreme Court struck down an Arkansas law that required teachers at public educational institutions, including universities, to file an annual affidavit listing all of their organizational affiliations, explaining that "the vigilant protection of constitutional freedoms is nowhere more vital than in the community of American schools." In *Keyishian v. Board of Regents* (1967) the Supreme Court struck down a requirement that faculty in the State University of New York system certify that they had never been Communists, explaining, "Our Nation is deeply committed to safeguarding academic freedom, which is of transcendent value to all of us. . . . [The First Amendment] does not tolerate laws that cast a pall of orthodoxy over the classroom."

26. Chemerinsky and Gillman, *Free Speech on Campus,* 82.

27. Association of American Law Schools, Statement by AALS on Efforts to Ban the Use or Teaching of Critical Race Theory, August 3, 2021.

28. Brief of Defendant-Appellants at 3, Pernell v. Fla. Bd. Governors State Univ. Sys. Nos. 22-13992 & 22-13994 (11th Cir. 2023).

29. Giulia Heyward, "Georgia's University System Takes on Tenure," *New York Times,* October 13, 2021, https://www.nytimes.com/2021/10/13/us/georgia-university-system-tenure.html; Ethan Sandweiss, "Indiana Universities Can Revoke Tenure If Profs Don't Foster 'Intellectual Diversity,' " NPR, March 21, 2024, https://www.npr.org/2024/03/21/1239991734/indiana-universities-can-revoke-tenure-if-profs-dont-foster-intellectual-diversi.

30. American Association of University Professors, *Declaration of Principles on Academic Freedom and Academic Tenure* (1915), https://www.aaup.org/NR/rdonlyres/A6520A9D-0A9A-47B3-B550-C006B5B224E7/0/1915Declaration.pdf.

31. William F. Buckley, *God and Man at Yale: The Superstitions of "Academic Freedom"* (Washington, D.C.: Regnery Gateway, 2021); David Corn, "Remember How Dinesh D'Souza Outed Gay Classmates—and Thought It Was Awesome?" *Mother Jones,* January 24, 2014, https://www.motherjones.com/politics/2014/01/dinesh-dsouza-indictment-dartmouth-outed-gay-classmates/; Ari Shapiro et al., "How Cancel Culture Became Politicized—Just Like Political Correctness," NPR, July 26, 2021, https://www.npr.org/2021/07/09/1014744289/cancel-culture-debate-has-early-90s-roots-political-correctness.

32. Kim Parker, "The Growing Partisan Divide in Views of Higher Education," Pew Research Center, August 19, 2019, https://www.pewresearch.org/social-trends/2019/08/19/the-growing-partisan-divide-in-views-of-higher-education-2/. It should be noted that trust in higher education among Democrats also has eroded. http://news.gallup.com/poll/508352/americans-confidence-higher-education-down-sharply.aspx

33. Emma Pettit, "Who Should Shape What Colleges Teach?" *Chronicle of Higher Education,* September 13, 2023, https://www.chronicle.com/article/who-should-shape-what-colleges-teach.

34. Advisory Comm. on the Univ. of Mich. Principles on Diversity of Thought & Freedom of Expression, Report of the Advisory Committee on the University of Michigan Principles on Diversity of Thought & Freedom of Expression, 2024, https://president.umich.edu/wp-content/uploads/sites/3/2024/09/advisory-committee-report_principles-on-diversity-of-thought-and-freedom-of-expression.pdf.

35. Jeffrey Adam Sachs and Jeremy C. Young, "America's Censored Classrooms 2023" (2023), PEN America, https://pen.org/report/americas-censored-classrooms-2023/.

36. *Pernell v. Lamb*, No. 4:22CV304-MW/MAF, 2023 WL 2347487 (N.D. Fla. February 22, 2023), *rev'd and remanded sub nom. Pernell v. Fla. Bd. of Governors of State Univ.*, 84 F.4th 1339 (11th Cir. 2023).

37. See *Epperson v. Arkansas*, 393 U.S. 97, 107 (1968) (describing the latitude of schools to determine their curriculum). This latitude is seen as the explanation for why there has been only a relatively small number of challenges to the laws prohibiting teaching of Critical Race Theory. See Hannah Natanson, "Few Legal Challenges to Laws Limiting Lessons on Race, Gender," *Washington Post*, March 17, 2023, https://www.washingtonpost.com/education/2023/03/17/legal-challenges-gender-critical-race-theory/.

38. See, e.g., *Connally v. Gen. Constr. Co.*, 269 U.S. 385, 391 (1926) (a law is unconstitutionally vague "when people of common intelligence must necessarily guess at its meaning").

39. *Nat'l Ass'n for Advancement of Colored People v. Button*, 371 U.S. 415, 433 (1963).

40. *Nat'l Ass'n for Advancement of Colored People v. Button*, 432–33 (citations omitted).

41. *Schad v. Borough of Mount Ephraim*, 452 U.S. 61 (1981).

42. Hannah Natanson, "A White Teacher Taught White Students about White Privilege. It Cost Him His Job," *Washington Post*, December 6, 2021, https://www.washingtonpost.com/education/2021/12/06/tennessee-teacher-fired-critical-race-theory/.

43. Eesha Pendharkar, "Teacher Fired for Lesson on White Privilege Loses Appeal," *Education Week*, October 26, 2021, https://www.edweek.org/teaching-learning/teacher-fired-for-lesson-on-white-privilege-loses-appeal/2021/10.

44. Ryan Quinn, "Indiana Governor Signs Bill Tying Tenure to 'Intellectual Diversity,'" *Inside Higher Ed*, March 14, 2024, https://www.insidehighered.com/news/quick-takes/2024/03/14/gov-signs-bill-tying-tenure-intellectual-diversity.

45. *Santa Cruz Lesbian & Gay Cmty. Ctr. v. Trump*, 508 F. Supp. 3d 521, 543–44 (N.D. Cal. 2020).

46. See Vanessa Miller, Frank Fernandez, and Neal H. Hutchens, "The Race to Ban Race: Legal and Critical Arguments against State Legislation to Ban Critical Race Theory in Higher Education," *Missouri Law Review* 88 (2023): 1.

47. Arizona Revised Statutes Title 15. Education § 15-717.02.

48. See *Matal v. Tam*, 582 U.S. 218 (2017).

49. *Rosenberger v. Rector & Visitors of Univ. of Virginia*, 515 U.S. 818, 829 (1995).

50. *Pernell v. Fla. Bd. of Governors of State Univ. Sys.*, 641 F.Supp.3d 1218, 1234 (N.D. Fla. 2022).

51. Dylan Salzman, "The Constitutionality of Orthodoxy: First Amendment Implications of Laws Restricting Critical Race Theory in Public Schools," *University of Chicago Law Review* 89 (2022): 1069; Dylan Saul, Note, "School Curricula and Silenced Speech: A Constitutional Challenge to Critical Race Theory Bans," *Minnesota Law Review* 105 (2023): 1311.

52. 457 U.S. 853 (1982).

53. 457 U.S. 853 (1982) at 864.

54. 457 U.S. 853 (1982) at 867.

55. *Pratt v. Indep. Sch. Dist. No. 831, Forest Lake, Minn.*, 670 F.2d 771, 777 (8th Cir. 1982).

56. *Chiras v. Miller,* 432 F.3d 606, 619–20 (5th Cir. 2005).

57. 793 F.3d 968 (9th Cir. 2015). It should be disclosed that Erwin Chemerinsky argued this case in the Ninth Circuit for the challengers to the Arizona law.

58. Ariz. Rev. Stat. Ann. §§ 15-111 to -112 (2011).

59. "Florida Educators and Students File Lawsuit Challenging 'Stop W.O.K.E.' Censorship Law," ACLU, August 18, 2022, https://www.aclu.org/press-releases/florida-educators-and-students-file-lawsuit-challenging-stop-woke-censorship-law.

60. We discuss the relationship of academic freedom and the First Amendment in chapter 2.

61. 547 U.S. 410 (2006).

62. See, e.g., *Pickering v. Bd. of Educ.*, 391 U.S. 563 (1968) (holding that a government employee's speech is protected by the First Amendment if it involves a matter of public concern and does not unduly interfere with the functioning of the workplace).

63. *Garcetti,* 547 U.S. at 421.

64. *Garcetti,* at 425.

65. *Garcetti,* at 438.

66. 746 F.3d 402 (9th Cir. 2014).

67. 746 F.3d 402 (9th Cir. 2014) at 406.

68. 746 F.3d 402 (9th Cir. 2014) at 412.

69. *Keyishian v. Board of Regents,* 385 U.S. 589 (1967).

70. *Sweezy v. New Hampshire,* 354 U.S. 234, 250 (1957).

71. *Meriwether v. Hartop,* 992 F.3d 492 (6th Cir. 2021).

72. 641 F.Supp.3d 1218 (N.D. Fla. 2022). The law said: "It shall constitute discrimination on the basis of race, color, national origin, or sex under this section to subject any student or employee to training or instruction that espouses, promotes, advances, inculcates, or compels such student or employee to believe any of the following concepts:

1. Members of one race, color, national origin, or sex are morally superior to members of another race, color, national origin, or sex.

2. A person, by virtue of his or her race, color, national origin, or sex is inherently racist, sexist, or oppressive, whether consciously or unconsciously.

3. A person's moral character or status as either privileged or oppressed is necessarily determined by his or her race, color, national origin, or sex.

4. Members of one race, color, national origin, or sex cannot and should not attempt to treat others without respect to race, color, national origin, or sex.

5. A person, by virtue of his or her race, color, national origin, or sex bears responsibility for, or should be discriminated against or receive adverse treatment because of, actions committed in the past by other members of the same race, color, national origin, or sex.

6. A person, by virtue of his or her race, color, national origin, or sex should be discriminated against or receive adverse treatment to achieve diversity, equity, or inclusion.

7. A person, by virtue of his or her race, color, sex, or national origin, bears personal responsibility for and must feel guilt, anguish, or other forms of psychological distress because of actions, in which the person played no part, committed in the past by other members of the same race, color, national origin, or sex.

73. 641 F.Supp.3d 1218 (N.D. Fla. 2022) at 1235.

74. 641 F.Supp.3d 1218 (N.D. Fla. 2022) at 1276.

75. 641 F.Supp.3d 1218 (N.D. Fla. 2022) at 1290–91.

76. Mike Gonzalez, "Conservative Efforts to Roll Back DEI in Higher Education Sweep through Another State," Heritage Foundation, June 1, 2023, https://www.heritage.org/education/commentary/conservative-efforts-roll-back-dei-higher-education-sweep-through-another.

77. "DEI Legislation Tracker," *Chronicle of Higher Education,* https://www.chronicle.com/article/here-are-the-states-where-lawmakers-are-seeking-to-ban-colleges-dei-efforts?sra=true (last updated Augus 30, 2024).

78. Jeffrey Sachs and Jeremy C. Young, "More Than Meets the DEI," Pen America, May 25, 2023, https://pen.org/more-than-meets-the-dei/.

79. "DEI Legislation Tracker."

80. Sachs and Young, "More Than Meets the DEI."

81. See "DEI Legislation Tracker." See also Chloe Appleby and Evan Castillo, "Diversity Statements Are Getting Cut from These Universities' Hiring Practices," Best Colleges, https://www.bestcolleges.com/news/diversity-statements-are-getting-cut-from-these-universities/ (last updated June 4, 2024).

82. Idaho Code § [67-5909C] 67-5909B.

83. "DEI Legislation Tracker." SF 2435's full text can be found at "Senate File 24," Iowa Legislature, https://www.legis.iowa.gov/legislation/BillBook?ga=90&ba=SF24 (last visited September 24, 2024).

84. See *Students for Fair Admissions v. President and Fellows of Harvard College,* 143 S.Ct. 2141 (2023). The admissions programs at Harvard College and the University of North Carolina violate Title VI of the 1964 Civil Rights Act and the equal protection clause of the Fourteenth Amendment in using race as a factor in admissions decisions to benefit minorities and enhance diversity.

85. Chemerinsly and Gillman, *Free Speech on Campus,* 82–110.

Chapter 5. Principles, Practices, Precautions

1. See Tony Banout and Tom Ginsburg, eds., *The Chicago Canon on Free Inquiry and Expression* (Chicago: University of Chicago Press, 2024).

2. Report of the Advisory Committee on the University of Michigan Principles on Diversity of Thought and Freedom of Expression, 2024, https://president.umich.edu/wp-content/uploads/sites/3/2024/09/advisory-committee-report_principles-on-diversity-of-thought-and-freedom-of-expression.pdf.

3. *Principles of Community,* https://diversity.berkeley.edu/principles-community.

4. Catherine E. Lhamon, "Dear Colleague Letter: Protecting Students from Discrimination, Such as Harassment, Based on Race, Color, or National Origin, Including Shared Ancestry or Ethnic Characteristics," White House, May 7, 2024, https://www.whitehouse.gov/wp-content/uploads/2024/05/colleague-202405-shared-ancestry.pdf.

5. See *Brandenburg v. Ohio,* 395 U.S. 444 (1969) (articulating the standard for incitement that is unprotected by the First Amendment); see *Counterman v. Colorado,* 600 U.S. 66 (2023) (articulating the standard for true threats unprotected by the First Amendment).

6. 141 S.Ct. 2038 (2021).

7. 141 U.S. at 2043.

8. Pet'r's Br. 7, *Mahanoy Area School District v. B.L.,* 141 S.Ct. 2038 (2021).

9. *Mahanoy Area School District v. B.L.,* at 2048.

10. *Mahanoy Area School District v. B.L.,* at 2045.

11. 138 S. Ct. 1876 (2018).

12. 138 S. Ct. 1876 (2018) at 1885.

13. 561 U.S. 661, 679 n.11 (2010) (citations omitted).

14. The law as to each of these requirements is summarized in Erwin Chemerinsky, *Constitutional Law: Principles and Policies,* 7th ed. (New York: Aspen, 2022).

15. 452 U.S. 640, 648 (1981).

16. Susan Svrluga, "Berkeley Free-Speech Fight Flares Up Again over Ben Shapiro," *Washington Post,* July 20, 202, https://www.washingtonpost.com/news/gradepoint/wp/2017/07/19/berkeley-free-speech-fight-flares-up-again-over-ben-shapiro/.

17. Sudhim Thanawala, "Multiple Arrests at Ben Shapiro Berkeley Protests," *USA Today,* September 15, 2017, https://www.usatoday.com/story/news/nation/2017/09/15/ben-shapiro-berkeley-protest-arrests/669071001/.

18. Jonathan Stempel, "UC Berkeley Must Face Lawsuit Alleging Bias against Conservative Speakers," Reuters, April 26, 2018, https://www.reuters.com/article/us-california-ucberkeley-lawsuit/uc-berkeley-must-face-lawsuit-alleging-bias-against-conservative-speakers-idUSKBN1HX2B4/.

19. UC Berkeley Public Affairs, "Settlement Reached in Free Speech Case," December 3, 2018, https://news.berkeley.edu/2018/12/03/settlement-reached-in-free-speech-case/; Alex Morey, "UC Berkeley Agrees to Pay $70k, Change Policies, in Speech Suit Settlement," FIRE, December 4, 2018, https://www.thefire.org/news/uc-berkeley-agrees-pay-70k-change-policies-speech-suit-settlement.

20. UC Irvine Policies & Procedures, § 900–15: UCI Major Events Policy, January 2019, https://freespeechcenter.universityofcalifornia.edu/wp-content/uploads/2021/05/UCI-900–15-Major-Events-Policy.pdf.

21. Frances Dinkelspiel, "UC Berkeley Spent Close to $4M on Security in Just One Month in 2017," *Berkeleyside,* February 6, 2018, https://www.berkeleyside.org/2018/02/06/uc-berkeley-spent-close-4m-security-just-one-month-2017.

22. UCLA Administrative Policies and Procedures, UCLA Policy 862: Major Events (effective date September 4, 2024), https://www.adminpolicies.ucla.edu/APP/Number/862.0.

23. UC Irvine Administrative Policies and Procedures, § 900–23: UCI Guidance concerning Disruption of University Activities, https://ucipolicy.ellucid.com/documents/view/138/?security=fc7492c09cc70a85f8803bce0006cc35e0c5ab9e (last reviewed September 2024).

24. UCI's Constructive Engagement Model, https://dos.uci.edu/freespeech/#:~:text=UCI%27s%20Constructive%20Engagement%20Model&text=It%20outlines%20principles%20such%20as,and%20adherence%20to%20university%20policies.

25. For examples of such resources, see UC Irvine, Resources to Support Academics Targeted by Online Harassment, January 2022, https://freespeech.uci.edu/

wp-content/uploads/2022/06/Resources-to-support-academics-targeted-by-online-harassment-0122.pdf.

26. 391 U.S. 563 (1968). See also *Perry v. Sindermann*, 408 U.S. 593, 597 (1973) (holding that the First Amendment limits the ability of the government to fire or discipline employees because of their speech activities).

27. *Pickering* at 568.

28. *Connick v. Myers*, 461 U.S. 138 (1983).

29. American Association of University Professors, *Statement of Principles on Academic Freedom and Tenure* (1940).

30. American Association of University Professors, *Statement of Principles on Academic Freedom and Tenure*, n.6 (1940).

31. Keith E. Whittington, "Academic Freedom and the Scope of Protections for Extramural Speech," *Academe* (Winter 2019).

32. Regents Policy on Use of University Administrative Websites, https://regents.universityofcalifornia.edu/regmeet/jan24/j3attach1.pdf.

33. See Erwin Chemerinsky, "Swastika Found Drawn on Flyer of Alan Dershowitz After His Berkeley Law Event," *Berkeley Law*, October 16, 2017, https://sites.law.berkeley.edu/inthenews/2017/10/16/swastika-found-drawn-on-flyer-of-alan-dershowitz-after-his-berkeley-law-event/.

34. Steven Davidoff Solomon, Opinion, "Don't Hire My Anti-Semitic Law Students," *Wall Street Journal*, October 15, 2023, https://www.wsj.com/articles/dont-hire-my-anti-semitic-law-students-protests-colleges-universities-jews-palestine-6ad86ad5.

35. Erwin Chemerinsky, "Dean's Message: Supporting Our Students," *Berkeley Law*, October 17, 2023, https://www.law.berkeley.edu/article/deans-message-supporting-our-students/.

36. Howard Gillman, On Statements, https://chancellor.uci.edu/communications/on-statements/index.php.

37. 143 S.Ct. 2141 (2023) (the admissions programs at Harvard College and the University of North Carolina violate Title VI of the 1964 Civil Rights Act and the equal protection clause of the Fourteenth Amendment in using race as a factor in admissions decisions to benefit minorities and enhance diversity).

38. See Brian Soucek, "Diversity Statements," *UC Davis Law Review* 55 (2022): 989 (explaining the constitutionality of diversity statements).

Index

Abbott, Dorian, 26-27

abortion rights: as deeply contested
issue, 106-107

academic freedom: AAUP statements
relating to, 67-68, 81, 92, 95, 182;
as applied to faculty members in
the classroom, 230-233; as applied
to government employees,
192-193; basic principles of, 6-9,
65-66, 116-117, 152, 207-208;
conservative concerns relating to,
182-183; controversies relating to
protection of, 71-89; court cases
relating to, 188-197; and DEI
statements, 110, 114; as distinguished from free speech, 68-70,
87-89; and extramural speech, 15,
119, 121-123, 125, 130-131, 133,
136, 142, 146, 147, 148, 149; and a
faculty member's efforts to recruit
students to support a particular
candidate or agenda, 85-86, 232;
and the First Amendment, 70,
87-89, 192, 193-194, 233; German
model of, 181; and guidelines
governing political statements by
departments and faculty members,
92-107, 205-206, 233-235; and
identity-based targeting of students,

84-85; key elements of, 83-84; laws
affecting, 173-180, 197-199; limits
to, 14; origins of the concept of, 82;
and peer review, 67, 111, 195, 242;
principles of, 205-206; and racial
epithets as used in class discussion,
75-77; and respect for diverse
viewpoints, 66-67, 116-117,
177-186, 202-204; as safeguard for
free expression, 11, 15; and
sensitive issues, 231-232; state
efforts to interfere with, 171-172;
and tenure, 67-68, 81, 92, 95,
180-181. *See also* Critical Race
Theory; "divisive" concepts;
extramural speech; free speech on
campus; *and names of individual
colleges and universities*

Academic Freedom Alliance, 113; and
controversy relating to discussion of
adult-child sex, 80; and Amy Wax's
racist comments, 152

admissions, rescinding of: based on
social media posts, 165-168

adult-child sex: controversy relating to
discussion of, in the classroom,
79-80

Alliance Defending Freedom (ADF),
19, 171

health professions: and student's
"violation" of standards, in social
media posts, 164-166
*Heffron v. International Society for
Krishna Consciousness, Inc.*, 217-218
higher education: conservative attacks
on, 5, 182-183. *See also names of
individual colleges and university*
high schools, free speech in, 11
Hill v. Colorado, 44-45
Hitler, Adolf: Stanford student
investigated for reading book by,
159-162
Hodge, Harlan, 168
*Hurley v. Irish-American Gay, Lesbian
and Bisexual Group of Boston*,
57-58

Idaho: and law relating to diversity
statements in academic hiring and
admissions, 201; and laws relating
to "divisive concepts," 177
incitement: criteria for, 7-8
Indiana public colleges and universities: and failure to teach "diverse
viewpoints" as basis for firing, 177,
187
Indiana University: extramural speech
as issue at, 134-140
institutional websites: and posts
relating to potentially divisive
issues, 94-99, 234-235
Iowa colleges and universities. *See*
University of Iowa
Irvin, Nick, 145
Islamophobia: as issue on college
campuses, 4, 71-72
Israel: diverse responses to Hamas
attack on, 3, 4, 89-92; encampments on campuses relating to the

response to the Hamas attack, 35;
as a Jewish state, 97
Israel-Palestine: tensions on campus
relating to, 82-83, 84-85, 89-92,
97, 105. *See also* Hamas attack on
Israel; Israel; pro-Palestinian organizations

Jackson, Ketanji Brown, 18
Jasinski, John, 168
Jehovah's Witnesses: Supreme Court
decision affecting, 29-30
Jewish Journal: Chemerinsky's
response to opinion piece in, 59;
opinion piece in, 59
Jewish students: diatribe directed at,
162-163; harassment of, 46, 54-55.
See also antisemitism on campuses;
Zionism/Zionists
Jewish Studies: as issue at UC Irvine,
39-40

Kalven, Harry, Jr., 102
Kalven Report: and the university's
role in political and social action,
102-103, 105, 236
Karega, Joy: antisemitic Facebook
posts by, 147-150
Kashuv, Kyle: and acceptance at
Harvard rescinded, 167
Kavanaugh, Brett, 85
Kemp, Brian: and law prohibiting
the teaching of "divisive concepts,"
177
Kennedy, Anthony, 192
Kennedy, Randall: on DEI state-
ments, 112
Kershnar, Stephen: and controversy
relating to discussion of adult-child
sex, 79-80

Title VI (1964 Civil Rights Act): as
applied to religious discrimination,
48-49, 162; Berkeley Law accused
of violation of, 59; criteria for
violation of, 49-51; and discriminatory learning environment
violation, 162; and the First
Amendment, 13-14, 51, 61-63;
harassment as defined under,
49-51; and issues relating to
antisemitism and Islamophobia, 4;
and Jewish Zionists as a protected
class, 97; and political statements
made by departments, 234. *See also*
nondiscriminatory learning
environments
Title IX (civil rights statute): as
applied to harassment, 52-53. *See
also* Office of Civil Rights;
nondiscriminatory learning
environments
transgender rights: as issue on college
campuses, 22, 24-25
trigger warnings, 232; as choice
protected by academic freedom, 74-
75
Trump administration: and ban on
teaching Critical Race Theory,
172-173; and cutoff of federal
funds to universities based on
alleged antisemitism, 63-64; and
executive order on combating race
and sex stereotyping, 173-175,
187-188; Muslim ban imposed
by, 104, 106; and opposition to
DEI, 115, 187; and withholding
of research funds for political
reasons, 5
Tufts University: encampments
at, 35

Tulane University: and student's
antisemitic diatribe as extramural
speech, 162-163
*Turner Broadcasting System v. Federal
Communications*, 26
Turning Point USA, 24

UC Berkeley: academic freedom as
issue at, 82-84; costs of campus
security at, 29; encampments at,
35; Free Speech Movement, 213;
lawsuit filed by law students in
support of Palestine, 56; protests at,
25; principles of community at,
209-210; public safety as issue at,
28-29; report on the university's
role in addressing controversial
issues, 93-94; response to lawsuit
filed by law students, 56-57;
restrictions on speakers at, 28. *See
also* Berkeley Law
UC Davis: DEI statements as required
by, 108; extramural speech as
issue at, 145-147; factors involved
in faculty hiring, 108; protests
at, 24
UC Irvine: and anticipating disruptions of campus activities, 222-225;
costs relating to encampment
at, 44; criteria for determining
which issues call for a response
from the administration, 106-107;
encampment at, 38-39; free
speech as issue at, 32-33; "Guidance concerning Disruption of
University Activities," 33-34; major
events policy at, 28, 31, 220-221;
and political advocacy in the
classroom, 86; response to
encampment at, 39-41